IN DEFENSE OF ISRAEL

A Memoir of a Political Life

MOSHE ARENS

BROOKINGS INSTITUTION PRESS

Washington, D.C.

Library of Congress Cataloging-in-Publication data
Names: Arens, Moshe, author.
Title: In defense of Israel : a memoir of a political life / Moshe Arens.
Description: Washington, D.C. : Brookings Institution Press, [2018] |
    Includes index.
Identifiers: LCCN 2017020199 (print) | LCCN 2017021698 (ebook) |
    ISBN 9780815731429 (ebook) | ISBN 9780815731412
    (cloth : alk. paper)
Subjects: LCSH: Arens, Moshe—Diaries. | Statesmen—Israel—
    Biography. | Aeronautical engineers—Israel—Biography. |
    Israel—Politics and Government—20th century.
Classification: LCC DS126.6.A735 (ebook) | LCC DS126.6.A735
    A3 2018 (print) | DDC 956.9405/4092 [B]—dc23
LC record available at https://lccn.loc.gov/2017020199

ISBN 978-08157-3141-2 (cloth : alk. paper)
ISBN 978-08157-3142-9 (ebook)

9 8 7 6 5 4 3 2 1

Typeset in Adobe Caslon Pro

Composition by Westchester Publishing Services

Contents

Preface

My story begins with a description of the events that took place in the Rumbula Forest, near Riga, Latvia, in November 1941. It was the beginning of the German extermination of Latvia's Jewish community. I was not there, but I might have been: I had left Latvia for the United States on September 7, 1939, a few days after the outbreak of World War II on September 1. I have lived with the image of Rumbula for many years; it underlies my determination that the Jewish people should never again be defenseless. I have devoted most of my adult life to doing what I can to strengthen Israel. This book is my story.

By profession I am an engineer. My professional career was devoted to the development of aeronautical engineering in Israel. As a founding member of the Department of Aeronautical Engineering at Israel's Institute of Technology, called the Technion, in Haifa, and as vice president of engineering at Israel Aerospace Industries, I played a leading role in educating a generation of Israeli aeronautical engineers and in providing the Israel Defense Forces with aircraft and missiles that would give it a qualitative advantage over the weapons fielded by Israel's enemies.

As defense minister I had the opportunity to shape Israel's defense policy: funding Israeli weapons system development projects, sending Israeli satellites into space, and making Israel fairly independent in supplying its armed forces with the equipment they required. I steered Israel through the First Gulf War, in 1990–91, and promoted the development of active missile defense technology. I introduced a number of reforms in the Israel Defense Forces to better prepare them for modern warfare. As foreign minister I sought ways to bring peace to Israel, a most difficult task in the Middle Eastern environment. Over the years Israel has become stronger, and some of the threats directed against the country at its birth have receded. I was privileged to be able to contribute to that process.

I end my story with a review of my research on the Warsaw ghetto uprising. After retiring from politics, freed of my obligations as defense minister, I took the opportunity to attempt to understand what happened during the Holocaust and under what circumstances Jewish resistance was possible—even though desperate and without hope of victory.

The existence of a strong State of Israel provides the assurance that what happened during the Holocaust cannot happen again.

ONE

Rumbula

On November 30, 1941, the first column composed of elderly men, women, and children, accompanied by fifty guards, was marched out of the Riga ghetto at 6:00 a.m. It was a cold winter morning, 7 degrees below freezing. The previous evening there had been a light snowfall. Not everyone could keep up with the pace set by the guards, and the column began stretching out, the oldest and weakest falling behind. Anyone not keeping up or stopping to rest was shot on the spot by the guards. Along the path followed by the column could now be seen the dead and the wounded. Spots of the victims' blood began to cover the snow.

Two days earlier the able-bodied men in the ghetto had been ordered into a four-block enclosure cordoned off by barbed wire, leaving the women, children, the elderly, and the infirm in the remaining ghetto area. It was from among them that a group had now been formed into columns and was being marched in the direction of the Rumbula Forest.

It was ten kilometers from the ghetto to the execution site chosen by the Germans on the edge of the forest. The first column arrived at Rumbula after three hours. The people were ordered to undress and deposit their clothing and valuables in designated locations. Dressed only in their underwear, they were then led to pits that had previously been prepared by Russian prisoners of war. In single file, ten at a time, they were ordered into the pits, where they were shot, falling on top of the bodies of those who had preceded them—many of those already in the pits still alive.

Fifteen thousand Jews from the Riga ghetto were killed on that murderous day, to be followed by another 10,000 eight days later. The executions had been planned and overseen by Friedrich Jeckeln, commander of SS Einsatzgruppe A. The *Einsatzgruppen*, literally "task forces," were death squads that followed the German army as it advanced into the Soviet Union and were tasked with killing the Jews in the areas that had fallen under German control.

I was not there that day, although I might have been, together with my mother, Roza, and my younger sister, Miriam. We escaped the fate of the Jewish community of Riga, among them many of my friends and schoolmates, because my father, Tevye, an enterprising industrialist, was in New York with my older brother, Richard, when World War II broke out. Concerned for our fate in war-torn Europe, he cabled us to join him and my brother immediately in America. So on September 7, 1939, seven days after the German invasion of Poland—the Baltic countries as yet untouched by the war—we took a flight from Riga to Stockholm, and in the Swedish port of Göteburg boarded the SS *Drotningholm* for our journey to New York, landing there in late September.

On that bloody day in Rumbula I was attending George Washington High School in the Washington Heights section of Manhattan, completely unaware of what was happening that day in Riga, the city in which I had grown to adolescence. Only some years later, as the dimensions of the Holocaust became apparent and details of the killings were published, did I learn the fate of the Jewish community in Riga. Since then, the scenes of the murders committed at Rumbula have haunted my thoughts almost as if I had been there. Hardly a day goes by that these thoughts do not enter my mind, accompanied by a feeling that a special obligation was imposed on me, as a survivor of the Holocaust, to do whatever I could to contribute to the security and safety of my people, the Jewish people. The German murder machine aimed at exterminating the Jews of Europe had also been directed at me and my whole family, and our good fortune had been to leave while there was still time. I have attempted to focus on that obligation for most of my life, so that what happened at Rumbula, at Babi Yar, in the Warsaw ghetto, at Treblinka and Auschwitz, and at the thousands of other locations in Europe where six million Jews were murdered by the Germans and their collaborators during the Holocaust, while the world stood by, could never happen again.

TWO

Betar

I was born in Kaunas, Lithuania, on December 27, 1925. I was a year and a half old when my family moved to Riga, Latvia's capital. Until our departure for America in September 1939, when I was almost fourteen, I had grown up in Riga, which had a Jewish community of close to 50,000. The Jews of Latvia, together with a population of Russians and Germans, constituted significant minorities among the Latvian population and were treated as such by Latvian governments, which granted them autonomy in matters of culture and education.

There was no trend toward assimilation among the Jews of Riga. They considered themselves a national and cultural group apart from the local Latvian population. Growing up in Riga meant growing up Jewish, not Latvian. The Jews of Riga were Zionists, religious, Yiddishists, and communists, or else occupied by their daily concerns and not identifying with any particular political trend. My father, Tevye, came from a religious family in Dvinsk (now Daugavpils), Latvia, who were followers of the Hassidic rabbi known as the Rogatchover Rov, but he had left religion behind as he went out into the world. He was an enterprising industrialist who had established chemical factories in Lithuania and Latvia and spent much of his time in New York building a yeast factory there. My mother,

Roza, came from a nonreligious family in Kovno (now Kaunas). She was a dentist who devoted herself to social welfare activities among the poorer Jews of Riga. Neither of them had a particular political orientation. They enrolled me in the Ezra school, a school for Jewish children where the language of instruction was German. By the time I had finished grade school I had decided to join Betar, the Revisionist Zionist youth movement, led by Ze'ev Jabotinsky, which had a strong chapter in Riga. The movement, founded in Riga in 1923, advocated paramilitary training for Jewish youngsters in preparation for the tasks awaiting them in Palestine and followed the political program of the Zionist-Revisionist movement led by Jabotinsky. It was no more than an intuitive attraction at the time, which over the years turned into a rational belief in Ze'ev (Vladimir) Jabotinsky's teachings.

The outbreak of the war on September 1, 1939, and my father's cable from New York asking my mother to leave Riga immediately and join him in New York, of course changed my plans. Seven days later we were on the way to New York.

America was a new and strange world for me. As I adjusted to the new environment I decided to pursue the decision I had taken in Riga and to look for a Betar chapter in New York. In this quest I was aided by my cousin Vivian Sudarsky, who had been a member of Betar in Riga and who had come with us to America. But finding Betar in New York was no simple matter. Who had ever heard of it, and who could steer us in the right direction? The New York *Daily News* in those days carried a column where readers' questions were answered. We sent in our question—where could we locate the Zionist-Revisionist youth organization Betar?—and the paper published a reply that directed us to Rabbi Louis I. Newman of the Reform Rodeph Sholom Synagogue in New York. Rabbi Newman, who had been a supporter of Jabotinsky, gave us the address of the offices of the Zionist-Revisionist organization in New York. It was located in small, dingy quarters on Lower Broadway. There we were told that a branch (*ken*) of Betar was located in the East Bronx. One Sunday my cousin and I, traveling by subway and on a succession of trolley cars, made the two-hour journey from Upper Manhattan to the Bronx ken of Betar. There we met a few dozen young people dressed in the American version of the Betar uniform—khaki rather than brown—doing close-order drill and singing Hebrew songs. We learned that there was another branch in

Brooklyn, but despite these two kens, the movement was no more than a small speck on the American Jewish landscape: Jabotinsky's Zionist-Revisionist movement had not made serious inroads into the American Jewish community, which in any case was largely non-Zionist at the time. The American Zionist Federation, led by the Supreme Court justice Louis D. Brandeis, at one time had had some popular support and wielded influence in the world Zionist movement. After the First World War the federation was part of the Zionist delegation to the Versailles Peace Conference. But the world Zionist leadership, led by Chaim Weizmann, did not find a common language with their American counterparts. With Brandeis and most of his associates in the American Zionist leadership being at odds with Weizmann, they ceased being active Zionists. The Zionist Organization of America, led by Rabbi Stephen S. Wise and now associated with the General Zionists in world Zionist forums, did cooperate with Weizmann, but it gradually lost the position of influence that American Zionists had had in the days of Brandeis (the General Zionists were a center-right Zionist movement that took its place between the socialist Zionists and the Religious Zionists in the World Zionist Organization). Jabotinsky, who had served on the World Zionist Executive after the First World War, established the Zionist-Revisionist movement in 1925. Although he visited the United States twice in the following years, he did not succeed in mobilizing a significant following there.

Toward the end of 1939 Aaron Propes arrived in New York. He had been one of the founding members of Betar in Riga in the wake of Jabotinsky's visit there in 1923. Jabotinsky would refer to him as the "first Betari." From Riga Propes had gone to Poland to lead the Polish Betar movement. Under his leadership Betar became the largest Zionist youth movement in Poland, numbering more than 70,000 members. What I did not know at the time was that in 1938 Propes had been replaced by Menachem Begin as leader of the Polish Betar, in response to pressure from the membership seeking a more militant approach in coordination with the Irgun underground then operating in Palestine. He had gone on to Romania and from there to Palestine. He was arrested by the British on arrival and released on condition that he leave the country. Now he had come to America.

War was raging in Europe. The occupation of Poland by the Germans and the Soviets had effectively brought an end to the activities of Betar there. Propes was now charged by Jabotinsky with building a large Betar movement in America that could take the place of what had been lost in Europe.

A meeting was called at a New York hotel to greet Propes on his arrival in America. A few hundred members of Betar and Zionist-Revisionist supporters came to listen to him with great expectations. He appeared in the brown Betar uniform and addressed the audience in Yiddish. He was soon going to learn how different America was from Europe, and how difficult the task that he had set for himself was. He would shortly learn English and begin his adjustment to the American scene. Part of that adjustment was his decision to organize a children's summer camp on the American model. It was to be a source of income and, hopefully, a training ground for youngsters who would join Betar. The first such camp was Camp Betar, held in Hunter in upstate New York in the summer of 1940. Some 200 families registered their children for the camp. I and some other members of Betar served as camp counselors and service personnel. The surroundings were great and the camp was a lot of fun.

In the summer of 1940 Hitler's armies seemed to be unstoppable. German and Soviet conquests had almost completely destroyed Jabotinsky's great youth movement. In Palestine the Zionist-Revisionist movement was split between the supporters of David Raziel, the commander of the Irgun, who advocated a cease-fire in the war against British rule in Palestine for the duration of the war, and Raziel's deputy, Avraham Stern, who insisted that the struggle against British rule must continue. The campers, including me, were barely cognizant of these world-shaking events. The camp was visited by refugees from Europe, Revisionists who had succeeded in escaping to America and found in this children's camp a temporary home away from home on the weekends. We, the youngsters, could observe their heated late-night discussions in Russian, German, and Hebrew. On occasion the camp was visited by a few Hebrew-speaking young men, the Irgun delegation that had been sent by Raziel to America. Of course they knew of the split in the movement in Palestine. Propes, fully aware of what was happening—receiving letters from Europe and Palestine with the latest news, meeting the Irgun emissaries—nevertheless found the inner strength to manage a children's camp that summer, which he was proud to show to Jabotinsky, who had arrived in New York in March.

Jabotinsky had traveled from London with Colonel John Patterson, who had commanded the Jewish Legion in World War I, to launch a campaign for the establishment of a Jewish army to participate in the war against Germany. In Manhattan Center, a building on West Thirty-Fourth Street, this great orator gave his last major speech to a mass audience. His adherents and admirers wanted to believe that he would succeed with the Jewish army, as he had twenty-three years earlier when he organized the Jewish Legion. But his health was failing. The last six months had brought him endless disappointments: Germany's victories, the blows to European Jewry, the destruction of his movement in Europe, the split in the ranks of the Irgun in Palestine. He had no doubt that Germany was going to be defeated and he was convinced that a Jewish army had to participate in the war. On his second visit to Camp Betar, in August, he arrived from New York City toward evening. After reviewing a line of campers in their Betar uniforms, he asked to retire to his room, where he collapsed and died of a heart attack.

In camp we stood guard over his body, which was covered with the Zionist flag, now the flag of the State of Israel. The next day we accompanied his casket to a funeral parlor on Second Avenue in New York, and went on to the funeral, attended by tens of thousands, at New Montefiore Cemetery in Queens. The sad news went out to all corners of the world: Jabotinsky was no more.

Camp Betar was in mourning. The Zionist flag flew at half-mast and we attached black ribbons to our Betar uniforms. Yet only many years later did I really understand the full impact of the death of Ze'ev Jabotinsky on his movement, the movement he had founded and led. He had taken it out of the World Zionist Organization, in protest against the leadership's readiness to accept the policy of the British government, which was constantly retreating from its obligation to the Zionists. Now it was isolated, adrift, without a recognized heir to the leadership role. He had been such a towering figure that nobody dared assume the mantle of leadership after his death.

His followers in Palestine, in war-torn Europe, in America, looked for ways to implement his teachings without his guidance, on which they had relied in the past. The first to continue the task that Jabotinsky had begun were the Irgun emissaries who had come to America at the beginning of the war, led by Hillel Kook (calling himself Peter Bergson). Aided by Arye Ben-Eliezer, Yitzhak Ben-Ami, Alex Rafaeli, Shmuel Merlin, and some of Jabotinsky's American followers, they created the Committee for a Jewish Army, which was shortly joined by many public personalities. Quickly learning the English language and appealing to the American public by the use of full-page ads in the press, within months they mobilized considerable support for the establishment of a Jewish army. We, the youngsters in the American Betar, watched with admiration the impressive efforts of these newly arrived Palestinian young men, and dreamed of becoming soldiers in the Jewish army.

But that summer, at the camp, something new was added to the daily routine: a course for the more mature members of Betar to be trained as instructors, if they were found qualified to be accepted. I was the youngest to qualify. The instructors' course was led by Yirmiyahu (Irma) Halperin, a legendary figure in the Betar hierarchy. He had organized a self-defense unit in Tel Aviv in the days of the Arab riots in the 1930s, had run Betar instructors' courses in Europe, and had commanded the Betar Naval Academy in Civitavecchia, Italy. He arrived in America shortly before Jabotinsky's death, as a third mate on a merchant ship crossing the Atlantic. At Jabotinsky's funeral he wore a naval captain's uniform of his own design. He was a picturesque character and a hard taskmaster, insisting on close-order drill, teaching infantry maneuvers with wooden guns, Morse code, and semaphore communications, giving lectures on Jewish and Zionist history, and above all, stressing punctuality and exactness—that was our daily routine for two weeks until we graduated as "instructors."

In the fall it was back to high school and Betar activities in the city. The following summer, 1941, Camp Betar was moved to Bloomingburg in the Catskill Mountains. That was the summer when the Germans invaded the Soviet Union and began the mass murder of Jews in the areas under their control. Not only were we in the camp unaware of what was happening to the Jewish people of Europe, but the whole free world seemed to have no inkling that hundreds of thousands were being murdered every month. Only a year later did the world begin to learn the truth about the German campaign to exterminate the Jewish people. And that news was treated with a considerable measure of indifference.

On December 7, 1941, the Japanese attacked Pearl Harbor, and President Franklin Roosevelt declared war against Japan and joined the war against the Germans. Young men were being conscripted into the U.S. armed forces, and so, one by one, the older boys in Betar departed for military service. Propes was left with the girls and youngsters, like me, who were not yet eighteen, to continue Betar activities in New York.

Toward the end of 1942 I began to comprehend the tragedy of the destruction of European Jewry. News was arriving from Europe, confirming the sporadic reports received earlier that had mostly been treated with skepticism, of the mass killings of the Jews in German-occupied Europe. The Irgun delegation switched its activities from calling for the establishment of a Jewish army to drawing attention to the fate of European Jewry and demanding that emergency rescue actions be taken. The Emergency Committee to Save the Jewish People of Europe, organized by them, enlisted the support of many prominent Americans, Jews and non-Jews. On March 9, 1943, the Emergency Committee presented a pageant entitled *We Will Never Die* in Madison Square Garden before an audience of 40,000. It had been staged by Ben Hecht, Billy Rose, Moss Hart, and Kurt Weill, outstanding American theater personalities. The participating actors included Paul Muni, Paul Henreid, Edward G. Robinson, and Stella Adler. After New York the pageant went on tour in the major cities of America. Accompanied by an energetic publicity campaign, it aroused awareness of the ongoing murder of Europe's Jews, but it took many months before any concrete results were to be obtained.

I graduated high school in February 1943 and had been accepted by the Massachusetts Institute of Technology to study engineering. Studies there had been accelerated to a three-semester-a-year tempo because of the war, with the first semester to begin in June. So as I awaited the beginning of my first MIT semester I spent a semester taking courses at the City College of New York. Once I started at MIT, I was away from Betar activities in New York, but I followed the campaign of the Emergency Committee, which had a chapter in Boston. I applied myself to my studies until I was called up for army service in August 1944.

From the induction center at Fort Dix I was dispatched to the infantry replacement training center in Camp Joseph T. Robinson, near Little Rock, Arkansas. Infantry replacement training centers were part of the

U.S. Army's plan to train replacements for infantry divisions whose ranks had been thinned by casualties sustained in combat. But by August 1944 the war was going well and it seemed doubtful that we, undergoing four tough months of infantry basic training, would actually see combat in Europe. A month before completing the scheduled training I received orders to report to an army unit at Pennsylvania State University, in State College, Pennsylvania, to resume my engineering studies as a soldier. This was part of a reconstituted Army Specialized Training Program, which had been set up to ensure adequate professional manpower for the United States in times of war or peace. The program had been abandoned some months earlier as the need for combat soldiers increased, and those in the program had been pulled from their studies and put into frontline units. Now it seemed that that need had passed.

But the Battle of the Bulge, the surprise German attack through the Ardennes Forest, which started in December 1944, changed everything. A week after I had been sent to Pennsylvania State University my unit at Camp Robinson was shipped off to Europe, without having completed the full training schedule, to be thrown in as replacements for the Ninety-Ninth Infantry Division, which attempted to stem the German advance and sustained heavy casualties, including among the replacement troops. It was pure chance that I did not share the fate of my comrades with whom I had trained.

In June, after the German surrender, I completed the army version of an accelerated engineering course, was transferred to the Army Corps of Engineers, and was shipped off to the 1507th Army Engineer Water Supply Company, stationed at Camp Shelby, Mississippi. The army authorities evidently believed that my engineering training would come in handy in this assignment, but it turned out to be completely irrelevant to my duties there. Camp Shelby was hot and humid—the soldiers stationed there called it "the asshole of the world." The company that I joined had just returned from an extended stay in Persia and was now preparing for the planned attack on Japan.

By now, the summer of 1945, the army was beginning to discharge soldiers who had had many years of service. The senior personnel of the company had been in service since the beginning of the United States' entry into the war and were entitled to go home. As they left, opportunities for promotion opened up for the newcomers. The result was a meteoric rise in the ranks for me. Within a few months, after a series of promotions, I rose to the rank of technical sergeant, at that time the second-highest noncommissioned rank in the U.S. Army. At the age of twenty I may have been the youngest soldier in the army to hold that rank.

The army was preparing for the final onslaught against the Japanese—the invasion of mainland Japan. My unit was to take part in this grand battle. But unbeknownst to the generals planning the invasion, scientists in New Mexico were putting the finishing touches on the atom bomb.

By August we were ready to head for Japan. Having received my last furlough to see my family, I was returning by bus to Camp Shelby when I heard on the bus radio that the atom bomb had been dropped on Hiroshima. I realized that the invasion of Japan would be canceled. Less than a month later Japan surrendered and the war was over.

It took another nine months before it was my turn to be discharged. The day after my discharge at Fort Dix, on June 30, 1946, I reported for duty to Aaron Propes at the Betar office in New York.

THREE

The Irgun

World War II was over and the Irgun's revolt against British rule in Palestine was going full force. For over two years now the Irgun and the Stern Groups had been attacking British installations in Palestine almost every week. No sooner had I been discharged from the U.S. Army than I was asked to join the Irgun, which had decided to organize secret cells outside Palestine and had now begun to function in America. I was duly sworn in, my hand on the Bible and a pistol. My first commander was Yosef Hakim, who had been active in the Irgun in Palestine in the late thirties, had been captured by the British, tortured, and released on condition that he leave the country. That is how he arrived in New York. Now he had been called back to active service. He was a dark, mysterious figure. His family hailed from Sudan. He fitted what I had imagined an Irgun fighter to look like. I went through a short course in the use of small arms, although it was not clear to me just what missions would be entrusted to me.

By September 1946 I was back at MIT to complete my engineering studies. I took a heavy course load so as to graduate as quickly as possible and received my engineering degree a year later, in September 1947. While in Boston I organized a local Betar branch and also inducted some of its members into the Irgun.

The Irgun delegation in America, headed by Hillel Kook, was doing a very effective job of supporting the underground in Palestine and promoting the establishment of what they called a "Hebrew" state in Palestine. In an attempt to gain the support of the American Jewish community, the delegation had decided to use a terminology that differentiated between what they began calling the "Hebrews" in Palestine and the "Jews" of America. This presumably was intended to make it easier for American Jews to lend their support for the struggle to establish a state in Palestine without in any way being associated with another nation that was taking shape in Palestine. This artifice was not only ideologically problematic but also turned out to be useless. As Israel, the Jewish state, was established and fought for its independence and survival, it enjoyed the support of the vast majority of American Jewry. No artificial divide between "Hebrews" and "Jews" needed to be created to arouse and sustain this support. We in Betar, just like those in the rest of the Zionist movement in America, believing in the unity of the Jewish people, rejected this divisive tactic that Kook had adopted. We found ourselves at odds on this issue with the American League for a Free Palestine and with the Hebrew Committee of National Liberation, which Kook and his people had established.

Differences of opinion between the Irgun leadership in Palestine and Kook and his organization in America regarding the distribution of the funds collected in America—most of which were going to fund the activities of the American League and the Hebrew Committee, which had established an "embassy" in Washington—resulted in the Irgun's dispatching of an Irgun emissary to New York with the task of raising funds specifically for the Irgun in Palestine. Yisrael Lifshitz, a member of Betar in South Africa, who had visited Palestine and met Begin, was entrusted with this task. In New York he established the Palestine Resistance Committee (PRC). Although we were not fully aware at the time of the differences that had sprung up between the Irgun in Palestine and Kook and his people, we saw Lifshitz as our direct line to the Irgun in Palestine, and went to work raising funds for the PRC.

In February 1947, under the pressure of the blows that Britain had suffered from the attacks of the underground, the British foreign secretary, Ernest Bevin, decided to turn the Palestine problem over to the United Nations. In May 1947 the UN General Assembly established the United

Nations Special Committee on Palestine (UNSCOP), which in September 1947 recommended that the Palestine Mandate be terminated and that Palestine be granted independence. The majority of the UN Special Committee members recommended that Palestine be partitioned into independent Jewish and Arab states. After deliberations the Jewish Agency decided to accept partition of Palestine as recommended by UNSCOP, even though the area assigned to the Jewish state was a truncated and disjointed part of western Palestine. The Arabs rejected the proposal. On November 29, 1947, the UN General Assembly decided on the establishment of a Jewish state and an Arab state in Palestine. The Jewish Agency, led by David Ben-Gurion, accepted the UN decision, while the Arabs rejected it.

The Irgun denounced the partition of Palestine, insisting that all of western Palestine should be allocated to the Jewish state. We in the American Betar naturally followed the Irgun line. Palestine had already been partitioned once in 1922, when the Churchill White Paper closed the east bank of the Jordan to Jewish settlement. Then, 78 percent of the area allocated by the League of Nations to Britain for the establishment of a Jewish state had been handed to Abdullah, the son of Sharif Hussein bin Ali. One partition was enough for us. In any case, the Irgun expressed great doubt as to whether Britain really intended to leave Palestine. As far as we were concerned the battle for a Jewish state in Palestine continued, and we claimed the right to all of the area west of the Jordan River. Unlike most of the Zionist movement, for us November 29, 1947, was not a day of rejoicing, since it involved the agreement by the official Zionist bodies to another partition of Palestine.

I had expected to leave for Palestine after graduating from MIT, but at the national Betar assembly in September 1947 I was elected to be the head of Betar in the United States; I was to spend the next twelve months in that post. Aaron Propes had decided to return to Europe and devote himself to organizing the remnants of the Betar movement that had survived the Holocaust. And so it fell to me to lead the Betar movement in America.

Leaving my engineering training behind, I threw myself into the task, aided by six excellent members of the executive who over the years became my close friends. Seymour (Simha) Rosenberg had been my first superior when I joined the ranks of Betar in the Bronx, shortly after arriving in America. He had served with the infantry in Italy, had reported to Propes on being discharged from the U.S. Army, and was now studying economics at City College of New York. Martin (Marty) Marden had been a member of the Bronx chapter, or *ken*, before the war, had served in Europe with an armored division, and had risen to the rank of captain. Yishayahu (Sy) Warsaw, the oldest among us, had served with the First Cavalry Division (dismounted) in the South Pacific. Ray Kaplan had been in a navy program during the war and was studying at MIT when we first met. We were both living in the barracks assigned to students who were veterans of the armed forces. No sooner had I made his acquaintance than I tried to talk him into joining Betar, giving him the pamphlet *This Is Betar* to read. He immediately sat down on the floor—there was a shortage of furniture in the barracks—and read it through. When he was finished reading he told me he was prepared to join Betar, and he joined the Boston ken that I had formed. On graduating from MIT he joined the executive in New York. The other members of the executive were David (Smitty) Smith, who was a student at Yeshiva College in New York and headed the Betar chapter there, and Dave Krakow. Krakow had joined Betar during the war and had kept things going while we were in the army—he eventually became my brother-in-law.

Our aim was first and foremost to recruit Jewish youngsters to our ranks and educate them in activist Zionism, and to prepare the older ones for aliyah (literally, "going up") to Palestine. By the time I had completed my tenure as head of the American Betar we had more than 1,000 members—some ten branches in New York City and branches in Boston, Philadelphia, Pittsburgh, Cleveland, Detroit, and San Francisco. It was a modest beginning, considering our ambitious goal to create a mass youth movement in America. Our thoughts were with the fighters of the underground in Palestine risking their lives attacking British targets in Palestine, with those who had been sentenced to death on the gallows by the British, and with the many others who were languishing in British prisons in Palestine or had been exiled to concentration camps in Africa. We were out in the streets demonstrating against British rule in Palestine, calling for a boycott of British goods, "invading" British consulates, and collecting money and weapons for the Irgun.

After the UN's partition resolution, fighting broke out in Palestine, with local Arab militias attacking Jewish traffic on the roads. It was the beginning of Israel's War of Independence. At the beginning of 1948 it was clear that the coming year was going to be critical for the future of the Jewish people and the Jewish state. All available forces would have to be mobilized to participate in the fighting in Palestine, which was becoming increasingly ferocious. Of course the American Betar would have to do its part and send members to Palestine to join the Irgun. The first American Betari to leave for Palestine, in June 1946, was Moshe Brodetzky. He had been an infantry officer in Europe, had been wounded during the fighting as the U.S. Army entered Germany, and had been awarded the Silver Star for gallantry in action. Shortly after being discharged he decided to avail himself of the GI Bill's provision of free education at a school of the veteran's choice, and matriculated at the Hebrew University in Jerusalem to study agriculture. Not long after his arrival in Jerusalem he joined the Irgun.

The Jewish Agency had set up a recruiting office in New York under the code name "Land and Labor," headed by Teddy Kollek, and provided transportation and certificates for entry to Palestine for volunteers. We had no problem using their good offices for transportation to Palestine, and they seemed to have no problem in assisting us, even though they knew of our political orientation.

Our first group was led by Ray Kaplan and included my future wife, Muriel Eisenberg. Of the group of twenty from Betar who were supposed to board the SS *Marine Carp* leaving New York for Haifa on May 5, 1948, about five backed out at the last minute. The group was to be contacted by an Irgun representative at the Haifa dock on arrival. All this was arranged through secret channels by the Irgun representative in New York, for Palestine at the time was still under British rule, and the Irgun was an underground organization. On May 15, while the *Marine Carp* was at sea, the British departed from Palestine and David Ben-Gurion proclaimed the Declaration of Independence of the State of Israel. On the *Marine Carp*, returning Israelis and American volunteers celebrated the birth of the Jewish state.

But as the boat docked in Beirut on its way to Haifa, the Lebanese army boarded the boat, ordered all males headed for Haifa off the boat, and transported them to a prison camp in Baalbek. The Betar girls arrived in Haifa the following day. For reasons not clear to this day, no one from the Irgun was there to greet the two girls. The boys who had been forcibly taken off the boat in Beirut harbor were released after five weeks of internment on condition that they return to the United States.

The next group we sent went on a vessel called *Altalena* and included two members of the American Betar Executive, Sy Warsaw and Dave (Smitty) Smith. The *Altalena*, a U.S. Navy wartime LST (landing ship tank), had been bought by the American League for a Free Palestine (the Irgun delegation in the United States) and was captained by Monroe Fine, an American volunteer who had been an LST commander in the Pacific. The Irgun in Europe had assembled a considerable stock of arms in France, some with the assistance of the French government, which were loaded onto the *Altalena* while it was docked in Port de Bouc, near Marseille. There, some 900 Irgun members, many survivors of the Holocaust, boarded the boat expecting to participate in Israel's War of Independence on arrival in Israel. The ship had been purchased in the United States in 1947 and had sailed for Europe, where it had awaited the arrival of the arms that had been assembled and the Irgun fighters before sailing for Israel. It departed Port de Bouc on June 11, 1948, and arrived at Kfar Vitkin, a beach village not far from Tel Aviv, on June 20, as had been agreed in negotiations between the Irgun and a representative of Israel's provisional government.

Two weeks earlier, the Irgun forces had been integrated into the Israel Defense Forces (IDF), except for those in Jerusalem, where the Irgun continued to operate independently but coordinated its activities with the IDF commander of the area. A UN-declared truce in the fighting between the IDF and the invading Arab armies had gone into force on June 11, the day the *Altalena* left France. Disregarding the earlier agreements and the urgent need for fighters and weapons to reinforce the Israeli troops in their battle against the invading Arab armies, Ben-Gurion, the prime minister of the provisional government, gave orders to surround those landing at Kfar Vitkin and to seize the arms that had already been unloaded. Menachem Begin boarded the *Altalena* at Kfar Vitkin and ordered the ship to continue on to Tel Aviv, expecting that the ship would not be attacked there. But Ben-Gurion gave orders to shell the *Altalena* as it stood off Tel Aviv. It was destroyed by artillery fire, and those who had to abandon the ship and were swimming toward the beach were fired on from the shore. Ben-Gurion insisted that he acted to prevent a coup d'état that he claimed Begin was trying to organize, although there is not a shred of evidence to support this claim. He used the opportunity that presented itself in order to attempt to liquidate the political opposition led by Begin.

All of the American Betar members on the *Altalena* managed to get ashore unharmed, and most of them joined the Irgun in Jerusalem and participated in the fighting there.

To many it was inconceivable that the Ben-Gurion government would give orders to fire on the *Altalena*. After we in New York received news reports of what had happened we looked for a means to demonstrate our protest at what seemed to us a criminal act committed against reinforcements that had arrived at a critical hour in Israel's War of Independence. After a demonstration in front of the offices of the Jewish Agency in New York, some of us forced our way into the offices, where we found Abba Eban, at the time a Jewish Agency emissary to the United Nations. He seemed to be as puzzled as we about the turn of events in Israel. In any case he was unable to give us an explanation nor was he prepared to offer excuses, and we left as we had come, having vented our anger but having achieved nothing.

Despite the *Altalena* incident we decided to send a third group to Israel. They left New York on a small navy surplus LCVP (landing craft, vehicle, personnel) craft that was owned by a former member of Betar from Belgium, who agreed to take the Betarim at no charge on condition that they supplement the crew on board. That little ship barely made it across the Atlantic, but finally put in at Marseille. There the Betar volunteers, assisted by the Jewish Agency, were sent on to Israel. By the time they arrived, the Irgun had ceased to exist as a fighting unit in Israel, and they joined the IDF.

In September 1948 I completed my one-year tenure as head of Betar in the United States. At the annual Betar convention, held in Pittsfield, Massachusetts, we elected Seymour Rosenberg to take my place, and I was free to go to Israel and join the ranks of the Irgun. My travel arrangements were made by Yisrael Lifshitz, who was the Irgun representative in

New York. I crossed the Atlantic on the Cunard passenger liner RMS *Mauretania*, landing at Southampton, and arrived in Paris in the middle of September, with instructions to report to Eli Tavin, the commander of the Irgun in the Diaspora. When I left New York I expected to join the Irgun forces in Jerusalem on reaching Israel, but by the time I arrived in Paris, the Irgun in Jerusalem had given in to an ultimatum from the provisional government to disband within twenty-four hours, and it did so on September 21.

The morning after I arrived in Paris, I reported to Eli Tavin. He had offices on 18 Avenue de Messine, an imposing building that had been acquired by the Hebrew Committee of National Liberation when some of its leaders established themselves in Paris after the UN partition resolution of November 1947. When they left for Israel after the establishment of the state, Tavin inherited their sumptuous quarters. From there he directed the activities of the Irgun forces in Europe.

"I need you here for our activities in Europe," he told me. "The Irgun in Israel has been disbanded and is now a political party, Herut, but the Irgun in Europe is continuing its activities. We will send you to Israel for two weeks and you will get to know our people there and then you will return to Paris for further orders." Stunned by this turn of events, I did not ask why the Irgun continued to function in Europe when it had been disbanded in Israel, but seeing myself as an Irgun soldier now under Tavin's orders I obeyed what I took to be a command from him, who was now my superior. Later I learned that the continued operation of the Irgun in Europe became a subject of discussion between Tavin and the Irgun leadership in Israel, one that eventually led to the cessation of Irgun activities in Europe.

Eli Tavin had become a legendary character in the Irgun. A graduate of the philosophy department at the Hebrew University of Jerusalem, he had been in charge of the intelligence section of the Irgun. Tavin was kidnapped in February 1945 by members of the Haganah, acting on orders of the Jewish Agency leadership in Palestine, which at the time was pursuing a policy of cooperating with the British in their attempt to suppress the Irgun. The Haganah, the official Jewish defense organization in Palestine at the time, engaged in the kidnapping of members of the Irgun. Tavin was tortured and held captive in a kibbutz, chained to a bed for months.

His release was a precondition set by the Irgun for the formation of the united resistance movement, Tnuat Hameri, in October 1945. This group, which included the Haganah, the Irgun, and the Stern Group, engaged in combined military actions against British rule in Palestine. Upon his release in September 1945, Tavin was spirited out of Palestine to Italy. There he took charge of the Irgun operation that led to the bombing of the British embassy in Rome in October 1946. From Rome he moved to Paris, where he commanded Irgun operations in Europe. His soldiers were primarily Holocaust survivors who had been members of Betar before the war, assisted by instructors sent by the Irgun in Palestine.

During my stay in Paris, awaiting transportation to Israel, I attended a convention of the European Betar. It was my first opportunity to meet members of our movement who had survived the Holocaust or who had managed to escape from the Soviet Union. It was a moving experience. In halting Yiddish I was able to communicate with them, and even address the gathering. Their leader was Gidon Abramowich, who had arrived in Europe as a soldier in the Jewish Brigade. Abramowich had given his documents to a survivor who used them to go to Israel, while he stayed in Europe and devoted himself to reviving the Betar movement there. He was their leader, and most of them referred to themselves as "Gidon's men." To my disappointment I found that a split had developed between those who had been recruited from their ranks by the Irgun, accepting the Irgun leadership, to whom they had now sworn loyalty, and the rest of the Betar movement, headed by Abramowich. Abramovich, himself a supporter of the Irgun, thought that there was no need for an additional hierarchy in the European movement, with its attendant split and rivalry. It was a recurrence of a similar situation that occurred in prewar Poland, when Irgun emissaries recruited Betar members over the objections of the official Betar leadership there, who believed that there was no need for another organization.

Overseeing the convention was Aaron Propes, who had been devoting all his time after leaving the United States to the revival of Betar in Europe. He invited me to his office at the Hôtel des Deux Mondes. There he suggested that I join the world leadership of the Betar movement. I was not sure that I deserved this honor, but explained to him that I could not possibly accept the offer as I was a member of the Irgun, under orders from Eli Tavin. Gradually my awareness grew that there was a tug-of-war going on between the Irgun and Betar: both groups were part of the Jabotinsky movement and shared the very same ideology, but they were commanded by different hierarchies. The Irgun, actually by now the Herut Party, was headed in Israel by Begin and his lieutenants and in Europe by Eli Tavin, still filling the role of an Irgun commander. Betar was headed by an old-timer, Propes, who had been a founding member of Betar in Riga in 1923. In 1938 Begin had replaced Propes as head of the Betar in Poland. Now, ten years later, as head of the Betar movement, Propes sought the recognition of Begin, the acclaimed leader of the underground, a recognition he failed to get. In the coming year this was to become clear to me. I took orders from Tavin but my heart went out to Propes.

After a few days Tavin booked me on a flight to Israel. Ever the underground operator, he had a cobbler embed a message in the heel of one of my shoes. The message was intended for Haim Landau, who had been a member of the Irgun high command and was now a senior member of Herut. The flight from Paris to Haifa was about ten hours. We landed at night. By taxi I continued my journey to Tel Aviv, where I delivered the shoe containing the message. After the heel had been replaced I went on to the Savoy Hotel, where I lodged for the rest of my stay in Israel. The Savoy was located on Hayarkon Street, near the beach. From that beach I could see the wreck of the *Altalena* offshore, a constant reminder of that terrible day when Ben-Gurion attempted to eliminate Begin and his associates.

Before I had a chance to gain a concrete impression of the Land of Israel, I already knew that it was everything I had dreamed of. I was ecstatic at every site and every view that I saw. Israel, the newborn Jewish state, had, of course, been our goal for many years, and now it was here—a dream fulfilled. But only partially. The territory under Israeli control was only a fraction of what we of the Irgun felt was rightfully ours, and we did not trust the Ben-Gurion government to complete the task of gaining control over all of the area west of the Jordan. We also felt estranged from a government that had fired on our people and made it clear that it did not trust us.

I had arrived during a truce in the fighting between the Arab armies that had invaded Israel on May 15, 1948, and the IDF. But within days of my arrival the IDF began an offensive against the Egyptian army in the south, capturing Ber Sheva on October 19. Israel had been gaining steadily against the invading Arab armies during the past few months, and in Tel Aviv the war already seemed far away. But when I went up to Jerusalem to see my comrades who had arrived on the *Altalena*, I found a city that still seemed in a stage of siege. Although the newly constructed Burma Road (Derekh Burma) from Kibbutz Hulda, in central Israel, to the city was passable, East Jerusalem, including the Old City and its Jewish quarter, were in the hands of the Jordanian Legion, and you could hear occasional gunshots. There was a feeling in the air that the truce might be broken at any moment.

Many of the Irgun soldiers in Jerusalem had not yet joined the IDF, even though the Irgun in Jerusalem had been disbanded. They were still using quarters in the Katamon neighborhood, which had served them as a base before they broke up. There I met Moshe Bodetzky, Sy Warsaw, and Dave Smith, learned of their experiences since arriving in Israel, and discussed with them our plans for the future. It was clear to us that the time had not yet come for each of us to go our own way. But what was our common way going to be?

It seemed obvious to us that as members of Betar our task had as yet not been completed with the establishment of the state. All of the Land of Israel had not yet been freed, and so it seemed that it was for us, the members of Betar, to contribute to the best of our abilities to achieve that aim. For such activity we found a convenient framework in the plans of the provisional government of Israel to establish "border settlements" that would contribute to the security of the country. Service in such settlements was considered equivalent to service in the IDF. In such a border settlement we would be facing territory that we hoped would in time become a part of the State of Israel. Such a settlement would also provide a framework to concentrate the members of the American Betar who were already in Israel and others whom we expected to arrive in the future.

At this time the Jewish Agency settlement department, headed by Levi Eshkol, allocated settlement locations to the various political parties whose youth was prepared to establish a border settlement. It had offered the newly established settlement department of the Herut Party a location in the Jerusalem Hills, on the southern border of the corridor leading from central Israel to Jerusalem, that the IDF had carved out during the fighting. Some members of the Irgun battalion in Jerusalem, which had been disbanded, declared their intention to establish a settlement in this location. I discussed this with Warsaw and Smith during my visit to Jerusalem and we concluded that joining them in the new settlement might be the opportunity we were looking for.

I drove out to see the place intended for the settlement. It was to be named Ramat Raziel after David Raziel, the man who commanded the Irgun before Begin. It was a scenic location in the mountains, some twenty kilometers from Jerusalem, near the abandoned Arab village of Dir Aban. It seemed an appropriate location for our plans. Later in Tel Aviv I arranged a gathering of members of the American Betar in Israel, discussed with them our future plans, and notified them that it was our intention to concentrate the American Betar members in Israel and those we expected to arrive in the future at the Ramat Raziel border settlement.

It was arranged for me to meet Begin. Maybe he was curious to meet me, the former head of Betar in the United States and now taking orders from Tavin in Paris. Maybe he just wanted to size me up. In any case, on the appointed day I was ushered into his office in a modern building on Tshernichowsky Street, in Tel Aviv, which had become the headquarters of the newly founded Herut movement. It was only a few months since he had left the underground. Even most members of the Irgun had never seen him in person until recently. He was the legendary commander of the underground army, called the Mefaked, "the Commander." That is how most addressed him even now that he had become a political leader. Veteran Irgun members with great exploits to their credit stood in awe of him, almost trembling in his presence.

I had one message that I wanted to transmit to him: to impress him with the activities of Betar in the United States and with my belief in the possibility of enlarging the activity of Betar there; to encourage a substantial aliyah of Betar members from the United States to Israel; and to explain the need for former Irgun members to be sent as emissaries from Israel to help Betar in the United States to achieve these goals.

Begin listened to me attentively, asking a number of questions about our movement in the United States. It was clear to me that he had been very impressed by the activities of Hillel Kook's organization, and attached only secondary importance to the activities of Betar in the United States. He probably thought that the organization that Kook and his associates had built in America could be used to support Herut as a political movement in the years to come. In this he was destined to be disappointed, for that organization fell apart after its leadership left for Israel.

In the beginning of November I flew back to Paris. Tavin's people put me up in a small hotel on Rue Lafayette named Le Grand Hotel Lafayette, and my service as an Irgun soldier in the Diaspora began. Tavin's "soldiers" used to meet for lunch at a Jewish restaurant in the Place de la République, referred to by its Irgun habitués as the "*der Pletzl*." There I met up with my comrades, some of whom were to become my close friends.

David Danon had, as a young boy, been one of the first fighters in the Irgun. He had been released from a British internment camp in Latrun when his father, a physician, obtained his release by showing the British authorities that he had been admitted to medical school in Geneva. Tavin had torn him away from his studies in Geneva and ordered him to Paris. In years to come he was to become a prominent scientist at the Weizmann Institute in Rehovot.

Louis Fogiel had survived the Holocaust together with his father and two brothers and was now in service with the Irgun under Tavin's orders. He had been a member of Betar in Belgium before the war. As the German army advanced into Belgium the family fled to France. There they were arrested and shipped off to the east. Mother and sister were separated and perished. The father and the three sons survived great hardships. Louis had been in charge of assembling the arms for the Altalena, but at Tavin's orders stayed behind as part of the team working with Tavin.

The first task Tavin assigned to me was to establish contact with a member of the Irgun, who was hiding out in London, as a first step to freeing a member of the Irgun, Monty Harris, who was serving a seven-year prison sentence in Britain. Harris had been preparing explosives in his apartment for use against military equipment that was scheduled for shipment from England to Iraq when he was arrested. He was tried and sentenced. Going to London was no problem for me with my U.S. passport. This was real cloak-and-dagger stuff. It had been arranged for me to meet "Yona," an Irgun member hiding out in London, at a London subway station. "Yona" was not at all encouraging as regards the object of my visit to London. Deciding to make another attempt, I called on Abraham Abrahams, one of the leaders of the small Zionist-Revisionist movement in Britain. I met him in his apartment in London. He was a middle-aged gentleman who obviously had no inclination to get involved in underground activity. Returning to Paris I informed Tavin that we did not seem to have the beginning of the contacts needed to get Harris out of prison.

Toward the end of December Begin, returning from a visit to America, spent a week in Paris. During that time he held lengthy consultations with Tavin and the senior personnel of the Irgun in Europe. It transpired that there had been an ongoing debate these past weeks between the former leadership of the Irgun, which was now the leadership of the Herut Party, a legal political entity in Israel, and the senior people in the Irgun in Europe, led by Tavin. Begin was of the opinion that now that the Irgun had been disbanded in Jerusalem there was no justification for continuing underground activities in Europe. Moreover, such activity might even endanger the legal status of the Herut Party in Israel. Tavin was stubbornly insisting that there was a continuing need for underground activity outside the borders of Israel, since the aims of the Irgun, the liberation of all of the Land of Israel, had not been achieved, and was unlikely to be achieved by a government led by Ben-Gurion. Obviously Begin had the final word in this matter. Tavin was ordered to cease underground activities in Europe and turn the store of weapons, including aircraft that the Irgun had acquired, over to representatives of the provisional Israeli government in Europe. For Tavin, who had been abducted by the Haganah, imprisoned and tortured for months, this was a tough pill to swallow.

Begin was now focused on Herut, the political movement he had created, and wanted to use the connections that Tavin and his people had developed in Europe in order to mobilize support for the Herut movement. One of his objectives was to gain control of the old Zionist-Revisionist establishment, especially the Betar movement. There was no love lost by the Irgun veterans for the leadership of the Zionist-Revisionist movement in Israel, which was competing with Herut in the upcoming elections in Israel, and who as far as they were concerned had made no contribution to the revolt against British rule in Palestine. Their aim now was to gain control of Betar, the youth movement. I, having headed the Betar movement in the United States, was now an asset in pursuing these plans. Without knowing it I had become a tool for an attempted takeover that I did not support.

On January 12, 1949, the Irgun in the Diaspora was officially dissolved. This act, not coincidentally, preceded the first Israeli elections held on January 25, elections in which Herut, led by Begin, participated. The election results were a disappointment to Begin and his supporters. Herut received fourteen seats in the Knesset, coming in fourth after Labor, Mapam, and the United Religious Front. From a peak of public support in May 1948, when the Irgun had emerged from the underground and launched the campaign to conquer Jaffa, their support had plummeted after the *Altalena* incident and in the wake of the success of the IDF under Ben-Gurion's leadership during the battles of the War of Independence.

Those of us reporting to Tavin were not told of the decision to dissolve the Irgun in the Diaspora. He continued his previous modus operandi, ordering me to proceed to North Africa and make contact with members of Betar there, help strengthen them, and prepare them for the possibility of having to defend the Jewish community against Arab riots. I was to be joined by David Danon, who had been ordered by Tavin to come to Paris. Now he was to proceed to North Africa with me. In time he became one of my best friends and, in later years, a prominent scientist at the Weizmann Institute of Science in Rohovot.

Our first stop was Tunis. There we found the headquarters of the Tunisian Betar and an active Betar organization, with chapters in all the towns in Tunisia that had Jewish communities. After meeting with the leadership of the Tunisian Betar and members of the Betar in Tunis, we set out to visit the Betar chapters: Sfax, Gabes, Sousse, and Mouknine. Everywhere we were welcomed as the Irgun emissaries from Israel, and all were eager to follow our instructions. On our return to Tunis I applied to the British embassy for a visa to Libya but was turned down for some reason. Leaving Danon in Tunisia I set off westward to Algeria and Morocco.

Tavin had given me some addresses in Algiers, my first stop. Only one of them seemed to be current, and at that address I found a middle-aged gentleman who seemed to have no information on a Betar organization in Algeria and could not provide me with any further leads. So I took the night train from Algiers via Oudja to Casablanca.

I had been provided with some names in the Melah, the poor Jewish quarter of Casablanca. I located two youngsters, but could make no progress when attempting to enlarge the circle. At this point I decided that I was wasting my time. I took a flight to Paris and informed Tavin that I had decided to return to Israel. He did not argue with me, and arranged for me to go to Naples where I boarded an immigrant ship bringing Libyan Jews to Israel. On landing in Haifa I took the bus to Tel Aviv, where I presented myself at the offices of the settlement department of the Herut Party. Mordehai Olmert, the head of the party's settlement department, arranged for me to join my comrades in Ramat Raziel.

FOUR

From Ramat Raziel to M'vo'ot Betar

Arriving in Ramat Raziel, I found our small group of American Betar members farming the vineyards abandoned by the former Arab inhabitants of the area. My future wife, Muriel Eisenberg, had obtained a release from the Israel Air Force under an arrangement existing at the time that membership of a border settlement was considered the equivalent of military service, and had joined the group at Ramat Raziel. The group of American Betar members was now part of a larger group of young people, most of whom had been in the Irgun in Jerusalem and had now decided to make their home in Ramat Raziel.

We took turns with members of other border settlements in the area manning military outposts on the cease-fire line. The outpost assigned to us was above Kibbutz Kiryat Anavim, facing the Jordanion Legion, which had taken up positions in what was referred to as the Radar outpost. It had housed a British radar installation in bygone days and had changed hands a number of times during the fighting, eventually ending up in Jordanian hands.

There had been a substantial change since my visit to the area in September of the previous year: Ramat Raziel, once in the line of fire, was now in the middle of the Jerusalem Corridor, a few kilometers north of the cease-fire lines that had been established after the Israel Defense Forces' (IDF) Operation Har in late October 1948, which had considerably widened the Jerusalem Corridor southward. In that operation the IDF captured the Arab villages of Bet Natif, Alar, and Ras Abu 'Ammar on the road to Bethlehem.

Ramat Raziel, by now some distance from the cease-fire lines, was hardly the ideal location for the aim we had ambitiously set for ourselves to increase the area under Israeli control. Nor did most of the settlers there share that ambition. We needed to move from there, establish ourselves as an ideologically coherent group, and find another location that would suit our plans. We named our group of Betar members from the United States and a number of others who had decided to join us Had-Ness (a single flag), after the principle enunciated by Jabotinsky, that we are devoted to one single ideal—the Jewish state.

That summer a world convention of Betar took place in Tel Aviv. Three representatives arrived from the United States—Seymour Rosenberg, Ray Kaplan, and Dave Krakow. Dave Smith, Yishayahu Warsaw, and I came down from Ramat Raziel to complement the U.S. delegation. It was to be the occasion for the Herut leadership to take over the Betar movement and replace the old guard, represented by Propes. For a while Herut had tried to establish a rival movement, named Bnei Etzel (sons of the Irgun), but it never took off; feeling the need of an allied youth movement, Herut leaders decided to take over Betar. My mind was focused on the future of our settlement group rather than the coup d'état taking place at the convention, but I was sorry to see Propes sacked. He had been in the original group in Riga, which, after hearing Jabotinsky speak, decided to form the Betar movement in 1923. Thereafter, in Poland, he had led Betar to become the largest Zionist youth organization in the country. In the United States he led Betar during the years of World War II. He was a fine man, an example of what a Betari should be. He went on to do sterling service for the State of Israel, promoting and directing large international Israeli festivals. In Betar he was missed.

While still at Ramat Raziel, Muriel and I decided to get married. On July 12, 1949, we were married on the roof of the rabbinate building in Jerusalem. Attending were all of the Had-Ness members; some of Muriel's relatives, who had come up from Tel Aviv; and Ben-Zion Netanyahu, the father of Yoni Netanyahu (who would fall in the Entebbe, Uganda, rescue mission, in 1976) and of Benjamin Netanyahu, the future Israeli prime minister. We were the first of our group to marry.

The settlement department of the Herut movement did not take kindly to our decision to leave Ramat Raziel. They were interested in strengthening Ramat Raziel and were afraid that our departure would weaken the settlement. But our minds were made up. As there was no alternate location available at the moment, we were transferred to Shuni, adjacent to the Betar moshav (cooperative community of farmers) called Nahlat Jabotinsky.

Shuni was an abandoned, decaying structure built in Ottoman times, at the foot of the Mount Carmel range, which had been used by the Irgun as a training base during the days of the underground. There we found another group waiting to put up a settlement, Bnei Zfat. They were former members of the Irgun, most of whom stemmed from the northern town of Safed. They were a fine group of young people who were easy to get along with.

Life in Shuni meant working a small vegetable garden we had planted on the shores of the Crocodile Stream in order to prepare ourselves for agricultural work, and finding day work in the area to make enough money to sustain ourselves. That entailed competing in the job market in Binyamina, such as it was, which was run by Kobo, a Georgian, who was the "boss" of the workers' organization, Histadrut. He was to be found in the local Histadrut labor exchange every evening, sitting behind a desk and assigning work for the next morning to those lucky enough to draw his attention among the crowd who thronged around his office seeking work for the next day. The available work was house help for the more wealthy housewives in Binyamina, picking oranges in the orange groves, and working on the gravesite of Baron Rothschild on a nearby hill.

Not far from Shuni there was a stone quarry operated by the Histadrut construction company Solel Boneh. At the time they were in the process of assembling new quarrying equipment from parts that had been shipped from abroad. I managed to land a job there working together with a large number of unskilled workers engaged in assembling the new quarry equipment. The parts for the equipment had arrived together with blueprints with instructions for the assembly. Here was an opportunity for me to demonstrate my skills as a graduate engineer. To the amazement of the other laborers, who thought that I was an unskilled worker like them, I read the blueprints and showed the others how the parts were to be assembled. In no time I had become an essential worker in this Histadrut enterprise. Each morning everyone waited for my instructions on how the different parts of the equipment were to be assembled.

While we were in Shuni, negotiations were going on between our Betar group, the Jewish Agency settlement department, and the settlement section of the Herut Party regarding the location where our settlement was going to be established. Among the locations that were offered to us was Mishmar Hayarden, a settlement that had been destroyed when it was overrun by the Syrian army during the War of Independence. It had come under Israeli control as part of the Israeli-Syrian armistice agreement of 1949. Its members had been members of the Zionist-Revisionist movement, so it seemed appropriate to all that we should be chosen as the group to resettle the place.

But we had different ideas. Mishmar Hayarden was located on the border with Syria, an internationally recognized border, and at the time we had no ambition to move that border eastward. So we turned down the offer; it was accepted by the group of Bnei Zfat with whom we had shared our quarters in Shuni. We insisted on a location that was astride the Israeli-Jordanian armistice line of 1949, in the expectation that from there we might be instrumental in moving forward and thus enlarging the area under Israeli control. Two of our members, Yishayahu Warsaw and Moshe Brodetzky, had discovered just such a location while patrolling the Judean Hills during our stay in Ramat Raziel. It was an abandoned Arab village, Ras Abu 'Ammar, sitting practically on the armistice line. It faced the Arab villages of Wadi Fukin and Hussan, in territory controlled by the Jordanian army, on the road leading to Bethlehem. What's more, it was only a few kilometers from the ancient fortress of Betar, where Bar Kochba had made his last stand in the second revolt against the Romans in A.D. 135. Not far from the ruins of ancient Betar was the Arab village of Batir, now bisected by the armistice line. Nothing could have been symbolically more suitable as a settlement site for a Betar group.

The approval of the Jewish Agency, which had retained its authority over all agricultural settlement activities after the establishment of the State of Israel, was required, and initially it did not approve of our choice;

only after weeks of negotiations did we obtain their agreement. The name we chose was M'vo'ot Betar, literally, "the approaches to Betar." Here, too, an argument ensued with the Jewish Agency, which seemed to be eager to demonstrate its authority. It was no more than an ego contest among unequals. Eventually the Agency was prepared to settle for the name M'vo Betar, meaning "approach to Betar," the settlement's actual current name. But among ourselves we continued to use the name we had chosen.

In the winter of 1950, while we were already in preparation for moving to our new settlement, Israel was hit with the worst snowstorm the region had seen in decades. In February we had heavy snows in the Binyamina area. The immigrant tent camp that had been set up on the road leading from Shuni to Zichron Yaakov, one of many that dotted the Israeli landscape at the time, was snowed in and inundated. It was a chance for us to come to the assistance of the distraught immigrants, whose tents had collapsed around them. We shoveled snow, put up tents, and assisted in any way we could; we felt that we were doing our bit in helping absorb the great aliyah that was arriving in Israel in those days.

April was the month chosen for us to make the move to M'vo'ot Betar. But before leaving Shuni I had a surprising job offer. The manager of the quarry, who had evidently been impressed by my technical talents, offered me a position as work supervisor of the quarry. The offer included a small house in the workers' quarter of Binyamina and advice to stay away from the "crazy" group in Shuni. He was surprised when I turned him down flat. I told him that I had other plans.

In April we loaded all our belongings, which now included a cow I had purchased in Karkur, onto one truck, while we traveled in a second truck, and we were on our way to the Judean Hills to found the settlement of M'vo'ot Betar.

It was a tortuous road that wound past Har Tuv, the moshav abandoned during the War of Independence; the Tegart fortress, built during the days of the British mandate, which was already serving the Israeli police; the abandoned Arab village of Dir Aban, now the city of Bet Shemesh; and on to the Catholic monastery of Bet Jimal. From the monastery the winding road passed the abandoned Arab village of Zakariyya, now the moshav Zacharya, and from there entered the Valley of Elah, where David slew Goliath. Through the valley, the road continued past Kibbutz Netiv

HaLamed Hey (named after the "thirty-five" who had rushed to the rescue of beleaguered Gush Etzion and were killed in an encounter with thousands of local Arabs), which recently had been settled by a group of veterans of the Palmah, the elite Haganah brigades. Leaving the kibbutz behind, we began the climb along a narrow unpaved road, originally a Roman road, our trucks negotiating the steep climb with some difficulty, until we finally reached the top of the mountain range at an altitude of about 800 meters. There the road led to our new home. It was a three-hour trip. We were the only vehicles on this lonely route.

We were greeted by an IDF platoon that had been guarding the area and was already all packed up to leave now that we had arrived. We were issued rifles, two mortars, a light machine gun, and ammunition, and received an orientation lecture from the second lieutenant in command. Standing on the road to Bethlehem, from which we could see the nearby Arab villages of Wadi Fukin and Hussan, he pointed out a carob tree about 100 meters to the south. "If you draw an imaginary line from that tree to the lime pit"—it could be seen about 200 meters to the east—"that is the armistice line," the second lieutenant said. "It delineates the areas under Israeli control from the areas under Jordanian control."

I looked around at our new home. Barren hills and rocks all over the place. In the distance, to the south, on the horizon I could make out the buildings of Massuot Yitzhak, one of the four settlements in the Gush Etzion settlement block that had been captured by the Jordanian army during the War of Independence, days before the establishment of the State of Israel. I could also see the famous oak tree that became a symbol of the Gush Etzion settlement block, lost during the war.

And then the IDF platoon took off, leaving us in charge. We had just enough time to distribute the rifles, pitch our tents, dig two latrines, post guards on the perimeter, and get ourselves settled before the sun set.

In the following weeks the Jewish Agency settlement department supplied us with some of the basic elements of a functioning agricultural settlement: a tractor and trailer, a chicken coop, seedlings for a vegetable garden, and beds to sleep on in our tents.

We were a small group composed of members of Betar from the United States, their Israeli girlfriends, and others who, attracted by our ideas, had joined us. Less than twenty, we were too few to man this outpost and simultaneously begin building our settlement. We were hoping to receive reinforcements from America, but they were slow in coming. Before we had a chance to take stock of the need for additional members we received a reminder of the dangers surrounding us.

We had no running water in the settlement, so we brought water up from the spring at the abandoned Arab village of Ras Abu 'Ammar, about a kilometer from our tent camp. Every morning two of us drove the tractor, pulling the trailer, down to the spring, filled a large container mounted on the tractor, and returned with our daily ration of water. For security the tractor driver was armed with a rifle and was accompanied by another armed member riding shotgun. One morning the tractor did not return from the trip to the spring, and we heard rifle shots from the area of the spring. I rushed down to the spring, and as I approached I could see the tractor and hear its engine, still running, but nobody was manning the tractor. Coming closer I saw one of the youngsters who had joined our group and had accompanied the tractor that morning. He lay on the ground, lifeless, his rifle gone. The driver was nowhere to be seen. My attempt to track down the assailants failed. They had evidently left the scene in a hurry, taking with them the driver. I expected that they would have fled southward, toward the armistice line.

The boy who was killed that day was seventeen-year-old Yoel Yehuda Potpovich from Tel Aviv, a member of Betar who had joined us a few weeks earlier. The missing driver of the tractor was David Keren, who had come to Israel from Finland and had joined our group. The rest of the day was spent in patrolling the area in an attempt to catch the assailants, but to no avail. But in the evening, after dark, David Keren suddenly entered our encampment without his rifle.

We learned from him that two armed Arabs, who had evidently scouted the area and learned of the daily trips by tractor to the spring, had ambushed them. After killing Yoel, they took his rifle and forced David to accompany them as they fled the area. They had not moved southward but rather northward, across the railroad tracks, deeper into the Jerusalem Corridor. Our patrols did not discover them. In the evening they let David go and he made his way back on foot to our settlement.

The incident made the newspaper headlines. The next day we attended Yoel's funeral in Tel Aviv. On our return we found that some twenty members of Betar settlements from all over the country had arrived to give us encouragement and to help out with guard duty.

The incident brought home to us the fact that our group was too small to handle the tasks of establishing the settlement while simultaneously handling the security situation. We obviously needed reinforcements right away.

Our reinforcement was Nili, a group of Betar members from South America, who had been awaiting their turn to establish a settlement and were now sent to us by the Herut settlement department. The ideological affinity between us helped to overcome the language barrier, and in no time we went about our tasks as a single group. A mixture of English, Spanish, Portuguese, and Hebrew soon became our means of communication.

Months went by as we began agricultural work in the area, started the Herculean job of clearing away some of the rocks, and built the first prefab huts and a dining hall—with our weapons always at the ready. The settlement department of the Jewish Agency began settling new immigrants from Yemen and Kurdistan in some of abandoned Arab villages on the surrounding hilltops, and we were asked to provide guard services for them. It was an additional burden on our small group, but it was also a source of income.

Many had heard about this "curious" group of Americans who had established a settlement so far from civilization. We had a visit from Yisrael (Sheib) Eldad, one of the leaders of the Stern Group, and had frequent visits from relatives of the settlers of Gush Etzion, who took advantage of our location to gaze at what could be seen on the horizon of the remains of the destroyed settlement, now in Jordanian hands. One day the head of the Jewish Agency settlement department, Levi Eshkol (and a future Israeli prime minister), arrived in a long black limousine to see for himself what and how we were doing. He seemed to be well impressed, and at the conclusion of his visit asked me why such a fine group of young people was associated with this "crazy" Betar movement. I expect that after I told him that we did not recognize the cease-fire lines as Israel's permanent borders, he was convinced that we really were crazy.

As time went by, although we frequently reconnoitered the area beyond the cease-fire line, it became clear to me that our aim of moving the cease-fire line was not realistic and that this task would have to be achieved by the IDF. That being the case, Muriel and I came to the difficult decision to leave M'vo'ot Betar and for me to return to my profession as an engineer.

Our first stop was a rented room in Tel Aviv. As I went looking for a job as an engineer, I soon found out that it was not going to be easy despite my MIT diploma. One obvious place to look for a job was Israel Military Industries, the primary source for locally manufactured weapons for the IDF. I was interviewed for a position there and seemed well received. But a few weeks later I was notified that I had not passed the security review. I needed no explanation to understand that my having been in the Irgun and my association with Betar were enough to disqualify me, despite my engineering credentials.

Eventually I found a position with an American engineering consulting company, Knappen, Tippetts, Abbett, McCarthy, that had been hired by the Tel Aviv municipality to upgrade the municipal water supply system. Here my political background was no impediment, However, I did not find the work sufficiently challenging, and decided that I needed to go back to school to refresh and upgrade my engineering competence.

The government had decided to offer all Mahal volunteers (those who volunteered for the IDF during the war) a trip to their point of origin. We decided that Muriel, already pregnant with our first child, should take up this offer, and that I should follow her to the United States to undertake graduate studies in engineering. Muriel flew back to New York and I followed a few months later, arriving in New York in September 1951. A few days after my arrival, on September 18, our first son, Yigal, was born.

FIVE

Engineer

Although I graduated from MIT with a bachelor's degree in mechanical engineering and had gotten reasonably good grades, I had not taken a deep interest in engineering. This was primarily because I had been wholly absorbed with Betar and the events in Palestine during my years at MIT, and also because my studies had been interrupted by my service in the U.S. Army. After my return from army service, all I wanted was to finish my studies as quickly as possible, leaving little room for immersing myself in any of the subjects. Now, after a number of years away from my chosen profession and never having really practiced it, it was my intention to return to graduate school and to master the subject.

When I arrived in New York in September 1951, it was too late to be admitted for the fall semester, so I would have to wait a year before returning to school. Fortunately, I did not have to search for a job: The manager of the American engineering firm for whom I had worked in Tel Aviv sent a warm recommendation to their headquarters in New York. They hired me immediately, and I spent a year designing water supply installations for U.S. air bases in Libya and Saudi Arabia. I knew that that was not the kind of engineering I would want to do in my professional career and was looking forward to returning to school and finding out what "real" engineering was all about.

I applied to the graduate schools of America's best engineering schools—MIT, my alma mater, and the California Institute of Technology (Caltech). I was admitted to both, and chose Caltech. It turned out to be a good choice.

In September 1952, Muriel, one-year-old Yigal, and I landed at the Burbank airport to begin a new chapter in our lives. As a U.S. army veteran I was entitled to accommodations in the veterans' housing quarters located in Temple City, not far from Pasadena, the location of the Caltech campus. A few days later I was attending classes at Caltech. I had chosen the Jet Propulsion option that was offered in the graduate curriculum, assuming that it would prove useful on my return to Israel.

Caltech was a revelation to me. Much smaller than MIT, the school provided an opportunity for intimate contact with the teaching and research staff. The fact that Caltech was home to the Jet Propulsion Laboratory, a center of aeronautical research, created an atmosphere of excitement about the new developments in this field. The engineering courses placed an emphasis on fundamentals, on rigorous derivation of engineering formulas, and the connection between engineering and physics and chemistry. It was a new world to me and it captured my imagination. I knew that I had come to the right place. My attitude to engineering in the years to come was shaped during the time I spent at Caltech. It was an inspiration.

In June 1953 I was awarded a master's of science degree in engineering. My grades had been excellent and the school urged me to continue my studies toward a Ph.D., offering me a full scholarship. Caught up in the excitement of my studies, I decided to accept and embarked on a doctoral program. But half a year into the program, with excellent grades in the courses I had taken, I had second thoughts on the direction I was taking. It seemed inconsistent with our plans to return to Israel. It would probably take three years to obtain the doctorate, which would mean a significant delay in our move. After deliberating on the subject for a whole night, I decided to drop my studies, go to the East Coast, and look for an opportunity to return to Israel. Muriel was in the advanced stages of her second pregnancy when we landed in New York in February 1954. There an advertisement in the *New York Times* caught my eye. The Curtiss-Wright Corporation, one of the major aircraft engine developers and manufacturers, was looking for engineers. This was an opportunity to obtain some practical experience in the area in which I had specialized. The following week I was at work, participating in the development of the J67 jet engine for the U.S. Air Force. And I was now the father of two boys. Our second son, Raanan, was born days after our arrival in New York.

The Curtiss-Wright plant was located in Woodridge, New Jersey. We found an apartment in Fort Lee, on the Hudson River across from Manhattan, and every weekday morning I drove to my new job, returning in the late evening. It was interesting and challenging work. However, I soon learned that Curtiss-Wright's competitor, Pratt & Whitney, was developing a similar but superior engine, the J57. Curtiss-Wright's J67 was already undergoing development testing when I arrived, and only minor modification were possible at this stage. There was no way of catching up with the competition.

However, two other possibilities opened up for using the J67. Both would use the J67 as the core of a turbo-ramjet engine for an aerial vehicle that would fly at a velocity three times the speed of sound, Mach 3, at an altitude of 60,000 feet. That was the direction the U.S. Air Force was taking at the time in search of a revolutionary combat aircraft that would be superior to Soviet aircraft. The other application was the supersonic transport (SST) aircraft, at that time in the early stages of development, which would provide commercial flight at three times the speed of sound. A turbo-ramjet engine would be suitable in both these applications, operating as a turbojet until the aircraft had reached a speed of Mach 2 and then having the air flowing into the engine bypass the turbojet engine and enter the afterburner, now operating as a ramjet, the optimal engine cycle at the higher speeds.

I was appointed to take charge of the development of the turbo-ramjet engine, named the XRJ55. It was intended to power the Republic XF-103 aircraft, in development at Republic Aviation Corporation in Farmingdale, Long Island. I traveled frequently to Tullahoma, Tennessee, where I supervised the testing of the J67 engine at the U.S. Air Force altitude simulation facility there, and to the Boeing Company in Seattle, Washington, which was engaged in the early stage of development of an SST.

At the same time I began searching for job opportunities in Israel. The Technion in Haifa offered me a position as research fellow in the newly formed Department of Aeronautical Engineering, and I decided to accept it. Now all we had to do was fix the date for our long-planned return to Israel.

My colleagues at Curtiss-Wright found it difficult to understand my desire to leave what seemed a promising career in order to go to Israel. On one of our many trips to Seattle, my superior, Ed Heaton, tried to talk me out of it, explaining that he, of Irish origin, although proud to be Irish, would not think of going back to Ireland. I'm not sure that I succeeded in explaining to him the difference between being Irish and being Jewish at this time. My mind was made up.

We were now five, our daughter Aliza having been born in May 1954. In December 1957, six years after we had returned to the United States, we boarded an Israeli passenger vessel, the *Shalom*, in New York for the two-week trip to Haifa.

The day after arriving in Haifa I visited the aeronautical engineering department at the Technion, on the lower Mount Carmel Slopes. It was located on what is now the Neve Shaanan campus. At the time it was one of a few buildings there; the rest of the Technion was still located in the old Technion building in the Hadar HaCarmel district. Yohanan Ratner, an architect and at the time the acting president of the Technion, had designed the building, which housed the Department of Architecture and the Department of Aeronautical Engineering. My office on the second floor had a great view of Haifa Bay. From here I intended to contribute to the establishment of a full-fledged aeronautical industry in Israel.

The first stage was teaching students the fields of my specialty—propulsion, preliminary design of aeronautical vehicles, and thermodynamics—imbuing them with enthusiasm for aircraft and missiles, and giving them the confidence that on graduation they would be capable of building a modern aeronautical industry from the ground up.

It turned out that there had been some differences of opinion regarding the need to establish an aeronautical engineering department at the Technion. Many assumed that the requirement for aeronautical engineers in Israel would be limited to aircraft maintenance in the Israel Air Force and for the aircraft operated by El Al, and concluded that such a small demand would best be met by sending a few students abroad to study the relevant subjects. David Ben-Gurion's vision went beyond that: he foresaw the need for engineers in the defense industry, which would require a substantial number of engineers trained in this discipline. He was supported by Sidney Goldstein, a world-renowned expert in aerodynamics, who at the time was serving as vice president of the Technion.

Once the decision to establish the Department of Aeronautical Engineering had been taken, the next step was to arrange for teaching staff. Goldstein arranged for two bright Hebrew University physics graduates, Avraham Kogan and Meir Hanin, to be accepted as doctoral candidates in aerodynamics at Princeton and Cornell, and for two Technion graduates, Yosef Singer and David Abir, to be accepted as doctoral candidates in aircraft structures at the Brooklyn Polytechnic Institute. Missing was someone to teach propulsion—me. When I arrived I found Kogan and Hanin teaching aerodynamics and Singer teaching aircraft structures, and I began teaching propulsion and preliminary aeronautical design.

In June 1958 the first class of Israeli-trained aeronautical engineers graduated: eleven men and one woman. They were the first of many classes in the years to come whose graduates would build the foundation of a thriving aerospace industry in Israel, which astonished the world aerospace community.

Not many in Israel at the time shared my dream of establishing a modern aeronautical industry in Israel. To most it seemed far-fetched and unrealistic. Unlike me, the teaching staff in the department had not had any experience working in a modern aeronautical industry. The students, although showing great interest in aircraft, did not dare to aim at actually participating in the design of aircraft in Israel.

An expert sent by the UN spent a few weeks at the Technion, counseling us on the teaching syllabus in the department. He was A. D. Young, a renowned aerodynamicist from England, who had contributed to the British war effort during World War II. He was Jewish and obviously had the best interests of Israel and the Technion at heart. In a conversation with me he asked what I expected our students to do after graduation. When I told him that I expected them to design and develop aircraft and missiles, he put his hand on my shoulder in a fatherly manner and told me to drop the idea. "We in England," he said, "who were pioneers of aircraft development in the past, today can no longer keep up with the U.S., the Soviet Union, and France in this field. You in Israel are not going to be able to do it."

But I was not discouraged, and kept urging my students to set their sights on a career in aircraft and missile design. I was not disappointed. The graduates, moving on to the Israel Air Force, Israel Aerospace Industries (IAI), and RAFAEL, the Israel weapons development authority, quickly became engaged in advanced aeronautical projects. Less than ten years later Israeli-designed missiles and aircraft were undergoing flight tests.

I had joined the Department of Aeronautical Engineering at the Technion with the rank of research assistant. After a year I was promoted to senior lecturer, the equivalent of assistant professor in the United States, and two years later I was promoted to associate professor. I had come to academic life without a doctorate and realized that my promotion was dependent on publishing the results of my research. At the Technion, as everywhere in academia, it was "publish or perish." So I published and lectured on my research in propulsion and flight mechanics, and was duly promoted. As a result I was addressed, as is usual in Israel, as professor, a status that in Israel and Europe is seemingly carried for life. Years later, when I was already in politics and had become the target of the usual political mudslinging, stories were planted in the press that I had not received a doctorate and thus must have been an imposter as a professor. The ignoramuses making such comments thought that a doctorate was a precondition for being appointed a professor at a university. It is true that the vast majority of professors at universities nowadays have Ph.D.'s, but not all, especially in engineering. I had been promoted to associate professor at the Technion even though I did not have a Ph.D. But that did not stop the mudslingers, who did not bother to check with the Technion, and whenever the occasion arose insisted that I was an imposter. In politics I learned to weather these gratuitous insults.

Israel Aerospace Industries was founded and run by Al Schwimmer, an American aircraft enthusiast who had helped bring aircraft and pilots to Israel during the War of Independence. Until 1962 IAI had been engaged in maintaining and modifying aircraft and assembling the French Fouga Magister jet trainer. Always eager to undertake innovative and ambitious projects, now Schwimmer was eager to take on this new challenge. He approached me with the suggestion that I move over to IAI as its chief engineer. This was the kind of project that I had been waiting for. To obtain my release from my duties at the Technion, the deputy defense minister, Shimon Peres, who was leading the preparations for the response to the Egyptian missile threat, wrote a letter to the president of the Technion, Yaakov Dori, asking that I be allowed to move to IAI, and Dori acceded to his request. It was the beginning of my nine years' tenure as IAI's chief engineer and head of its Engineering Division. During this time IAI turned into a first-class aeronautical industry.

In November 1962 I took up my post as IAI's chief engineer. I continued lecturing at the Technion one day a week, and for the rest of the week I would commute daily between our home in Haifa and the IAI plant next to Ben Gurion airport. IAI engineers were at that time engaged in two projects: the Boeing 377 Stratocruiser conversion and the Gabriel sea-to-sea missile. The first was an overambitious brainstorm of Schwimmer's to convert commercial aircraft to military use; the other was an attempt to develop the first sea-to-sea missile in the Western world, which would provide the Israeli navy with the answer to the Styx, the Soviets' sea-to-sea missile.

Schwimmer had picked up a number of used Stratocruiser commercial aircraft with the grandiose idea to convert them to military use for the Israel Defense Forces (IDF) by making the following modifications: a hinged tail that could be opened to introduce a tank or vehicles into the body of the aircraft; fitting the body with rails that would permit parachuting vehicles through the aircraft's cargo doors; modifications that would permit soldiers to parachute from the aircraft; and the attachment of JATO (jet-assisted takeoff) rockets to enable takeoff from short air strips. In other words, an aircraft that would meet multiple IDF requirements in one package. It was too much for one aircraft and could not possibly succeed. In time the hinged tail was developed and made to work, and an ejection system was installed for the parachuting of vehicles from the aircraft. During the Six-Day War the aircraft was used to parachute supplies to Israeli forces in the Sinai, but thereafter the aircraft was only used for occasional transportation missions before it became obsolete.

The Gabriel missile was quite another matter and eventually became a resounding success. It had its origins in the Luz, a tactical ground-to-ground missile developed by RAFAEL for use by the IDF's infantry. However, the IDF felt it had no need for such a weapon. At IAI it was now being modified for use as a seaborne missile for the Israeli navy. The brains behind this project was Ori Even-Tov, a brilliant engineer who had worked at RAFAEL and moved with the project to IAI. Schwimmer was eager to add the missile to the IAI's inventory of projects, and when I arrived at IAI he asked me to take on its supervision. The missile, now renamed the Gabriel, was solid-rocket-propelled and semi-active-radar-guided. The main additional feature needed for it to fulfill its naval mission was an altimeter, which would permit it to skim above the waves as it approached the target.

In addition to Even-Tov, the program had another advantage—the support of Colonel Moshe Kashti, the director general of the Ministry of Defense, who made sure that the necessary funding would be made available for the project, even at times when its success was far from certain. Kashti was a believer in the importance of local engineering development, and used his position to allocate the necessary budgets at a time when the navy was not given high priority in the IDF's plans.

Development flight tests of the Gabriel were held near Atlit. Every few months we would camp there and watch the missile being launched at a target at sea, and each time we would see the missile dive into the sea instead of hitting the target, and it would be back to the drawing board. But finally, months of painstaking work began to pay off. The Gabriel skimmed over the sea surface and hit the target! But that was only the beginning. A fire-control system had to be developed, a job that was subcontracted to an Italian company. The missile launcher was developed by the IAI engineering division. Equally important, vessels on which the Gabriel system would be mounted were ordered from a shipyard in Cherbourg, France. Under the leadership of Rear Admiral Shlomo Erel, the Israeli navy was undergoing a revolution and entering the missile age. During the Six-Day War, when Charles de Gaulle declared an embargo on the shipment of arms to Israel, the French government refused to deliver to Israel five missile boats that had been ordered in France and were stuck in Cherbourg. On a stormy Christmas Eve in 1969 the boats were spirited out of Cherbourg by Israeli navy crews and made for Israel.

During the Yom Kippur War, a squadron of these missile boats commanded by Captain Michael (Yumi) Barkai, firing Gabriel missiles, conducted the first missile encounters in naval history and scored overwhelming victories over the Syrian and Egyptian fleets. In the years to follow the Gabriel became Israel's most important export product.

Since I had moved to IAI from the Technion, the graduates of the Technion Aeronautical Engineering Department had become aware of the intense engineering development activities at IAI. Whereas at first the best graduates were attracted to RAFAEL rather than to IAI, now many were eager to join IAI, and with them IAI's engineering capabilities grew apace.

In 1965 we began the design of the first Israeli-designed aircraft, the Arava. It was the brainchild of Joseph Szydlowski, the Jewish owner of Turbomeca, a French small-engine developer and manufacturer located in Pau in the Pyrenees. He was a frequent visitor to Israel. On one of his visits he spoke to Schwimmer about the commercial potential of developing a small turboprop aircraft that would have STOL (short takeoff and landing) capabilities, and for which he had just the right Turbomeca engine—the Astazou turboprop. It did not take much convincing before Schwimmer took the bait. Here was a project of our own design with commercial possibilities.

The Arava was a small (12,500-pound takeoff weight) twin-tail STOL utility transport with a hinged tail for cargo loading, with fixed undercarriage. To Szydlowski's chagrin the Canadian Pratt & Whitney PT6 turboprop engine was found better suited for the aircraft than his Astazou. Its first flight took place in November 1969. The second prototype of the aircraft was destroyed in flight due to a flutter problem of the wing struts. We lost three of the four-man flight test crew: Avraham Hacohen, IAI's chief test pilot; Aharon Ozeri, the flight test engineer; and Eitan Shpigel, the flight technician. Dave Levine, a former Marine F4 pilot who had joined IAI and was the copilot on the flight, managed to bail out.

Joseph Czinczenheim, a brilliant French Jewish aeronautical engineer, volunteered his services to lead the investigation of the cause of the crash and identified the flutter problem. The struts were redesigned and the aircraft was certified and went into production. A total of 103 Aravas were produced and sold to the Israel Air Force and to customers around the world. Dov Saar, a graduate of the first class of Technion aeronautical engineers, led the project.

Before we had completed the development of the Arava, another project suddenly appeared. In the United States in 1968 the Rockwell Corporation put its Jet Commander executive jet program up for sale. Schwimmer could not resist the temptation to get into the executive jet business, and IAI acquired the program. I sent a team of engineers, headed by Yehuda Yaakobi, to Oklahoma City, where the Jet Commander had been manufactured, to take over the program and transfer it to Israel. It became the precursor of the IAI Jet Commodore and eventually an IAI line of executive jets.

The French arms embargo created a severe problem for the Israel Air Force. It was dependent on the French for combat aircraft and also for spare parts for maintenance. Fifty Dassault Mirage 5 aircraft that had been ordered and paid for were held up in France. With typical Israeli ingenuity it was decided to produce the aircraft in Israel, using plans of the aircraft and its engine. Now produced at IAI and dubbed the Nesher, the first aircraft off the production line flew in 1971, and the Nesher became operational in the Israel Air Force in 1972.

But we intended to improve on the performance of the aircraft. American jet engines were considerably superior to French engines. If we could replace the French Snecma (Société nationale d'études et de construction de moteurs d'aviation) Atar engine with an American engine, we could significantly boost the aircraft's performance. There was an engine that fit the bill: the General Electric J79, which in principle could be inserted into the fuselage of the Mirage 5. For this we needed the agreement of the U.S. government. Gerhard Neumann, the legendary head of GE's engine division, came to visit. A German refugee, he had spent the war years in China with Colonel Claire Chennault's Flying Tigers, a volunteer squadron that fought with the Chinese Air Force in 1940–41. On arriving in America he worked for GE, eventually becoming the head of the Engine Division. Schwimmer and I had a good meeting with him. He was all for the project if the U.S. government agreed. When we got that agreement in 1969, the project to build a prototype Mirage 5 powered by the J79 took off. I appointed Yaakov Ben-Basat, one of my former students at the Technion, to run the project, which was code-named Technolog. In

September 1970 the "Technolog" aircraft took to the skies, piloted by the Israel Air Force's Danny Shapiro. He reported that the aircraft was much better than the Mirage 5 powered by the French engine.

That is how the program to develop a fighter for the Israel Air Force, which would be based on the Mirage airframe, began. It was to be named Kfir. Further improvements, in addition to the engine change, were made along the way in the avionics. The avionics package—the aviation-related electronics—was replaced, and the aerodynamic shape was changed by the addition of small canard (airfoil) surfaces mounted on the air intakes. The latter were designed by Avraham (Kerem) Kaflawi, a brilliant aeronautical engineer, also one of my former students. While serving as an officer in the Israel Air Force he had designed the replacement of the French Snecma Atar engine in the Super Mystère aircraft by the Pratt & Whitney J52. After leaving IAI for the United States he developed the now-famous Predator unmanned aircraft. I and the team that developed the Kfir aircraft received the Israel Defense Prize in 1971.

The day after the first flight of the Technolog, Colonel Kashti, the director general of the Defense Ministry, invited me to his office. Obviously impressed by the success of the Technolog program, he congratulated me on our success reengining the Mirage 5. He went on to ask me what capabilities I would need to design an Israeli fighter aircraft from scratch. Since that had been my goal for some years, I was prepared to answer this question. I told him we needed a wind tunnel to test models of a new aircraft, and we needed funding for a preliminary design section that would begin studies of alternate configurations of the next Israeli fighter aircraft. He agreed to allocate the necessary funds. The wind tunnel was duly built and the preliminary design section began studying fighter aircraft configurations. That was the beginning of what, some years later, was to become the Lavi fighter.

Kashti's confidence in the capabilities of our engineers was not shared by some of the senior air force staff, who suggested that further developments of the Mirage aircraft should be subcontracted to Dassault Aviation in France, this despite the tenuous relations between Israel and France on matters of defense at the time. We managed to deflect these suggestions, and the job of developing the Kfir fighter was given to IAI.

At this point we were handling a number of ambitious engineering projects: Arava, Jet Commander, Kfir, and the Gabriel, which was being developed in a separate plant by a dedicated and talented team run by Ori Even-Tov. It was more than the engineering manpower available to us was able to handle, and I had to resort to bringing engineers from abroad on a temporary basis, the so-called job-shoppers, to fill the gap. I even had to subcontract some design work to England. A few experienced Jewish engineers joined us on a voluntary basis. Outstanding among them were Joseph Czinczenheim, who had worked for Dassault, and Gene Salvey, who had worked for North American Aviation in the United States. Both spent more than a year with us and made invaluable contributions to our projects.

IAI's Engineering Division had grown almost exponentially under my direction, and the company had matured into an aerospace outfit capable of competing with the best. We had established ourselves in the field of missiles, civilian aircraft, and fighter aircraft—becoming, in the process, a source of wonder in the eyes of the world's aeronautical community. But IAI management had not kept pace with this development. The company was run by Schwimmer, an ambitious visionary eager to undertake any project that came along. He had good relations with Peres and the top brass in the Defense Ministry and was able to arrange for the financing to keep the company going even in tough times, despite the many skeptics in the Finance Ministry and especially in the Israel Air Force regarding the activities at IAI. This relationship was reinforced by Schwimmer's deputy, Asher Ben-Yosef, whose only qualification for the job seemed to be his political connections, but who could contribute nothing on the technical, financial, or management level. It became clear to me that I had little chance of advancing at IAI beyond my present position. I even had the feeling that with the growing respect for my achievements in the engineering and scientific community in Israel, Schwimmer and Ben-Yosef began to feel that they would be better off if I were to leave IAI. So I decided to leave.

After almost ten years as head of IAI's Engineering Division, I left the company with a feeling of great satisfaction. My Technion students and I had established an aerospace company, and my dream of helping to create an advanced defense industry in Israel that would make a significant contribution to the strength of the country had been realized. When in later years, after having filled senior positions in government, I was on occasion asked which phases of my career had given me the greatest satisfaction, I replied without hesitation that my position as head of IAI's Engineering Division in those formative years had filled me with the greatest pride and given me the greatest satisfaction.

SIX

Politics

I never intended to become a politician. After discharging my duties to Betar and the Irgun, I had planned to work in Israel as an engineer. At the Technion and thereafter at Israel Aerospace Industries (IAI) I had realized my ambition of using my engineering capabilities to contribute to Israel's security. Menachem Begin and the rest of the Herut leadership knew me well and had followed my achievements at IAI. On a number of occasions I was approached with an offer to appear on the Herut list of candidates for the Knesset, and I politely refused. While I was at IAI, going into politics was the farthest thing from my mind.

On leaving IAI I had another offer. Zvi (Chera) Zur, a former Israel Defense Forces (IDF) chief of staff, was assistant to Defense Minister Moshe Dayan and functioned as a czar in charge of all Defense Ministry activities not directly related to the IDF. We knew each other well, since he was responsible for all defense research and development projects. He now called me in and asked me to take on the job of head of the Israeli Atomic Energy Commission (IAEC). Professor Yisrael Dostrowsky, of the Weizmann Institute of Science, who for years had headed the IAEC, was now leaving the position. After thinking about it for a few days I told Zur that I would accept the appointment. He said that it would take a few weeks before it was officially announced; in the meantime I should become acquainted with the entire operation being conducted by the commission. I had spent some time with Dostrowsky and his subordinates going through an initial learning process when I was again called in by Zur, who informed me that Golda Meir, who as prime minister was also the chairman of the commission, did not agree to the appointment. Zur seemed embarrassed as he explained to me that he and Dayan had assumed that her agreement to an appointment proposed by them would be no more than a formality; they were astounded that she should decide to veto the appointment. I learned later that Meir, who did not know me personally, did not like my past political associations and preferred to have someone in the job with whom she would feel more "comfortable."

On leaving IAI I established a consulting firm named Cybernetics to advise government institutions and commercial firms on matters of strategy and systems analysis. My schedule was not as busy as it had been at IAI. My political views had not changed. I voted Herut and hoped that the day would come when Herut would come to power. When one day I was approached by Haim Landau, an old friend from my Irgun days and a senior figure in Herut, to become active in the party, I agreed to become a member of the Herut Central Committee and the Herut Executive Committee. Menachem Begin, the leader of Herut since it was founded in 1948, having failed to come to power time after time, had adopted a strategy of broadening the base of his political party and attracting fresh faces to the list of Knesset candidates. He had formed a united list, Gahal, with the Liberal Party in the Knesset elections. Adding me to the active membership of Herut, and eventually to the list of Herut Knesset candidates, fitted right in with this strategy.

A more important embellishment for Herut was Ezer Weizman, an illustrious Israel Air Force commander who joined Herut on leaving the IDF in 1969, in effect taking a leadership position second only to Begin. This move was greeted with enthusiasm by the Herut membership, who realized that the addition of this popular general to the ranks of Herut would broaden the party's appeal to the voters. He was immediately given a post as minister of transportation, representing Herut in the national unity government led by Golda Meir. His tenure as minister was short because in 1970, after Meir had agreed to an American peace initiative calling for an Israeli withdrawal to "secure and recognized borders" (the Rogers Plan), Begin decided that the combined faction of Herut and the Liberal Party (Gahal) should leave the government.

Weizman was less than enthusiastic about leaving the government. Always seeking the limelight, he now began engineering a coup in Herut against Begin. At the 1972 Herut convention he failed in his attempt to oust Begin and left the party in disgust. He thought that I—like him, a relative newcomer to the party—was a member of the anti-Begin coalition he had formed. Although I believed that in a leadership position Weizman broadened the party's electoral appeal, I did not support his move to replace Begin and was certainly not prepared to leave the party with him.

In preparation for the Knesset elections that were scheduled to take place in the fall of 1973, Landau suggested that I appear on the list of Herut candidates. At the time the list was composed by a nominating committee, which itself was nominated by Begin and approved by the Herut Central Committee. I assumed that Landau felt confident that I would be placed in a "safe" spot on the list. But at that time the Ministry of Defense was looking for a chief scientist to replace Professor Arye Dvoretzky, who was leaving the position. That was a position that I as a scientist was interested in, and would have preferred to going into politics. I asked to meet with Dayan, the defense minister, to find out whether I was the preferred candidate for the position. At his villa in Zahala, I told him that I had an offer to appear on the list of candidates for the Knesset but would forgo politics for the chief scientist position. He was noncommittal, saying that I was indeed one of the candidates for the position, but nothing had been decided as yet. So I informed Landau that I would agree to appear on the list of Herut candidates.

In preparation for the elections, a list uniting the right-wing parties—Herut, the Liberals, the Free Center (led by Shmuel Tamir), the National list (led by Yigal Horwitz), and the Movement for Greater Israel—was formed and named Likud. I ended up as number thirty-two on this united Likud list. Under Israel's system of proportional representation, it meant that the Likud would have to receive more than a quarter of the votes for me to be elected to the Knesset. It seemed a marginally safe position.

The elections had to be postponed because of the Yom Kippur War; they were held on December 31, 1973, a few weeks after the truce that ended the war. The appearance on the Likud list of Ariel Sharon, the hero of the Yom Kippur War, helped Likud obtain thirty-nine seats in the Knesset. The Likud had gained five seats while the Labor Alignment led by Golda Meir obtained fifty-one seats—a loss of five Labor seats, but it still allowed them easily to put together a working coalition. But for the first time in Israel's history Labor was facing a formidable opposition, led by Begin.

Here I was in the Knesset, a Likud backbencher and a member of the Finance Committee. Considering my background I was probably more suited to be a member of the Foreign Affairs and Defense Committee, but there were many with more seniority than I to fill the few slots available for Likud members on this prestigious committee.

I had my first introduction to Israeli politics as a member of the Finance Committee. The chairman of the committee was Yisrael Kargman of the Labor Party, a former worker at the Ata textile plant who had been the head of the workers' committee there. He ran the Finance Committee with an iron hand, making sure that all proposals submitted by the Ministry of Finance were duly approved by the committee. The opposition within the committee was led by Yohanan Bader, a veteran Herut MK (member of the Knesset) who was very erudite and wise and knew more about economics than all the rest of us on the committee put together. His views were respected by all, but after everyone had his turn in the discussions the coalition majority always prevailed.

I came into the Knesset together with Yitzhak Shamir, one of the leaders of the Stern Group (Lehi), which had battled valiantly against British rule in Palestine. I had known Shamir only from afar and he was a hero for me. Now we came to be close associates. It was the beginning of many years of political collaboration.

The Yom Kippur War was on everyone's mind, especially the failure to mobilize the reserves in time, even though there had been so many indications of an impending attack by the Egyptian and Syrian armies. This failure was what had made the war so costly in lives of soldiers lost. The whole country was grieving this loss of Israel's young men.

Israel had scored a great victory that would deter Arab armies from attacking Israel again in the years to come. Although the IDF was caught by surprise in the south and the north, it had managed to recover, and within eighteen days it had advanced to within 101 kilometers of Cairo, had encircled the Egyptian Third Army east of the Suez Canal, and was within artillery range of Damascus. But the Israeli public's attention was focused not on the victory but on the failure to mobilize the reserves in time, despite the many indications that Egyptian and Syrian attacks were in the offing.

On November 21, 1973, the Golda Meir government had appointed the Agranat Commission of Inquiry to investigate the initial stages of the war. Although it was obvious that the responsibility for not mobilizing the reserve forces in time lay with the political echelon—Prime Minister Golda Meir and Defense Minister Moshe Dayan—the committee chose to put the blame on IDF chief of staff David (Dado) Elazar and called for his dismissal. The man who had led the IDF to a brilliant victory was sacked, while Golda Meir and Moshe Dayan were absolved. It was a miscarriage of justice.

The many protests across the country finally led to the resignation of Golda Meir and her government on March 28, 1974. Although Meir had maintained her nerve during the first critical days of the war and helped steer the IDF to victory, the country could not forgive her for not having called up the reserves in time—she had depended on her defense minister, Dayan. The Labor Party hierarchy chose Yitzhak Rabin to form another government. Shimon Peres was appointed defense minister in Rabin's government. Peres, who knew me well from my days at IAI, now asked me to take on the position of chief scientist in the Ministry of Defense. I had had my eye on the position, but now it would entail my resigning from the Knesset. I didn't think I could do that without obtaining Begin's approval. Begin made no bones about the fact that he did not like the idea. I accepted his verdict and resigned myself to staying in the Knesset.

As the next election approached there was a feeling that maybe this time, finally, there would be a change of government and the Labor Party would be brought down. Shmuel Tamir, the leader of the Free Center party, an old friend of mine but a longtime opponent of Begin, told me that as long as Begin led the Likud we would never come to power. Although Tamir was an astute politician, his bias against Begin blinded him to the political changes taking place and the opportunities they represented. He chose to leave the Likud and join Dash, a new party led by Yigael Yadin, a former IDF chief of staff. Ariel Sharon, also pessimistic regarding the results to be expected in the coming elections, had decided to resign his seat in the Knesset and serve as an adviser to Rabin. I went to see him at his farm in the Negev in an attempt to convince him to run again on the Likud ticket. He was obdurate. "I believe Begin, but I don't believe in Begin," he told me. He decided to form a new party, Shlomtzion, to be headed by him. So the Likud was going to run without Tamir and without Sharon. But Weizman, smelling victory, had decided to rejoin Herut and took on the job of chairman of the Likud's election campaign.

This time the Herut candidates for the Knesset were not chosen by a nominating committee as in the past, but were elected by the Herut Central Committee. The great old timers, Landau and Bader, did not put forth their candidacies. Possibly they thought that they might not be elected to sufficiently high places on the list, or maybe they felt that they had done their bit and the time had come for them to retire. They probably did not anticipate that this would be the Likud's turn to come to power. It was sad to see these old warhorses, who had contributed so much, stand aside at this crucial moment.

I did not campaign to seek votes for my candidacy. It almost seemed at the time to be below my dignity. But evidently I had become popular within the ranks of Herut and was elected to the number three slot, right after Begin and Weizman. The final composition of the Likud list of candidates was composed by interspersing candidates from the Liberal Party and the other Likud component parties among those elected by Herut. Thus I ended up as the seventh on the list of Likud candidates. It turned out to be the beginning of my rise to prominence in Israeli politics.

In the election campaign I took the job of running the campaign in Tel Aviv. I divided Tel Aviv into seven sectors: Northwest, Northeast, Center, East, South, Jaffa, and the areas across the Yarkon River. I assigned someone to take charge of covering each of these sectors, to arrange for parlor meetings in each and every one of them regularly until Election Day, and then to mobilize our activists on Election Day to bring voters to the polls. I had our people do house-to-house polling, choosing for this purpose a voting district in East Tel Aviv where the results in the previous election had been similar to the national score. The results indicated that the Likud was going to win this election and turned out to be more accurate than the polls published in the press. On Election Day I was confident—with good reason, it turned out. The results in Tel Aviv were a landslide for Likud. That night it was clear that the Labor Party had suffered its first defeat in Israel's history, and that the Likud would form the next government. Begin would be the next prime minister of Israel. A sensation.

Begin assembled a coalition quickly. Sharon, who had succeeded in obtaining only two seats in the Knesset, immediately decided to merge his faction with Likud. Adding the National Religious Party and Agudat Yisrael, Begin had the sixty-one votes for a majority in the Knesset. It was a slim majority, but it was enough.

Another surprise came shortly after the results of the election became known. Begin announced that he would appoint Moshe Dayan, who had been elected on the Labor Party ticket, as foreign minister in his government. I was shocked. Not only did Dayan's views not coincide with the positions of the Likud, but I, like many, saw him as the man primarily responsible for the failure to call up the reserve units in time prior to the Yom Kippur War. Was he going to be rewarded now by a position in a Likud-led government? I did not want to be associated with that kind of a maneuver and decided to resign my position as a newly elected Likud MK.

Begin had suffered a heart attack after the election and was taken to Tel Aviv Ichilov Hospital. I was still clearing up the Tel Aviv campaign headquarters when I heard the news and decided to rush over to Begin's bedside to inform him of my decision to resign in protest against his decision. When I was ushered into his ward, I saw him in bed in pajamas, pale as a ghost. I simply did not have the heart to tell him of my decision. After a cursory conversation with him about the state of his health, I left. I had changed my mind.

Why did Begin pick Dayan to be his foreign minister? Begin was aware that for many years he had been pictured in the foreign media as a terrorist and warmonger, a fanatic who could not be trusted. Now that he was the prime minister of Israel, he would have to overcome this image in his relations with the world. One of his first moves, even before assuming the office of prime minister, was to send Shmuel (Muki) Katz, who had been a member of the Irgun high command in the underground and was fluent in English, as an emissary to Washington to meet with the media and try to correct the false image of Begin that had taken root there. Appointing Dayan as his foreign minister he thought would be of immense importance in forging international relations, because of the wordwide positive reputation that Dayan enjoyed, a reputation that had not been tarnished outside Israel by his leadership failure during the Yom Kippur War. Begin remarked that foreign dignitaries would be "checking the pleats of their pants" before entering Dayan's office. He did not trust anyone in his political entourage to do for Israel's image what he thought Dayan could do, and thus strengthen his own hand in the world.

Dayan was only too eager to take the position Begin offered, which involved crossing party lines. He felt that he was in need of rehabilitation after the Yom Kippur War and thought the position offered him by Begin would serve that purpose.

But we learned shortly that Begin entered the prime minister's office intent on arriving at a peace agreement with Egypt, and evidently he felt that Dayan's presence in the Foreign Ministry was an essential element in the moves he was planning to make.

Forming the new government involved selecting the ministers, with each coalition party selecting its ministers. Herut was to have three ministers. It was up to Begin to nominate them and for the Herut Central Committee to approve their nomination. Obviously, two of the Herut ministers were going to be Begin, the prime minister, and Weizman as defense minister. They filled the top two slots on the list elected by the Herut Central Committee and were going to be approved automatically. Who was going to be Herut's third minister? To the surprise of many on the committee, assembled in the Jabotinsky House on King George Street in Tel Aviv, Begin nominated David Levy as Herut's third minister. Begin's announcement was followed by calls from the audience that I should rightly be the third Herut minister. In preferring Levy, Begin obviously felt that it was politically important to have Levy, of Moroccan origin and a resident of the development town Bet Shean, as a member of the Herut representation in the government. To the calls demanding that I be the third Herut minister, Begin replied that I would receive an appropriate appointment in due time. I was not perturbed and told my supporters that I had no objections to Begin's decision, and it was not brought to a vote.

Shamir, who had also not been chosen to be a minister, was given the job of Speaker of the Knesset. Although the position of Speaker has assumed a status of considerable importance in recent years, at that time it was considered a largely ceremonial position. I asked Shamir why he had accepted this seemingly meaningless post. He threw up his hands and replied that that was the only position available.

I had been selected to head the Knesset's Foreign Affairs and Defense Committee. It was and still is the most prestigious Knesset committee. In the first meeting of the committee one could see the full impact of the change that the elections had brought to the Israeli political scene. Its members included many of Israel's past illustrious military leaders who were now in the opposition: Yigal Alon, Meir Amit, Yitzhak Rabin, Haim Bar-Lev. Its chairman was a former member of the Irgun.

The committee was supposed to receive reports from government ministers and officials on matters of defense that were not available to the general public, information that should remain secret. It quickly became apparent to me that some committee members passed on some of this information to the media. Once the information reached the committee there was actually no knowing where it would end up. To deal with this unpalatable situation I decided to set up a number of subcommittees that would focus on specific areas. There, the number of members I appointed was limited, and I believed that I could trust them to keep the information they received to themselves. That worked, and the system of subcommittees is working to this day.

When I called Yitzhak (Haka) Hoffi, the head of the Mossad at the time, to testify before one of the subcommittees, he told me that he had never divulged information on the Mossad's activities to the Knesset and he did not intend to start now. I felt that it was incumbent on the committee to supervise the Mossad's activities, but he would not relent. I turned to Begin, who as prime minister was the immediate superior of the head of the Mossad, and asked him to order Hoffi to report to the committee. Begin, who was very punctilious in observing the proper relations between the government and the Knesset, agreed with me and told Hoffi to appear before the committee. Thereafter Hoffi duly reported to the committee whenever he was asked to do so, as did his successors in the job in the following years.

Another innovation that I introduced as committee chairman was to develop relations with the parallel parliamentary committees in other democracies. Meetings were held with the U.S. Senate Foreign Relations Committee and the Defense Committee of the German Bundestag.

When Begin broadened the coalition by adding the Dash party, headed by Yigael Yadin, another ministerial portfolio for Herut became available in the government. He called me and asked if I wanted to take the position. He mentioned in passing that if I decided not to take the position he would offer it to Haim Landau. I did not hesitate for a moment and turned down the post. Landau, a member of the Irgun high command during the days of the underground—and an old friend who had pulled me into politics—had decided not to run in the Herut internal elections, possibly because he did not anticipate that this time the Likud would win. Thus he missed what would surely have been a ministerial appointment in a Likud-led government. He was certainly deserving of this appointment. I told Begin he should appoint Landau, and continued as chairman of the Foreign Affairs and Defense Committee.

Begin had his mind set on reaching a peace agreement with Egypt. The appointment of Dayan as his foreign minister was a clear indication of the direction he had chosen. Soon after Begin assumed the office of prime minister, he sent Dayan on an exploratory mission to Morocco to meet with King Hassan, where Dayan suggested that a high-level Israeli-Egyptian meeting be arranged. Begin himself traveled to Romania to meet with Nicolae Ceauşescu, the Romanian president. There he suggested that Ceauşescu pass on to Anwar Sadat, the president of Egypt, a message that he was seeking to arrive at a peace agreement with Egypt and suggested that a high-level Israeli-Egyptian meeting be arranged. It turned out that Sadat was prepared for such a meeting.

Quickly the process moved into high gear. In November 1977, five months after Begin had formed his government, Sadat accepted Begin's invitation to come to Jerusalem and address the Knesset. Almost overnight he was there.

The following month Begin met Sadat in Ismailia. When no progress was made in the negotiations, President Jimmy Carter decided to step in, and in September 1978 invited Begin and Sadat to Camp David in an attempt to arrive at an agreement between them. After ten days of intensive negotiations the Camp David Accords were signed by Begin, Sadat, and Carter. Begin had agreed to return the entire Sinai peninsula to the Egyptians, and remove all Israel settlements, as well as the Israeli air and naval bases there.

I was shocked. "He threw in everything but the kitchen sink," I said to myself. I was prepared for a territorial compromise in the Sinai peninsula. That would have been a price worth paying for a peace treaty with Egypt. But to concede everything? This was unprecedented in international relations. Egypt, which had attacked Israel four times and had been beaten four times, was going to be compensated for its aggression by gaining back everything it had lost in its wars of aggression. What kind of a precedent was this setting for future and past aggressors? After being defeated, was the aggressor to pay no price for his aggression? To me it made no sense.

What made Begin agree to this? In the past he had talked about retiring to one of the settlements in the Sinai, one of the settlements he now agreed to abandon. He had taken with him to Camp David Dayan and Weizman, each one for his own reasons intent on reaching an agreement with Sadat, almost regardless of the price. It was significant that Begin had not asked any of his own comrades to accompany him on his fateful journey to Camp David. He must have felt that they would be opposed to far-reaching concessions. He did not consult me, even though I was the chairman of the Knesset's Foreign Affairs and Defense Committee.

The fact that the Sinai Peninsula, which had not been part of Mandatory Palestine, was not, as far as Begin was concerned, a part of the Land of Israel must have made it easier for him. As became clear in the later negotiations on the Palestinian issue, he was not prepared to give an inch when it came to any part of what to him was the Land of Israel. Strategic considerations were evidently not uppermost in his mind, when weighed against his fervent desire to reach a peace treaty with Egypt. Proving that he was not the warmonger he had been depicted to be at home and abroad may also have been a consideration for him. To clear his conscience he telephoned Sharon from Camp David to ask for his opinion regarding the military implications of a complete withdrawal from the Sinai Peninsula. Sharon gave his assent from a distance.

On his return to Jerusalem Begin brought up the Camp David Accords for discussion in the cabinet, where they were duly approved. According to

Israeli law, that was sufficient to make them binding. Nevertheless, Begin—looking for a demonstration of support for the large concessions he had agreed to—decided to bring them to the Knesset for discussion and approval. He had also told Carter that the agreement to remove the Israeli settlements in the Sinai would be subject to the approval of the Knesset. The Knesset approved by a large majority.

The public supported him wholeheartedly. The terrible cost of the Yom Kippur War and the fear of another round of fighting had created an immeasurable longing for peace among most Israelis. Yet being realistic they had not expected it, and here Begin had brought about the seemingly impossible. Why haggle about the territorial price to be paid?

The Labor Party was aghast. They would never have been prepared to make the kind of concessions that Begin had made at Camp David. But now that Begin had done it, could they oppose the peace that he brought back with him?

Who in the Knesset was prepared to vote against it? Some Herut stalwarts like me. Actually, the majority of the Herut Knesset members voted against. Some Labor Party hawks, Shlomo Hillel and Shoshana Arbeli-Almozlino, also voted against. There were a number of abstentions. Yigal Alon, the hero of Israel's War of Independence, abstained, as did Yitzhak Shamir, now the Speaker of the Knesset. But a strong majority voted to approve the Camp David Accords. It was a great victory for Begin.

Before the vote Begin had tried to convince a number of Herut Knesset members to support the Accords, but he did not appeal to me, knowing, I suppose, that I was steadfast in my opposition. In conversations with me Shamir said that he was opposed to the agreement, but ended up abstaining. When I asked him why he had abstained, he replied that as the Speaker of the Knesset he thought it would have been inappropriate for him to cast an opposing vote.

Some in the Likud thought that I, as chairman of the Foreign Affairs and Defense Committee, had no business voting against the agreement. Weizman said that I should vacate the position. Begin could have ordered me to do so, but he did not. I continued in the job and maintained cordial relations with him.

Palestine Liberation Organization (PLO) terrorist activity originating in Lebanon kept tensions high on Israel's northern border. Following a terrorist attack on a bus on the coastal road in which thirty-eight Israeli civilians were killed, the IDF launched operation Litani, crossing into southern Lebanon in March 1978. There, Major Saad Haddad, an officer of the Lebanese Army, decided to ally himself with Israel and organized the "Free Lebanon Army," which took charge of a strip of territory bordering on Israel. Much of the committee's time was spent keeping an eye on the situation in Lebanon. I set up a subcommittee to deal with the situation there. Yigal Alon declined my suggestion that he head this committee, and I personally took charge of it.

In February 1980 the government decided on the development of an indigenous Israel fighter aircraft, Lavi. This had been my dream in the days when I had worked at IAI, and I had prepared the groundwork for such a project. I had no doubt that the IAI engineers had the capability to come up with a first-class fighter. The program had my enthusiastic support. After discussing the project in my committee, I proposed that we pass a resolution of support for the program, and it was passed with one dissenting vote; Yitzhak Rabin was the sole opponent. Seven years later, after two Lavi prototypes were already undergoing flight tests, Defense Minister Rabin led the battle in the government that led to the cancellation of the program. He had never been a great supporter of local weapon development.

Shortly thereafter, in May 1980, Weizman, who was defense minister, resigned from the government, claiming that he resigned because he was dissatisfied with the budget allocated to defense. However, in no time it became clear that he wanted to bring down the Begin government and believed that his resignation would trigger the fall of the government. He was up to his old tricks, trying to replace Begin. It did not work this time, either.

With Weizman's resignation, Begin was looking for a new defense minister, and he chose me. I had evidently established a good reputation as chairman of the Knesset's Foreign Affairs and Defense Committee, and he must have felt that the appointment would be generally approved. There was only one problem: me.

By that time the IDF had already completed a substantial part of the withdrawal called for by the Israeli-Egyptian peace treaty signed in March 1979, up to a line connecting El Arish with Ras Muhammad on the Red Sea. The most difficult part—withdrawing from the eastern Sinai, which involved abandoning air bases and also the town of Yamit—was still ahead. I had disagreed with the terms of the treaty, but had by now accepted them as givens. I realized that our commitments defined by the treaty had to be met. But I did not want the responsibility for carrying out this task.

Begin invited me into his office. His trusted aide, Yehiel Kadishai, ushered me in and then left us alone. The news of the impending offer had already been making the rounds, so I knew what was coming. Begin suggested that I take the position of defense minister. I knew that for me it would be an honor and a privilege to assume responsibility for the security of the people of Israel—to fill the position that in past years had been held by David Ben-Gurion, Levi Eshkol, and Moshe Dayan. But my mind was made up. I told Begin that, as he knew, I had not agreed to the terms of the Camp David Accords. Although I understood that the treaty was now a fait accompli, I was not prepared to be responsible for the final stage of the withdrawal.

"I don't understand your opposition, Misha," Begin interjected. "Sinai is not the Land of Israel; it is not the Land of Israel according to the Bible, Chief Rabbi Goren has declared that it is not the Land of Israel, and Jabotinsky never claimed that it was the Land of Israel. So why are you opposed to the withdrawal from Sinai?"

I saw no point in explaining to him that my objection to turn all of the Sinai over to the Egyptians had nothing to do with whether the Sinai was or was not part of the Land of Israel, but rather was based on strategic considerations and the precedent that was being set by rewarding aggression. So I left it at that. It was clear to me that Begin had a rather dogmatic position on the concession he had been prepared to make in order to achieve a peace treaty with Egypt—he was prepared to concede territory that was outside the borders of Mandatory Palestine. By his definition this was not the Land of Israel; he was not prepared to give an inch of areas within the borders of what had been Mandatory Palestine. This became clear when during the negotiations leading up to the signing of the peace treaty under Carter's tutelage he rejected pressure to make even the most minor concessions in the Gaza Strip. The myth that Sadat refused to accept Begin's offer of the Gaza Strip is without any foundation. As far as Begin was concerned the Gaza Strip was a part of the Land of Israel and not up for negotiations.

Although Sharon was angling furiously for the defense minister job, Begin decided to keep it for himself. For the rest of this government, a time of dramatic security events, Prime Minister Begin was also defense minister.

Successive PLO attacks against towns and village on Israel's northern border and against areas in southern Lebanon under the control of Major Haddad led to Israeli retaliations, and eventually to a U.S.-brokered truce in July 1981. I followed these events closely and became convinced that the continued presence of PLO forces in southern Lebanon had created an untenable situation, which would require an Israeli military move that would free northern Israel from the threat of PLO attacks.

The continuing civil war in Lebanon pitted the Christian forces, led by Bashir Gemayel, against the Syrian forces operating in Lebanon. Naturally Israel's sympathy was with the Christian forces, and a close relationship, managed and promoted by the Mossad, developed with Gemayel. Some of his fighters received training in Israel, weapons were transferred to his forces, and Gemayel himself visited Israel. On one occasion it was arranged for me to meet him in the home of a Mossad official in Israel. I could see that he was a charismatic leader. Israel's support of the Christian forces culminated in an Israel Air Force attack on two Syrian helicopters that were used in an attack on the Christian town of Zahle in the Beka'a Valley.

Finding an ally in a neighboring Arab country looked like a potential breakthrough. The Christians, led by Bashir Gemayel, seemed organized and motivated. They were opposed to our enemies, the PLO and the Syrians. It was easy to see why the Mossad got caught up in the idea of such an alliance. As became clear the following year, we were insufficiently aware of the complexity of the Lebanese political scene, the weakness and divisiveness of the Christian community there, and the lengths to which the Syrians were prepared to go to maintain their hold on Lebanon. For a while it looked promising.

The Iraqi dictator Saddam Hussein had built a nuclear reactor southeast of Baghdad with French help. It was intended as a step to make Iraq a nuclear power. Menahem Begin saw it as potentially an existential threat to Israel. In June 1981 the Israel Air Force, on orders from Begin, destroyed this Iraqi nuclear reactor. A superbly executed mission put an end to Hussein's dream of becoming a nuclear power. It was Begin's decision all the way. Putting aside doubts and reservations coming from all sides and prepared for the opposition that would inevitably come from Washington, Begin decided to act. It was a historic decision. Preparations for the mission were a close-held secret. I was not privy to the decision. When the aircraft safely returned from their mission Begin called me to inform me.

Within weeks of the destruction of the Iraqi nuclear reactor, Israelis went to the polls. The attack was a subject of the election campaign since Shimon Peres, the leader of the Labor Party, insisted that it had been a mistake. Labor recovered from the drubbing it had taken in the last election, but still lost to Likud 48–47 in Knesset seats.

While Begin was negotiating a new coalition agreement, the conflict with the PLO in Lebanon was escalating. After two weeks of PLO rocket and artillery attacks on northern Israeli towns and villages that were followed by Israeli retaliatory strikes, Philip Habib, President Ronald Reagan's emissary to the Middle East, negotiated a truce between Israel and the PLO that went into effect on July 25, 1981. Begin's second government was sworn in on August 5, 1981. Sharon had succeeded in pressuring Begin to appoint him as defense minister, and now replaced Begin in the job. I continued as chairman of the Knesset's Foreign Affairs and Defense Committee.

On October 6, 1981, Anwar Sadat was assassinated in Cairo. The news reached me as I was attending a gathering at the residence of the president, Yitzhak Navon. He had preceded me as chairman of the Foreign Affairs and Defense Committee and had invited me to a meeting of former chairmen. We were all aghast. Who was going to succeed Sadat, and what was going to happen to the Israeli-Egyptian peace treaty? Within days it became clear that the Egyptian vice president, Hosni Mubarak, took over as president quickly and that it was his intention to adhere to the treaty. Some of the warmth that had characterized the relations between the leaders of the two nations until then dissipated somewhat, but in the years to come Mubarak was scrupulous in observing the provisions of the treaty and met with Israeli leaders in Egypt, but with the exception of attending Yitzhak Rabin's funeral in Jerusalem he refrained from visiting Israel.

Maybe because he had some pangs of conscience about the withdrawal from Sinai and the abandonment of Israeli settlements there, Begin decided to introduce a bill in the Knesset that would apply Israeli law and administration to the Golan Heights—in effect, annexing the area captured by the IDF in the last days of the Six-Day War to Israel. On December 14, the law passed by a large majority. It aroused considerable anger in Washington. Relations with the Reagan administration were already strained by the attack on the Iraqi nuclear reactor and the ongoing battle that the American Israel Public Affairs Committee (AIPAC) was waging in Congress against the sale to Saudi Arabia of five Boeing AWACS (airborne warning and control system) aircraft, which Israel claimed would constitute a danger to Israel. The sale passed the Senate by a bare 52–48 vote, leaving much bad feeling behind. After the Iraqi nuclear reactor raid, Washington showed its displeasure by suspending the delivery of F16 aircraft to Israel. Now it was angered by the Golan law, and there was talk in Washington of "punishing" Israel. Incensed, Begin summoned the U.S. ambassador, Sam Lewis, and told him that there "was no force on earth that can bring about its rescission. . . . We are not your vassals, we are not a banana republic." In time tempers cooled, and it was generally agreed that the raid on the nuclear reactor had been an important act that benefited Israel and the United States.

Begin had assumed that the 15,000-strong Druze community in the Golan Heights would welcome incorporation into Israel, That did not turn out to be the case. They refused to accept Israeli identity cards, insisting that they were Syrian citizens and expected Syrian sovereignty over the Golan Heights to be restored. I saw it as an intelligence failure on our part. I held hearings in the committee and it turned out that no one in the intelligence community had been dealing with the Druze community in the Golan Heights. The government had naively assumed that they would gladly be joined to the 100,000-strong Druze community in Israel, whose sons serve in the IDF. In any case, the intelligence community had not been consulted, and no work had been done in preparation for the decision to incorporate the area into Israel. The allegiance of the Golan Druze to Syria continued in the years to come. They enjoyed all the benefits of living in Israel and the opportunities that offered, but insisted that they did not want to be Israelis, but were, rather, Syrians. We had ignored their close connection with Syria, their families in Syria, and the opinion of their religious leaders.

Shamir was now the foreign minister. One day, after a meeting of the Herut Executive Committee, he approached me suggesting that I should accept an appointment as Israel's ambassador in Washington. I had no doubt that the idea came from Begin, and assumed that Begin was hesitant to offer the position to me directly after my rebuff when he had asked me to become defense minister.

A few months earlier I had told Begin that I thought it was a mistake that, after the 1977 Likud electoral victory, our ambassadors in Washington continued to be adherents of the Labor Party. We need someone who can explain our views to the administration, Congress, and the American public, I told him. "Are you interested in the position?" he asked. I told him that I was not. But I was puzzled by the fact that after the Likud took over, Simha Dinitz, a Labor stalwart appointed by Golda Meir, continued as ambassador, and that after him Efraim (Eppie) Evron, also identified with Labor, had been appointed. I assumed that these appointments reflected Begin's admiration for the seasoned Labor officials and his lack of confidence in the abilities of his own people. Now he must have concluded that the time had come for a change.

It was a challenge. It was exciting for me to think of returning to the United States as the representative of the State of Israel. The United States was where I had come of age as a teenager and young adult. I decided to accept.

On January 20, 1982, after the agreement of the U.S. government had been obtained, it was officially announced that I had been appointed to be Israel's next ambassador to Washington. Eight days later, when Secretary of State Alexander Haig arrived in Jerusalem for his second visit in two weeks in an attempt to smooth some of the ruffled feathers of recent months, Begin invited me to the meeting, presenting me to Haig as Israel's next ambassador to Washington.

Shamir arranged for a small farewell gathering for me. In his speech he expressed his admiration for my readiness to leave a senior position on the political scene to become a "civil servant" in the Foreign Ministry. Of course it was said tongue-in-cheek, as the ambassadorial position in Washington was, and still is, considered to be a very senior position that is coveted by many. To take up the ambassadorial appointment I had resigned from the Knesset. It was to be a step of some consequence in my future political career, as became clear after I returned to Israel from Washington a year later to become defense minister.

Before my departure for Washington I asked to see Sharon, now the defense minister, to discuss the Lavi project. He invited David Ivri, the commander of the Israel Air Force, to the meeting. They knew that the project was very close to my heart. I told them I didn't believe the funding that the project would need in the years to come would be made available and suggested that while I was in Washington I would try to obtain U.S. financial support for the program. They heard me out but showed no enthusiasm for my suggestion. I could not tell whether it was because they felt sure that the funding from the Israeli government would be forthcoming or because they doubted my ability to obtain U.S. support. Nevertheless I took off for Washington determined to seek U.S. financial support for the Lavi project. I would succeed beyond my wildest dreams.

In early February my wife, Muriel, and I were seen off at Ben Gurion airport by Foreign Ministry officials, some friends, and our nineteen-year-old daughter, Rutie, who was attending the IDF officer candidate school. A photograph taken on that occasion appeared on the front page of the *New York Times* the following morning. To the newspaper's readers, it served as a first introduction to the State of Israel's new ambassador.

SEVEN

Ambassador

As Israel's ambassador to the United States, I had to give up my American citizenship. I filled out the necessary forms and handed them in to Bill Brown, the deputy chief of mission at the American embassy in Tel Aviv. I knew it had to be done and I did it willingly. I was proud to be an Israeli citizen, and the Israeli passport was enough for me. And yet, I felt sentimental about my American citizenship. I had come to America at the age of fourteen on a Latvian passport at the beginning of World War II. Going to America had saved my life. I received my education in the United States, attending MIT, the best engineering school in the world. I had served in the American army, receiving U.S. citizenship while I was in uniform. After being discharged from the army I had finished my studies at MIT on the GI Bill of rights, at the expense of the American government. My graduate studies at the California Institute of Technology had been the formative years in my engineering career. I admired and loved America, and I owed America a great deal. But I had left the United States because I wanted to make my contribution to the establishment and the security of the Jewish state. That was the most important thing in my life. For many years now I had felt myself to be 100 percent Israeli. Now I was turning the final page on the American chapter of my life.

I was an amateur diplomat. I had not studied international relations or political science and had no prior experience in the field of diplomacy. I was a political appointee coming to Washington in the footsteps of professional diplomats who had represented Israel in the past, men such as Abba Eban, Simha Dinitz, and "Eppie" Evron. In preparation for my new role I had a long discussion with Yitzhak Rabin, also a previous political appointee in that post, and with Evron on his return to Israel just before my departure. I had already learned that diplomatic protocol called for the departing ambassador to leave before the new ambassador arrived. I read the books written by three former ambassadors: Eban's *An Autobiography*, Rabin's *Service Book*, and Benjamin Franklin's *Autobiography of Benjamin Franklin*; Franklin served as the new nation's first ambassador to France during the years of the American Revolution. I mentioned this at a small farewell reception that Sam Lewis, the American ambassador, gave for me, which was attended by Eban, Rabin, and Dinitz. I told them that I did not intend to review their books, but could only say that of the three ambassadors, Franklin was the most modest.

On our way to Washington Muriel and I stopped off in London and had dinner with our ambassador to the United Kingdom, Shlomo Argov, and his wife and then went to the theater. He had served at our embassy in Washington, and spending an evening with him provided further insight as to what awaited me there.

I arrived in Washington at a time of crisis in the relations between the United States and Israel. The destruction of the Iraqi nuclear reactor by the Israel Air Force in June 1981 had angered Washington. When Washington announced its intention to sell five Boeing AWACS (airborne warning and control system) aircraft to Saudi Arabia, Israel objected that this would cause harm to Israel's defense capability. In October the Reagan administration won the battle that the American Israel Public Affairs Committee (AIPAC) fought in the Senate against approval of the sale by a narrow majority, but the fight left some bitter feelings behind in administration circles. Then came Begin's Golan bill that annexed the Golan Heights, causing additional tension between Washington and Tel Aviv. The administration signaled its displeasure by suspending the delivery of F16 aircraft to Israel.

It took me only a few days to size up the situation. President Ronald Reagan was basically friendly to Israel, as was his secretary of state,

Alexander Haig—unlike Secretary of Defense Caspar Weinberger, who did not hide his hostility. Most of the anger at Israel was concentrated among Reagan's immediate staff—James Baker, the president's chief of staff; Edwin Meese, counselor to the president; and William Clark, the president's national security adviser—and they seemed to be pulling the strings. Vice President George Bush, too, was cool toward Israel. This group looked upon Israel as a small country that should be grateful for the assistance it was getting from the United States and not cause any trouble. They were offended by the influence Israel was capable of wielding in Congress.

In the embassy I found an excellent team: Major General (Mendy) Meron, the military attaché; Danny Halperin, the economic minister; and Nachman Shai, the embassy spokesman. The deputy chief of mission (DCM) was Yaakov Nahshon, a former Herut member of the Knesset (MK) who was finishing his term in Washington. In those days the ambassador in Washington had the prerogative of choosing the DCM, and that was at the top of my agenda after receiving the appointment. I had met Zvi Rafiah, who had been the embassy's liaison officer with Congress at the time of my recent visit to Washington. He accompanied me during my appearances before congressional committees and I was very impressed by the connections he had made there. Now he had returned to Israel, retired from the Foreign Service, and established a consulting office. I asked him to return to Washington to be my DCM, but he turned me down. So who was it going to be?

I had met Benjamin Netanyahu and he had impressed me. He seemed to be doing an excellent job of organizing a conference on terrorism in Jerusalem in memory of his brother Yoni, who had fallen at Entebbe. He had succeeded in mobilizing a number of American personalities to attend the conference. I had known his father, Ben-Zion Netanyahu, from the time he had run the Zionist-Revisionist office in New York in the 1940s and assumed that his son and I were on the same wavelength ideologically. So I asked him to come to Washington to be my DCM, and he accepted. It seemed like a gamble at the time—he was young and lacked experience in the diplomatic world. But it paid off. He turned out to be an excellent DCM.

When Netanyahu arrived in Washington a few months after me he joined the team of Meron, Halperin, and Shai, who worked with me throughout my stay as ambassador. Not all of them were of my political persuasion, but we worked together in a common cause. I could not have asked for a better team. For years thereafter Washingtonians would tell me that Israel had the A-team at the embassy at the time.

I presented my credentials to Reagan within days of my arrival in Washington. My next stop was Howard Squadron, the president of the conference of major Jewish organizations. I met him in his law offices in New York and told him that after presenting my credentials to the president of the United States, I now came to present myself as Israel's ambassador to the American Jewish community.

My first stop in Congress was to pay my respects to Senator Danny Inouye, the senior senator from Hawaii. Of the many friends Israel had in the Congress, he was the best. He supported Israel without any reservations. His feelings toward Israel bordered on the messianic. Whatever we needed, we could always turn to him. He was a hero of World War II; an officer in the Nisei regiment, composed of Americans of Japanese descent, he had lost an arm during the fighting in Italy.

"What happened there at Camp David?" he opened the conversation after I sat down. "I thought you were expert negotiators," he said with a smile. He evidently shared my feeling that we had entered the negotiations with Egypt with a strong hand, after a great victory in the Yom Kippur War, and had ended up giving in to all the Egyptian demands. He probably knew that I had voted against the agreement. I knew I had found a soul friend. It was the first of many subsequent meetings with him. We remained close friends for many years, until his death.

I set myself the objective of establishing close contact with the administration. My target was Alexander Haig, a former four-star general who was now Reagan's secretary of state. I asked to meet him privately, without any of his aides present—a rather audacious move. To my surprise, he agreed. One evening I was whisked to a back entrance of the State Department headquarters in the Harry S. Truman building and directed to his office.

I explained to him that the reason I wanted to see him was that Begin was very anxious about the possibility of Egypt's not sticking to the terms of the Israel-Egyptian peace treaty now that Israel was completing the withdrawal from Sinai. Begin felt that that the United States was the key to continued Egyptian adherence to the terms of the treaty, since Hosni Mubarak, the Egyptian president who had succeeded Sadat, was intent on fostering Egypt's relations with the United States. Begin had made so great a concession at Camp David because he was under pressure from President Jimmy Carter; he was facing the Palestine Liberation Organization (PLO) terrorist threat from Lebanon; and now he was concerned that the Reagan administration would begin to apply pressure on Israel to retreat from Judea and Samaria, rather than insisting that Egypt stick to the terms of the peace treaty it had signed with Israel. Haig heard me out without interrupting, and then simply said: "Not on my watch." After a further discussion about the situation in Lebanon we parted on a first-name basis. I had obtained a valuable assurance and made a friend. I reported the conversation to Begin, and I sensed in his reply that he was relieved.

I made the same point when I appeared a few days later on the ABC news program *Nightline*, anchored by Ted Koppel. As the months went by I was a frequent visitor on that program as well as other TV news programs, and I became a familiar face to television audiences throughout the United States. From the feedback I received, I realized that such appearances created an impression not only on the public at large and members of Congress, but also on people in the administration. My television appearances were just as important as my official meetings, and maybe even more so.

My contact with Begin was generally by use of coded telegrams. On occasion we would talk on the telephone. We were quite sure that our calls were being monitored and tried to be circumspect, occasionally using code words that were probably not very successful in disguising the true meaning. Thus Begin would refer to Lebanon using the code word "land of the cedars"—surely understood by anyone who was listening in.

Shortly after my arrival in Washington I called a press conference to present myself to the media there. On that occasion I stated my opinion that the situation with the PLO active in southern Lebanon close to our northern border was untenable and that it was only a question of time before Israel would have to take military action to neutralize this threat.

At the embassy I established a routine of morning staff meetings with Meron, Halperin, Yaakov Nehushtan (a former Herut Knesset member), Shai, and the information officer, Harry Horowitz, where we reviewed the recent events and decided on the tasks each one of us would undertake that day.

I took it upon myself to visit a member of Congress almost every day. It wasn't long before I became a well-known personality in both houses of Congress and had made many friends along the way. Most of the support for Israel in the Congress came from the Democrats. Among the Republicans there were stout friends of Israel and others who were rather cool to Israel. Reagan himself was typical of Israel's friends. With him it was a gut feeling of friendship and admiration for Israel. He saw it as a small country embodying the American ideals of freedom, liberty, and democracy, facing great odds from surrounding enemies and courageously fighting them off. There were others among the Republicans who shared his feelings. On the other hand, some Republicans, like Vice President George Bush, saw Israel as a small country that was acting too big for its britches, which instead of displaying gratitude for the assistance it was getting from the United States kept asking for more and was making things difficult for the United States in its relations with Arab countries, while manipulating members of Congress to serve its interests. Their feeling for Israel was cool, sometimes bordering on hostility. Israel supporters in the Reagan camp were Haig and Jeane Kirkpatrick, the American ambassador to the UN; in the Bush camp were Caspar Weinberger, the secretary of defense, and the Reagan staffers, Baker, Meese, and Clark.

On April 19 the residents of Yamit in the Sinai, and their supporters from all over the country who had come to join them, were evacuated by force by army units under orders from Sharon. I watched it on television from afar. It was painful. This was the job I would have had to do had I taken up Begin's offer to become defense minister. I did not regret my decision. By completing the withdrawal from Sinai, Israel had met its obligations undertaken in the framework of the peace treaty with Egypt. Now that we had paid the price of the ticket, exorbitant as I held it to be, I believed that we should do whatever we could to arrive at the final destination: true peaceful relations between Israel and Egypt. As it turned out—the irony of fate—it finally fell to me, when I was foreign minister some years later, to solve one remaining stumbling block that held up the complete execution of the Israel-Egyptian peace treaty: the evacuation of the Taba one-square-kilometer area next to Eilat.

At the end of May Sharon visited Washington. I accompanied him to his meetings with Weinberger and Haig. In the meeting with Haig Sharon whipped out a map showing the deployment of PLO forces in southern Lebanon and emphasized the danger that they posed to Israel, sketching out possible Israeli moves to counter this threat. It has been alleged that at this meeting Sharon obtained a green light from Haig for the military operation Israel started twelve days later. There is no foundation to this story as I can testify. The two seemed to get along well together; Haig heard Sharon out but made it clear that the United States was opposed to such a move by the Israelis.

On June 3, eight days after Sharon's visit, Shlomo Argov, our ambassador in London, was very seriously wounded when he was shot at point-blank range on a street in London by three Palestinian gunmen. All hell broke loose. Israel saw in the attempted assassination of its ambassador a violation of the cease-fire that had been arranged by Philip Habib in July 1981. The next day the Israel Air Force raided PLO targets in Lebanon and the PLO retaliated by bombarding towns and villages near Israel's northern border.

On June 6 the Israel Defense Forces (IDF) entered Lebanon in a military operation named Peace for Galilee to restore quiet to northern Israel. The intention was to put the PLO rockets out of range of Israel's border with Lebanon, which required the IDF to move to forty kilometers north of the Israeli-Lebanese border.

President Reagan happened to be in Europe at the time; Haig and Clark were with him. In Reagan's absence Vice President Bush assembled a crisis management team in Washington, which, after discussing the situation, concluded that the United States should support a resolution to be introduced at the UN Security Council condemning Israel and threatening sanctions against it. On June 8 Reagan, in London, was advised of the decision and was told that his advisers in Washington unanimously approved the move. Haig interceded and convinced Reagan that the resolution should be vetoed. With only minutes to spare before the UN vote was to be taken, Haig telephoned Jeane Kirkpatrick and ordered her to veto the resolution.

The day before I had received a call from Kirkpatrick. She sounded frantic. She asked to meet me privately at a café in Washington. When we met she told me that Bush had taken charge of the situation and was pushing through a decision directed against Israel's move into Lebanon. She was at her wits' end. She disagreed with the decision, but at the UN she would have to follow the orders she received from Washington. This confirmed my impression that Bush was not particularly friendly to Israel, but there was little I could do. The following day I was greatly relieved when the resolution condemning Israel was vetoed by Kirkpatrick.

The episode made it clear to me that there were countercurrents in the administration regarding U.S. policy toward Israel. Reagan's inner circle, which included Clark and the vice president, were not friendly, whereas Haig and Kirkpatrick were strong supporters.

The ensuing days were busy for me. The IDF successfully engaged the Syrian Air Force and destroyed the Syrian surface-to-air missiles deployed in the Beka'a Valley while the IDF approached Beirut, and calls were heard from all sides for an immediate cease-fire. I appeared regularly on ABC's *Nightline*, NBC's *Meet the Press*, CBS's *Face the Nation*, and Public Broadcasting's *MacNeil-Lehrer Report*.

By June 8 the IDF had advanced to within fifteen kilometers of Beirut, and in mid-June the PLO forces were surrounded in an enclave in West Beirut. By this time the potential of the military operation was becoming clear: force the PLO to evacuate its forces from Lebanon and link up with Bashir Gemayel's Phalange Christian militia. What had started as a campaign to free the citizens of northern Israel from the threat of rocket and artillery fire had moved on to create the setting for a dramatic change that might free Lebanon of the presence of PLO forces and of Syrian tutelage and clear the way for an Israeli-Lebanon peace treaty.

This only became clear to me as the days went by, as we in the embassy were effectively left in the dark as to what the plans were. In order to understand just what was going on I asked Meron to fly back to Israel and go on to Lebanon, visit our forces there, and return to Washington with a clear picture of exactly what was unfolding so that we in Washington could explain Israel's position and plans. By the time he returned the picture was clear. Sharon was aiming to expel the PLO from Lebanon, force the Syrians to leave Lebanon, and create a situation where the Christians under Bashir Gemayel's leadership would take over leadership of Lebanon and establish peaceful relations with Israel. The IDF was now in East Beirut, the

PLO under Yasser Arafat was bottled up in West Beirut, much of the Syrian Air Force and their surface-to-air capability had been destroyed, and IDF units were astride the Beirut–Damascus highway, in effect cutting the Syrian connection to much of Lebanon. Israel was paying a mounting toll in casualties for these achievements. It was a grandiose plan that might just succeed. It was not hard to explain in the United States. Who would not agree to all foreign forces leaving Lebanon—the PLO, the Syrians, and also the IDF—and leaving Lebanon to the Lebanese? I was busy making this case morning, noon, and night on TV, and at meetings with members of Congress. But the administration insisted that there should be an end to the fighting and that Israel should agree to an immediate cease-fire. Philip Habib, Reagan's Middle East envoy, was busy shuttling back and forth between Israel and Lebanon attempting to arrange such a cease-fire.

It was at this juncture, on June 21, that Begin arrived in Washington for a meeting with Reagan. Begin had broken his hip climbing out of the bathtub at home a few days earlier and was now in constant pain and walking with the aid of a walker. His bodyguards would lift him out of the car on his arrival and he would then proceed on foot using the walker. I was amazed at his fortitude—his willingness to undertake such a difficult trip under these circumstances, and his ability to function even though physically handicapped. Originally Reagan's staff had suggested that the two meet without any note takers, but it was finally agreed that Begin would be accompanied by me, and Reagan by the U.S. ambassador in Israel, Sam Lewis.

Begin walked into the Oval Office using his walker and was greeted cordially by Reagan—"Call me Ron," Reagan said, "and I will call you Menachem." After both had been seated in front of the fireplace, and Lewis and I had taken the seats reserved for us, pad and pencil in hand, Reagan took some file cards out of his breast pocket. Before beginning to read from them he said somewhat shamefacedly, in his accustomed self-deprecating humor, "This is better than coming home at night and remembering that I had forgotten to say something, or worse, that I had said something I should not have said." And then he proceeded to read from the cards. In addition to some words of friendship and courtesy there was the insistence that the fighting in Lebanon must stop and that further loss of life must be avoided.

Begin did not need any prepared statements. Addressing Reagan as Mr. President, not as Ron, he launched into a long explanation of the dangers facing the people of Israel from the PLO terrorists in Lebanon and the reasons why the Peace for Galilee operation had become a necessity and why the job that had been started and was now close to completion had to be finished. Reagan was evidently not prepared for an extemporaneous exchange of views, and left it at that. We now left the Oval Office and proceeded to a larger meeting in the Cabinet Room. Begin had a rather harsh exchange with Weinberger, one of the more prominent spokesmen of those in the administration who advocated punishing Israel for its invasion of Lebanon.

The following day Begin met with a group of senators in a meeting that did not go well. His lecture on the situation in Lebanon and the Peace for Galilee operation was not well received, and a debate on Israeli settlements beyond the 1949 armistice lines ensued. One of the senators who challenged Begin was James Abdnor, a Republican senator from South Dakota, who was of Lebanese descent. "Mr. Prime Minister," he called out to Begin, "I have an old aunt in Lebanon and she has not been heard from since your invasion of Lebanon. I fear for her life."

There was nothing that Begin could say in response, but I buttonholed the senator after the meeting and asked for details of his aunt, telling him that we would try to locate her. Her name was Juria Abdnor and her village was Ayn Arab. I asked Major General Yehoshua Saguy, the head of IDF Intelligence, who had accompanied Begin to the meeting, to get this information to the IDF in Israel and ask that they try to find her. It turned out that Ayn Arab was in the Beka'a Valley, near the battle lines of the Israeli and Syrian forces, and not under IDF control at the time, but a special team was sent to the village, which found the old lady in good shape and brought her to Israel. The next thing I knew, our youngest daughter, Rutie, who was serving as a second lieutenant in the IDF and was posted near the Lebanese border, told me in a phone conversation that an old lady carrying a basket of cherries had been brought in by the army and that she was on her way to America. Juria Abdnor was delivered to the office of Senator Abdnor a few days later. Although obviously happy to see his aunt alive and well, it seems he did not know just what to do with her, and I believe that sometime afterward she was on her way back to Lebanon.

The next day Begin was in New York for a meeting with Jewish leaders. From his suite at the Waldorf-Astoria I called Haig, who was at the U.S. mission to the UN, staying at the same hotel. "Al, we have the head of IDF Intelligence here, and if you like I'll bring him over to give you a briefing on the situation in Lebanon," I told him. "You know, we're winning."

"You guys are always winning," he responded. "Come on over."

Begin, who overheard my side of the conversation, expressed his amazement that Haig and I were on a first-name basis. "Just like that, 'Al' and 'Moshe'?" he said. Within a few days it became clear that this friend of mine and of Israel was not going to stay in his post at the State Department.

Philip Habib was in Beirut trying to put together a cease-fire, while Sharon was continuing to apply pressure on the embattled PLO forces in West Beirut. The administration was pleading with us to interrupt the fighting and give Habib a chance. On June 25 I was in Haig's office in the State Department to relay a message from Jerusalem that the IDF would not enter Beirut for at least forty-eight hours and that Israel would notify the United States before it decided to do so. Haig seemed to understand the Israeli determination to finish the job and expel the PLO from Lebanon, but of course he presented the administration's position that Israel must cease the bombardment of West Beirut. As we parted he confided to me that he was now on his way to the president and expected that he would be leaving his position as secretary of state. That afternoon Reagan announced that he had accepted Haig's resignation and was nominating George Shultz to succeed him.

Haig's nemesis had evidently been William Clark, the national security adviser and a close friend of Reagan's from the days when he was governor of California. Clark was preeminent among Reagan's aides and had clashed with Haig on matters of foreign policy. So with Haig's resignation we had lost a good friend at Foggy Bottom—but who was George Schulz, the man taking over from Haig? He had been president of the Bechtel Corporation, which was doing a lot of business with Saudi Arabia, and had been quoted as favoring an "even-handed policy" in the Middle East. There seemed to be reason to worry. Within a few days, as I got to know him, it became clear that there was no reason to worry. He was a good friend of Israel, and became a good personal friend of mine. Shultz was sworn in on July 16, after being confirmed by the Senate. For ten days after his resignation Haig continued as acting secretary of state.

Arafat and his PLO cohorts were surrounded in West Beirut. It was now generally accepted that they would have to leave Lebanon. Amid discussions about the conditions of their departure there were intermittent cease-fires, with Sharon insisting that the pressure must be kept up to get them to depart. This pressure took the form of bombardment of their positions from the air, from the ground, and from the sea, which resulted in inevitable civilian casualties and aroused great anger in Washington. There was talk of the need to punish Israel and even impose economic sanctions. Every day I was called to appear on television to defend Israel's position. "A country that is prepared to sacrifice the lives of its sons for its defense is not going to give in to economic pressure," I said.

Saturday, July 17, the day after Shultz was sworn in, he invited me to meet him at the State Department. I was the first ambassador to be received by him. It was a good sign. Our meeting—the first of many more during the critical weeks that followed—was friendly. He and his wife, "Obie," invited Muriel and me to their house in Bethesda for dinner, and we went out together to the Kennedy Center to see a show. We became close friends.

On August 2 I was asked to come to the Oval Office to see the president. He was furious. On the desk before him he had a photo of an infant whose arms were wrapped in bandages. It had been reported that this infant had been injured in West Beirut by Israeli bombardment. Reagan looked at me, pointed to the picture, and said, "This must stop." All I could say was that I would check the circumstances of this infant's injury. It actually turned out that the infant had been hit in East Beirut by rocket fire that originated with the PLO, and not by Israeli fire. But it was clear to me that the reports of the suffering of the civilian population in West Beirut due to the siege and continued Israeli bombardment were arousing great anger. We were in danger of losing the support of the president, who during the past weeks had gone along with Israel's incursion into Lebanon and had resisted pressure from his inner circle to condemn Israel and even impose sanctions. I concluded that it was imperative for the IDF to cease its attacks on West Beirut and scrupulously adhere to a cease-fire. I cabled my views to Begin, Shamir, and Sharon and asked to come to Jerusalem to present the situation as I saw it from Washington. Begin agreed, and on August 8 I left for Tel Aviv.

The day I landed I was asked to attend a meeting of senior ministers, chaired by Begin, to present my case. Sharon, Shamir, and Yosef Burg, the interior minister from the National Religious party, were also there. I explained that since the start of operation Peace for Galilee we had been fortunate in having the support of Reagan, even though there were some people around him who were strongly opposed to Israel's entry into Lebanon and were suggesting that the United States "punish" Israel. But now the lengthy siege of West Beirut, the intermittent violations by us of the cease-fires negotiated by Philip Habib, and the daily reports reaching the president's desk of civilian casualties had brought the president to the point of anger and exasperation. I told them we were on the point of losing the president and strongly recommended that we agree to an immediate cease-fire and observe it scrupulously. "The president is a friend of Israel and we must retain his goodwill," I concluded.

At first there was a stunned silence. Then Sharon opened up. No way was there going to be a cease-fire in Beirut, now that Arafat and his terrorists have been trapped. The pressure had to be kept up so that he understands that he has to leave. A cease-fire now would prevent us from completing what we had begun. That was the sense of his remarks. No one replied; no one countered his position. Begin just listened. Shamir did not say a word. Sharon, obviously, was the ultimate authority as far as military matters were concerned. All obviously considered him to be the only one who really understood the military position in faraway Beirut. I had the impression that they felt they had no choice but to accept his verdict. My counterarguments fell on deaf ears. The meeting broke up. It looked as if I had come in vain.

The next morning Begin invited me to attend the government meeting and asked me to report on the situation in America. No sooner had I finished than a message arrived from Reagan expressing outrage at the continued bombardment of West Beirut. At this point the government decided to end the raids in Beirut; they would be renewed only if it became necessary. Then came a telephone call from Reagan, but there was a problem with the connection. But Begin got the message. He called Reagan back to inform him that a complete cease-fire had been ordered by the government. What a telephone call from the president of the United States can do!

The next day I went to Beirut by helicopter to visit with our forces there. Standing in the ruins of what was left of a building on the line separating Christian West Beirut and Muslim East Beirut, I met with Major General Amir Drori, commander of the northern front, who was commanding the IDF forces that had entered Lebanon, and Brigadier General Amos Yaron, commanding the IDF ground forces in the Beirut area. Things were quiet at the time, although there was great destruction all around us. All were awaiting the conclusion of the negotiations Philip Habib was feverishly carrying out for the evacuation of Arafat and his PLO forces and the Syrian troops besieged in West Beirut. Encircled by the IDF, Habib was now trying to arrange for their peaceful evacuation.

A meeting was arranged for me with Bashir Gemayel, commander of the Maronite Christian militia. We had met on one of his secret trips to Israel more than a year ago. We were almost old friends. Now he was the leading candidate to become Lebanon's next president, and our hopes for attaining a peaceful agreement between Lebanon and Israel were resting on him. I was already back in Washington on August 23, when the Lebanese parliament elected him president of Lebanon.

Begin, obviously worn out by the last few months, decided to take a vacation at the Carlton Hotel in Nahariya, a small, modest establishment near the Lebanese border. But it was not to be a pleasant vacation. On September 1 he had two visitors who managed to upset him: Bashir Gemayel, the Lebanese president-elect, and Sam Lewis, the American ambassador.

Begin was burdened by the heavy toll in the lives of Israeli soldiers the IDF operation in Lebanon had taken in the past three months. He expected that Gemayel—in gratitude for the effort Israel had made to drive the PLO out of Lebanon and to reduce the Syrian presence there, an operation that had paved the way for his election as Lebanon's president—would accede to Begin's demand that the time had now come for Lebanon to make peace with Israel. But Gemayel was weighed down by the challenges facing him in his new position: gaining legitimacy in the heterogeneous society of Lebanon, and finding his place among the leaders of the

Arab world. It is not time yet, he told Begin, who was enraged by this message. The two were worlds apart and parted in anger.

Sam Lewis came with a message from Reagan: the Reagan plan to bring peace to the Middle East. Shultz, the new secretary of state, felt that Israel's operation in Lebanon and the eviction of the PLO from the country had opened a window of opportunity for making peace between Jews and Arabs. Weeks of secret consultations with his advisers and associates had produced a plan that was intended to serve as a starting point for negotiations between Israel and the Arab world. It included a freeze on Israeli settlements in Judea, Samaria, and Gaza, and self-rule for the Palestinians in these areas. But Schultz had no idea of what was going through Begin's mind at this juncture. As far as Begin was concerned this was a time for weaning Lebanon away from the Arab world—not the time to restore the prestige of the PLO, which had just been defeated, by offering the Palestinians an improvement over what had been agreed at Camp David. He rejected the plan out of hand. "Don't worry, we know how to take care of ourselves, and we will," he called out to the hapless Lewis as he was departing.

Shultz, with the best of intentions, had spent a month putting together a peace plan that he believed would serve everyone's interest—Israel's, the Arabs', and the United States'—but he had failed to understand Begin's state of mind.

I was completely surprised by Shultz's initiative. Shultz had made sure to keep its preparations secret, and I came in for some criticism in Israel for not having alerted Jerusalem to what was coming its way.

On September 4 Arafat and his cohorts departed Beirut harbor and moved to the northern Lebanese port of Tripoli. Over a year later, in December 1983, they were forced to leave Tripoli after being besieged by dissident PLO forces supported by the Syrians. This time they left for Tunis. From there they were rescued ten years later by the Oslo Accords.

The eviction of the PLO from Lebanon had not been the announced objective of the Peace for Galilee operation, but it took shape as the fighting continued and the potential fruits of such an eviction became clear. It was clearly in the best interests of Israel and Lebanon. Philip Habib, Reagan's envoy, had invested tremendous effort to reach an agreement for the PLO's departure among all the parties involved. Now it was a fact. The eviction of the PLO, the ejection of some of the Syrian forces from

Lebanon, and the election of Gemayel as Lebanon's president were the direct result of Israel's military operation. At the moment it seemed to have been worth it. But just for the moment.

Within ten days the picture changed. On September 14 Bashir Gemayel was assassinated. What should have been clear to all was crystal-clear to Hafez el-Assad in Damascus: The Israeli plan hinged on one man. If he was made to disappear the plan would collapse like a house of cards. So they killed him. These are the rules of the game in the Middle East. The assassination set in motion a series of events that eventually ended my tenure as ambassador to Washington and brought me to the Defense Ministry in Tel Aviv five months later.

Two days after Bashir Gemayel's assassination, forces of the Maronite Christian militia entered the Sabra and Shatila Palestinian refugee camps in Beirut and carried out a massacre, killing hundreds of defenseless men, women, and children. There was wide television coverage showing scenes of the carnage. It was devastating.

The next day was Rosh Hashanah. Muriel and I attended services at the Adas Israel Congregation in Washington. The rabbi, Stanley Rabinowitz, invited us to his home for a festive meal. Before we had finished I received a call asking me to come to the State Department immediately. There awaiting me were Shultz and Undersecretary of State Larry Eagleburger. Both looked deadly serious. Skipping any formalities, Shultz turned to me. "The president has instructed me to demand that Israeli forces get out of Beirut," he said. "Israel, against all our advice, took control of the city, and now it is the scene of a massacre." Still under the impact of the grisly scenes I had seen on TV, I was almost speechless. "I will transmit your message," I replied, and took my leave.

It was obvious to me that what happened at the Palestinian refugee camps had to be investigated thoroughly, and that only an announcement that the matter was being investigated by us would allow us to ward off at least some of the allegations regarding Israeli responsibility and complicity in the massacre there. I cabled to Begin, Sharon, and Shamir my view that it was essential that an inquiry committee be set up immediately. There were similar calls from all directions.

Things began moving quickly. On September 20 Reagan announced that a Multinational Force (MNF) composed of U.S. Marines and French and Italian troops would be deployed in Beirut. The following day Amin Gemayel, Bashir's brother, was elected as Lebanon's president, and on that day the Israeli cabinet decided to withdraw IDF forces from Beirut, in coordination with the deployment of the MNF there. The next day Amin Gemayel was inaugurated as president, and on September 24 Begin announced the establishment of the Commission of Inquiry into the Events at the Refugee Camps in Beirut, to be headed by Supreme Court Justice Yitzhak Kahan to investigate the massacre at Sabra and Shatila. Four hundred thousand demonstrated in Tel Aviv the following day, calling for Begin's resignation. The extended military operation in Lebanon, the mounting casualty toll, and now the Sabra and Shatila massacre were all bringing to light a deep division in Israeli society about the conduct of the Peace for Galilee operation by the government. It still controlled a majority in the Knesset, but was facing massive opposition among the public.

Almost daily I was invited to appear on TV to explain recent events and Israel's position. On September 27 the *Washington Post* ran an article titled "Arens for the Defense" by Donnie Radcliffe. She quoted me regarding the massacre: "We have before us an event of unparalleled tragedy. . . . We've never had that kind of tragic event with the ramifications and the things that were said between the U.S. and Israel, between Americans and Israelis. In that sense it's a singular event in our relationship." Complimenting me on my appearances as ambassador, she wrote, "His performance since he arrived in Washington has earned him admiration," and quoted Ted Koppel of ABC: "He is very straightforward, very tough and never beats around the bush." It was nice being complimented, but the weeks after the Sabra and Shatila massacre were my toughest time in Washington. Arthur Goldberg, the former Supreme Court justice who had become my friend in Washington, tried to comfort me by quoting a Greek philosopher: "There is nothing terrible that lasts forever. Or even for long."

The appointment of the inquiry commission had provided something of a respite as everyone waited for the commission's findings. It gave me a chance to turn my attention to matters I considered of great importance: increasing U.S. financial assistance to Israel and obtaining funding for the Lavi fighter aircraft program.

Since the Yom Kippur War Israel's defense budget had consumed an inordinate percentage of Israel's resources. In 1974 Israel's defense expenditures consumed 30 percent of Israel's gross national product. And although the yearly defense budget decreased gradually over the following years, it continued to represent a heavy burden on the Israeli economy and induced a rampant inflation and kept the economy from growing. Shultz, a professor of economics, was concerned and was eager to be of assistance. He invited the Israeli finance minister, Yoram Aridor, and explained to him that this rate of inflation could not continue and had to be curbed. About two years later his advice was finally taken and an energetic program that included special U.S. financial aid brought inflation in Israel under control.

With the assistance of our economic counselor, Danny Halperin, I turned to Congress seeking an improvement in the annual aid package Israel received from the United States. This aid was provided primarily through the Foreign Military Sales program in the form of loans to purchase American weapon systems. These loans to Israel, although of great importance in bolstering Israel's defense capability, also required Israel to allocate annually the interest payments for the maintenance of these loans. Our request was that at first, economic aid in the form of grants would be provided to cover the cost of the interest payments, and that in the future the money for purchasing equipment in the United States would be provided as grants. It was an indication of the great bond of friendship between the United States and Israel that within a few years this goal was achieved. In the past the United States had provided Israel annually with about $3 billion in grants for the purchase of weapon systems in the United States, and the loans from previous years have been repaid.

More ambitious—even audacious—was our request for assistance in the development of the Lavi fighter program. The Lavi was intended to be an Israeli-designed and Israeli-produced fighter aircraft second to none. It was particularly close to my heart. Its designers had been my students at the Technion and had worked for me while I was the chief engineer of IAI. We had begun the early preliminary design of an Israeli fighter aircraft during my tenure there, while we were working on the Kfir fighter, the modification of the Mirage. I had full confidence in the team, led by

Ovadya Harari, my former student, to succeed in this venture and launch Israel into the first rank of fighter aircraft developers, in line with Boeing, Lockheed, and General Dynamics in the United States, Dassault in France, and the developers of the MiG aircraft in the Soviet Union.

One of the two major American jet engine manufacturers, Pratt & Whitney of Hartford, Connecticut, had sufficient confidence in the Lavi project to develop at their own expense an engine suited to its requirements, the PW1120 turbofan engine. The Grumman Aircraft Engineering Corporation, in Bethpage, Long Island, was a subcontractor for the initial manufacture of the aircraft's wings. There was only one problem with the project: Israel did not have the resources to fund the development on its own. American assistance would be required, assistance beyond what was available within the framework of the $3 billion annual Foreign Military Sales program made available to Israel, whose funds had to be expended for purchases in the United States. My challenge was to convince Congress and the administration to permit Israel to use a substantial part of this aid for the development of the Lavi in Israel. I was able to get permission for Israel to use $250 million of annual U.S. aid for the development of the Lavi aircraft in Israel rather than for purchases in the United States.

Admittedly, this was not easy. Not only was the Lavi going to be a direct competitor to the F16 aircraft produced by the General Dynamics Company of Fort Worth, Texas, but the Israel Air Force was itself considered to be a significant potential market for the F16, a market that would be lost to the F16 once the Lavi entered production. In addition, the United States gave permission to U.S. defense companies to participate in the program and to transfer technology to it. It was an unprecedented level of U.S.-Israel cooperation.

I succeeded in convincing Shultz that this was a very important program for Israel and therefore worthy of exceptional American support. I assume he must have convinced Reagan of the same. Moreover, I suspect that Shultz, who like the rest of the administration was not enamored of Sharon, was interested in advancing me on the Israeli political scene, and thought that the Lavi project would not only benefit Israel but also give me a boost politically, which would be to America's advantage. In Congress I had many friends and it was easy to gain sufficient support for my request. Thus it came to be that the United States extended extensive assistance to the development of an Israeli fighter aircraft that was a potential competitor to an American fighter aircraft.

On November 10 Begin left Israel for what was intended to be an extended trip to the United States, which was to conclude with a meeting with Reagan in Washington. I greeted him at Kennedy Airport. He looked wan and tired. He had by now discarded the walker and was using a cane. I flew with him to Los Angeles, where he was to address the Council of Jewish Federations. Not long after our arrival, Begin was informed that his wife, Aliza, had died, and he decided to return to Israel immediately. It was left to me to address the audience assembled to hear him. I was a poor substitute, but had no choice under the circumstances.

Aliza (Aala) Begin had been Menachem Begin's faithful companion for more than forty years; they married in 1939. Together they had fled Warsaw as the German army approached in September 1939 and found refuge in Vilna, then under Lithuanian sovereignty, hoping to be able to go on to Palestine from there. When the Soviets took over Vilna, Begin was arrested, tried, and sentenced to penal servitude in a Siberian gulag, while his wife succeeded in getting to Palestine. They were reunited when Begin, released from the gulag one year later, arrived in Palestine as a soldier in Anders' Polish army in exile. She was with him hiding out in the underground when he commanded the Irgun in its fight against British rule in Palestine, and during the many years he led the opposition in the Knesset. He was very attached to her, and her death shook him up. On the night in May 1977 when it was announced that he had finally won an electoral victory and that he was going to be the next prime minister of Israel, he gave expression to his admiration and love for his wife when he quoted the prophet Jeremiah: "I remember how faithful you were to me when you were young, you loved me as if you were my bride, you followed me through the desert, where nothing had been planted." In the months after her death he was a different man, seeming to have lost much of the energy that characterized him. Within a year he resigned and retired from politics.

I spent the next two weeks seeking ways of improving relations between the administration and the Israeli government. Washington insisted on implementation of the Reagan plan, which had been rejected by

Begin. I cabled Begin, with copies to Shamir and Sharon, suggesting the Israel government announce a three-month freeze on settlement activity in Judea and Samaria in order to relieve some of the tension. I did not realize that at that point Sharon already saw me as a potential candidate to take over the Defense Ministry if he should be forced to quit as a result of the Sabra and Shatila incident, and might use the content of the cable to block such a possibility. He leaked the contents, which resulted in accusations that I had gone soft and was prepared to give in on an important issue of principle: the right of Jews to settle in all of the Land of Israel. As it turned out the ploy did not work

On February 8 the Kahan Commission issued its report. It was a bombshell. It found Israel indirectly responsible for the consequences of the Maronite militia's entry into the Palestinian refugee camps of Sabra and Shatila, and recommended the removal of Sharon from the position of defense minister, as well as disciplinary action against a number of IDF senior officers. Two days later the Israeli government accepted the commission's report, and three days later Sharon resigned as defense minister, remaining in the government as minister without portfolio.

That day New York City had been hit by a snowstorm. I had gone to New York to attend a cousin's funeral and was unable to return to Washington as flights were canceled. Snowed in at the Regency Hotel, I was reading Saul Bellow's *Ravelstein* when I received a call from Israel. It was Dan Meridor, the cabinet secretary. "Begin wants you to take on the job of defense minister," he told me. It was the second time that Begin offered me the position. I assumed that he had not called me directly out of concern that I might turn him down again, and had asked Meridor to speak to me. This time I was not going to turn him down. I didn't hesitate, and accepted. "But Begin wants you to come right away," Meridor said.

"I'll do the best I can," I replied. It was clear that Begin was eager to have a defense minister in place as quickly as possible.

My next call was to Muriel in Washington to tell her the news. I would be leaving for Israel within two days and she would be left with the job of packing up our things and sending them to Israel. She was not overjoyed to hear this.

When flights finally resumed I returned to Washington. I bade farewell to my friends and made some last-minute arrangements. Senator Howard

Metzenbaum, one of my many friends in the Senate, wanted to host a farewell dinner for me with other senators, but I had to excuse myself and explained that I was in a rush to get back to Israel. In the morning I took the shuttle to New York and from there flew via El Al to Israel. I had been ambassador for twelve months.

As deputy chief of mission, Netanyahu took charge of the embassy on my departure. He had done an excellent job and I recommended to Begin and Shamir that he be appointed ambassador to replace me. They thought that he was too young and inexperienced to fill this most senior and important of Israeli diplomatic posts. I disagreed, and saw no need for this talented young man to be appointed to a minor diplomatic post before being considered sufficiently experienced to be appointed Israel's ambassador in Washington. They insisted on appointing one of Israel's experienced diplomats to replace me: Dr. Meir Rosen, who had accompanied Begin to the Camp David negotiations as the Foreign Ministry's legal adviser, and was serving as Israel's ambassador to France. No doubt it was a good choice.

Netanyahu preferred not to remain as DCM in Washington, and after some lobbying on my part he was appointed as Israel's ambassador to the UN. During his four-year tenure he turned out to be one of Israel's best representatives in that post. His frequent appearances gave him considerable publicity back in Israel and paved the way for his election to the Knesset on his return to Israel. It was the beginning of a brilliant political career. As of 2017 he is Israel's longest-serving prime minister.

Although I am frequently complimented or accused, as the case may be, for being responsible for Netanyahu's becoming prime minister, it really should be apparent that his great talent and capabilities would have made him a leading political figure in Israel in due time even if I had not appointed him to the Washington embassy staff in 1982.

EIGHT

Defense Minister

On March 2, 1983, I was sworn in as defense minister in the Knesset. From there I was driven directly to the Defense Ministry in Tel Aviv. After a short military parade in the Defense Ministry courtyard, I went up to my second-story office and began dealing with a number of urgent problems that awaited me.

Although not a former senior military officer like some of my other predecessors in the job—Ariel Sharon, Moshe Dayan, and Ezer Weizman—I came well prepared. I was acquainted with Israeli defense issues and had given them a lot of thought during my years at Israel Aerospace Industries (IAI) developing weapon systems for the Israel Defense Forces (IDF), and the five years I served as chairman of the Knesset's Foreign Affairs and Defense Committee.

I decided to keep a watchful eye on the progress being made on the Lavi fighter project, and was disappointed to hear that the U.S. Department of Defense was holding up the signing of contracts with U.S. subcontractors of the project, including the contract with the Grumman Corporation, which was producing the Lavi wing made of composite material. On April 17 I called Shultz to ask for his help in clearing this hurdle, and within two days the problem was solved. I could see that Caspar Weinberger, the secretary of defense, no great friend of Israel, was trying to put obstacles in the way of the program, but it was clear that Shultz, with the support of the president, had the upper hand.

The most urgent problem facing me was disentangling the IDF from Lebanon—now 30,000 soldiers deployed at the gates of Beirut, on the Beirut–Damascus highway, and throughout central and southern Lebanon. It was exacting an almost daily toll on our soldiers and seemed to serve little useful purpose. And yet, as I told a reporter on my arrival in Israel who asked me when we would leave Lebanon, we didn't want to leave with our tail between our legs. We had a right to expect that there would be some assurance that we would not return to the situation that prevailed in northern Israel before the Peace for Galilee operation.

There was some reason to hope that this goal would be achieved in the negotiations taking place between Israel and the Lebanese government, which had begun after the accession of Amin Gemayel, Bashir Gemayel's brother, to the Lebanese presidency. Amin differed from his brother Bashir. He did not have Bashir's charisma and his popularity, nor his courage, and yet now that he had been elected after his brother's assassination, the outcome of the negotiations depended on him. On our side the negotiations were led by Major General Abrasha Tamir, who headed a national security planning section set up by Sharon in the Defense Ministry, and Dave Kimche, the director general of the Foreign Ministry under Shamir. Tamir was a veteran soldier with a record going back to Israel's War of Independence; Kimche had held a senior position in the Mossad when Shamir appointed him to be the director general of the Foreign Ministry. The goal was for the agreement to provide for peaceful relations between Israel and Lebanon and for the withdrawal of the IDF and Syrian forces from Lebanon. The Lebanese wanted the IDF out of Lebanon, and Israel wanted a peace agreement with Lebanon and the Syrians out of Lebanon. It would take the arrival of George Shultz and some intense shuttle diplomacy by him to get an agreement signed, but it did not take long before it ended up in the ashcan of history.

On April 19, nine days before Shultz was due to arrive in Israel, the U.S. embassy in Lebanon, located in West Beirut, was attacked by a suicide bomber. The attack killed sixty-three people, seventeen of them Americans. Meant as a signal, sent from Damascus, that Americans were not wanted in the area, it was an introduction for Shultz to the rules of the game in the Middle East. It followed the assassination of Bashir Gemayel seven months earlier and was not to be the last such signal.

For over a week, Shultz, by now an old friend from my days in Washington, shuttled back and forth between Jerusalem and Beirut. On one of his visits here, Shultz, his wife O'Bie, Muriel, and I had dinner together at the King David Hotel in Jerusalem. I could tell that after his visits to Arab capitals Israel seemed like familiar territory to him. "When I come here," he confided to me, "I feel like I'm coming home."

On May 5 he brought the text of an Israel-Lebanon agreement to Jerusalem that he said the Lebanese had approved. It fell short of a peace treaty between the two countries, as Israel had demanded, but it did provide for the termination of the state of war that had existed between Lebanon and Israel since Lebanon participated in the all-Arab attack on Israel on May 15, 1948. It provided for a phased withdrawal of IDF forces from Lebanon and a parallel withdrawal of Syrian forces from Lebanon. It did not give Israel the degree of military control it sought in southern Lebanon, but provided for the establishment of a special security zone there in which the Lebanese army would be responsible for preventing attacks on Israel. Now it was up to the Israeli government to sign off on the agreement.

I knew it was not going to be easy. Sharon was adamantly opposed, claiming that we would be throwing away the fruits of the campaign that had been waged under his direction. To others in the government it was something of a disappointment, after having set our sights high and having paid a heavy price in casualties. And yet, to me it was clear that this was the best we could get at the moment.

The evening before the government meeting on May 6 that was to discuss the agreement, I decided to meet with Begin to make sure that he would steer the government meeting to a decision accepting the agreement. I asked Shamir to join me. We met at the prime minister's residence, where I explained to Begin that it was essential that we accept the agreement: It would allow us to withdraw our forces from Lebanon and begin a process of normalization of the relations between Israel and another Arab country. Begin asked a few questions, but did not argue. When we left I said to myself, "Mission accomplished."

Throughout the entire evening Shamir had kept his own counsel. "Why didn't you say anything?" I asked as we walked out into the street.

"It wouldn't have made any difference," he answered laconically.

The next morning, while Shultz impatiently awaited the outcome at the King David Hotel in Jerusalem, the government spent seven hours discussing the agreement, and then approved it, by a vote of 17 to 2.

That afternoon, in my presence, Shultz put through a call to Reagan to inform him of the result. Then he passed the phone to me. "Mr. President," I said, "in this land of miracles your secretary of state has brought off a real miracle." Shultz was beaming. He had worked hard this past week, had overcome seemingly impossible odds, and had succeeded in bringing an agreement to signature. But it was not yet by any means a done deal.

On May 17 two parallel signatures of the agreement took place. The Arabic and French versions were signed in the Lebanese coastal town of Khalde, and the Hebrew and English versions were signed in the northern Israeli town of Kiryat Shmona. The signatories were Antoine Fattal, who had been nominated by Amin Gemayel to represent Lebanon in the negotiations; Dave Kimche for Israel; and Morris Draper, Philip Habib's deputy, for the United States.

The Syrian dictator, Hafez el-Assad, made it clear that if Amin Gemayel did not want to follow in the footsteps of his assassinated brother, the agreement had better not be implemented. Amin Gemayel got the none-too-gentle hint. It was clear that the Syrians, who had suffered some severe blows from the IDF during the Israeli incursion into Lebanon, now, backed by the Soviets, were intent on recovering their dominant position there. Some months later the Lebanese government repudiated the agreement.

Certain personnel decisions had to be taken at this time regarding the IDF. First was the implementation of recommendations of the Kahan Commission of Inquiry, and, second, the appointment of a new chief of staff.

The Kahan Commission, in addition to calling for Sharon's departure from the position of defense minister, recommended that Major General Yehoshua Saguy not continue to hold the position of head of the intelligence branch of the IDF, and that Brigadier General Amos Yaron, who had commanded the infantry brigade in the Beirut area, not serve in the capacity of a field commander in the IDF for the next three years. The day after assuming the position of defense minister I informed Saguy that he would be replaced. He seemed stunned. It became clear to me that he and many others had assumed that the recommendations of the Kahan Commission would not be taken literally. I had decided to follow them to the letter. I held up Yaron's promotion for a year but permitted him to take on the position of head of the IDF's personnel division in his present rank of brigadier general. He was promoted to major general a year later. Saguy left the army. Now it was urgent to find a replacement for Saguy. I had been impressed by Major General Ehud Barak, one of the youngest generals in the IDF. He was intent on reaching the top in the IDF, and was concerned that this appointment rather than a field command might interfere with his plans. A little convincing and arm twisting brought him around. Eventually, he did end up as chief of staff—I appointed him during my second tenure as defense minister. But it turned out that his ambitions went way beyond leading the IDF. No sooner had he left the IDF than he joined the Labor Party as a minister in Rabin's first government, eventually becoming prime minister. Strange are the ways of politics and the military in Israel.

In April, Lieutenant General Rafael (Raful) Eitan was to complete his fifth year as chief of staff of the IDF, a record for length of service in that position. His bravery had become legendary in Israel. He had fought in all of Israel's wars, had been wounded, and had fought on. During the Yom Kippur War he commanded IDF troops in the Golan Heights as Syrian tanks broke through and reached the outskirts of his command post. Troops under his command repulsed them, threw them back, and then took the offensive that brought the IDF within artillery range of Damascus. He had been criticized by the Kahan Commission, but no action had been recommended against him. He was now free to return to his farm in Moshav Tel Adashim in the Jezreel Valley. Now I had to decide on his successor. There were three obvious candidates: Avigdor (Yanosh) Ben-Gal, Dan Shomron, and Moshe Levy. All three were major generals, and by all accounts worthy candidates for the position. I decided to consult my predecessor, Sharon, and the outgoing chief of staff, Eitan, and received conflicting recommendations. Sharon recommended Shomron but added that under no conditions should it be Ben-Gal. Eitan said the opposite: he recommended Ben-Gal, and under no conditions should it be Shomron. It was an indication of how deep the likes and dislikes ran among our generals. I interviewed all three and decided on Moshe Levy, who had been serving as deputy to Eitan. Because of his great height he was nicknamed Moshe-and-a-Half. Born in Tel Aviv to a family that had emigrated to Palestine from Iraq, he was to be the first non-Ashkenazi to head the IDF in the thirty-five years of its existence. The IDF had served and continues to serve as a melting pot for the many communities that make up the people of Israel. Levy's appointment was a sign that this cultural consolidation process had reached right to the top of the defense establishment.

I asked the other two candidates to stay on, telling them both that they would have another crack at the job in future years. Shomron decided to stay and became the next chief of staff after Levy. Ben-Gal decided to leave the army. That was a loss. He had been one of the IDF's best generals. As commander of the Seventh Armored Brigade he had stemmed the Syrian advance in the Golan Heights during the first days of the Yom Kippur War, when his forces were outnumbered and outgunned. He and Raful were among Israel's most popular military heroes. At one time during a period of tension with Syria, Begin in a radio broadcast called out to Assad: "Watch out, Assad! Raful and Yanosh are waiting for you!" All of Israel was sorry to see Yanosh end his service in the IDF.

An obvious lesson to be drawn from the Yom Kippur War was that the ground forces—armor, infantry, artillery, and the engineers—needed to be trained and equipped to fight in an integrated manner. The IDF needed a central ground forces command that would see to it that they were trained and equipped accordingly. But ten years later nothing had changed. The heads of the individual services still reported directly to the chief of staff and ran their own show. The idea of a ground forces command had been kicked around for years but had not been implemented, having run into the opposition of most of the senior IDF officers, who feared that their authority would be abridged by such a change. I was intent on bringing about this change, and appointing a new chief of staff presented an opportunity to do so.

When I informed Moshe Levy that I intended to appoint him as chief of staff, I told him that I had one condition: the establishment of a ground forces command. He thought for a moment and then replied that as long as this change would not affect the authority of the field commanders of the northern, southern, and central sectors he would go along with it. In other words, the ground forces command would have authority over training and equipment acquisition, but not over combat operations. Fair enough, I said, let's do it. Thus was brought about the first major structural change in the IDF since its inception.

The appointment of the IDF's chief of staff must be formally recommended to the government by the defense minister and then approved by the government. I notified Begin of my choice and his approval was seemingly automatic. Since returning from Washington I had realized that in all matters of defense he relied totally on me, not asking to be involved. The government duly approved my recommendation, and on April 19 Levy was promoted to the rank of lieutenant general and became the IDF's chief of staff. It turned out to be an excellent choice. He was a good soldier—capable, straight, and honest. He was married to a member of Kibbutz Beit Alfa in the Jezreel Valley, and on completing his four-year term he returned to the kibbutz to work in the cotton fields.

Now my attention turned to my former employer, IAI, Israel's foremost defense industry. Its major project at this time was the development of the Lavi fighter aircraft. My former students and employees were working on this all-important project. As ambassador in Washington I had succeeded in obtaining American support for the program, both financial support and technological cooperation. Now it was up to them.

I wanted to be sure that the general manager of IAI was somebody I could trust and depend upon. That man was Shalom (Zigi) Ariav, who had been the manager of IAI's manufacturing division during the time I had directed the engineering activities there. He had left IAI in the meantime and, with two other former IAI employees, had established a successful international aircraft trading firm. I needed him to come back to IAI to serve as general manager. I reached him by telephone while he was in the United States and told him to come back, that there was an important job awaiting him. He had one condition: that the chairman of the board not be active in the day-to-day activities of the company. David Ivri, a former commander of the Israel Air Force, had recently been appointed to that position. He had been an excellent air force commander and was not likely to take a back seat as chairman of the board. It was not a pleasant task, but I told him that he would have to vacate the chairman position, and I appointed Arye Grosbard, a businessman, member of Likud, and aircraft enthusiast, to the job. Ivri returned to the IDF as Levy's deputy chief of staff.

My appointment as defense minister was greeted with enthusiasm by some members of my embassy team in Washington, who wanted to continue working with me at the Defense Ministry. Major General "Mendy" Meron, the defense attaché in Washington, decided to return to Israel with me, and I appointed him to the position of director general of the Defense Ministry. Also deciding to return with me from Washington was his deputy there, Lieutenant Colonel Shimon Hefetz, and he became the deputy to my military adjutant. From among the candidates for that job I chose Brigadier General Danny Yatom, in later years to become head of the Mossad. Also joining me from the Washington team was Nahman Shai, who had been the embassy spokesman; he now became the spokesman of the Defense Ministry. Benjamin Netanyahu remained in Washington as the deputy chief of mission. I urged Begin and Shamir to appoint him ambassador but could not convince them that he was up to the job. They claimed that he was too young and inexperienced.

"Do you think he needs to serve as ambassador to Cyprus before he can be ambassador in Washington?" I asked, but I could not convince them. When Shamir became prime minister he agreed to appoint Netanyahu to be Israel's ambassador at the UN. The rest is history.

I had always been impressed by the loyalty of the Druze community in Israel to the State of Israel, and by the service of their sons in the IDF. Among Israel's minority communities, the young Druze and Circassian men are called up for compulsory military service, unlike the Muslim and Christian Arab young men. They used to serve in a Druze infantry battalion that had been set up especially to facilitate their service in the IDF. Upon becoming defense minister I asked whether Druze and Circassian soldiers had the opportunity to serve in other branches of the IDF if they so desired. They answer was negative. A policy based on a degree of caution regarding non-Jewish soldiers in the IDF had denied them access to these opportunities until then. In my view all those taking the same risks in military service had to be given the same opportunities. I instructed Levy to allow Druze soldiers to choose among all branches of the IDF instead of obliging them to serve in the Minority Battalion. That has been IDF policy ever since. Gradually the number of Druze soldiers who preferred service in units other than the Druze battalion grew. The Druze battalion was disbanded in 2015. Today Druze soldiers can be found serving in all branches of the IDF, and Druze officers have reached its highest ranks.

At the end of May the biannual air show opened at the Le Bourget Airport in Paris, an event no aeronautical engineer would want to miss. I intended to go and visit the IAI stand there and brag a little to my aeronautical colleagues about the Lavi. Now that the project had the funding it needed, it had made great progress. I had the full backing of Shultz, and whenever a problem appeared with transfer of U.S. technology to the project I would call him and the problem would be fixed within forty-eight hours.

But Begin asked me not to go; I was distraught to see that he actually pleaded with me. I saw that he did not want to be left with the burden of dealing with security problems, even for a few days. I did not appreciate that this was an indication of a more serious crisis to come. I promised to limit my stay to two days, and he reluctantly assented. I had a great time in Paris. I took great pleasure in meeting the CEO of Dassault Aviation, Benno Vallières. Now I had the opportunity to gleefully tell him about the Lavi, an aircraft that would be superior to any of the aircraft in the Dassault stable.

As a visitor to the air show I was the guest of the French defense minister, Charles Hernu. Israel's relations with France had not been particularly good ever since de Gaulle declared an embargo on the shipment of French arms to Israel on the eve of the Six-Day War. To my surprise, Hernu had prepared a royal reception for me at the French Defense Ministry—a full dress parade of French troops in the courtyard of the ministry. After reviewing the parade we spent an hour in his office discussing possible cooperation between France and Israel. All this was duly reported in the press. The following day I was invited to meet the French foreign minister, Claude Cheysson. Just in case I was under the impression that I was witnessing a renewal of the French-Israeli romance of yester-year, he took pains to let me know that French foreign policy was not made in the Defense Ministry, but rather in the Foreign Ministry. Make no mistake about it, he emphasized.

Shortly after the signing of the May 17 agreement with Lebanon it became clear to me that the Lebanese government was not likely to implement it. As a matter of fact, they never even ratified it. The Lebanese army, composed of soldiers from the different religious communities in Lebanon, was no more than a parade army. In addition to the army there were a number of militias, each one loyal to one of Lebanon's religious communities, operating at will. They took no orders from the Lebanese army, which was incapable of imposing its authority. Under these circumstances I decided that we could wait no longer and that the IDF had to begin evacuating Lebanon. I asked Levy to present to me some alternatives for a redeployment of our forces in Lebanon. Within a few days he came back with three alternatives: a redeployment to the Litani River in southern Lebanon, along the Zahrani River north of the Litani, or along the Awali River north of the Zahrani. My primary concern was to keep northern Israel out of range of rocket fire from Lebanon, and chose the Alawi River as the line defining the redeployment to the south. It meant leaving the Beirut area and the Shouf Mountains, populated by Druze and Christians. On July 14 Levy announced that the IDF would withdraw to the Awali Line. Six days later the withdrawal from the vicinity of Beirut began.

The Americans continued to believe in the Lebanese government and in the Lebanese army. It was not to be America's last misapprehension of Middle Eastern reality. The Americans acted as if Lebanon was an independent sovereign state, not realizing that the Amin Gemayel government looked to Damascus before it took any action, and that the Lebanese army was incapable of dealing with any of the local militias. By now it was, in effect, the Syrians who ruled Lebanon, and they were not about to cooperate. The Syrians were now in cahoots with the Lebanese Druze, led by Walid Jumblatt. They armed his militia, encouraging it not to cooperate with the Lebanese government or its army and to attack Christian targets in the Shouf Mountains, as well as the area where the American Marines were located in Beirut.

Walid Jumblatt had not always been a Syrian stooge. His father, Kamal Jumblatt, had at one time led Druze opposition to Syrian domination in Lebanon. Assad had him assassinated in 1977. Walid took over leadership of the Druze in Lebanon and subsequently met with Assad in Damascus. At their meeting Assad made a point of reminiscing about Walid's late father. That was enough to change his son's position. He mourned his father but understood the rules of the game. He would have to take orders from Assad from now on.

I decided to go to Beirut to appeal to the Christian leadership there to try to reach an agreement with the Druze so as to avoid internecine bloodshed and to strengthen the hand of the Lebanese government against Syrian pressure. On August 16 Muriel and I were flown by an Israel Air Force helicopter to Juniye, a Christian-dominated town north of Beirut, and from there we were driven to East Beirut, controlled by the Christian Phalange militia. There I was met by an honor guard of the Christian militia and greeted by its commander, Fadi Frem. From there we were taken to a fancy French restaurant—the men in uniform, guns in their holsters, and the women dressed in the latest fashion. In this crazy country it looked like some people were still living it up. At a press conference I said, "We believe it is very important to reach an agreement between the Christian and Druze communities and the Central Lebanese government before we [the IDF] leave the Shouf." My meetings with more than a dozen leaders of different Christian denominations—Maronnite, Greek-Orthodox, Greek-Catholic—seemed to produce no results. They were either incapable of taking a united stand, or else they considered my proposal pure fantasy.

I paid a courtesy visit to Pierre Gemayel, the father of the Gemayel brothers, in the village of Bikfiya on Mount Lebanon, and laid a wreath at the grave of Bashir Gemayel. I met with Camille Chamoun, a former president. I visited Charles Malik, a former Lebanese representative at the UN. He was suave, erudite, very friendly—a gentleman of the old school, probably wondering how he was going to survive in the jungle that Lebanon had become. In the evening we flew back by helicopter to Tel Aviv. My visit caused quite a stir, but it had been in vain. The Syrians were raging mad and the Lebanese prime minister, Shafik Wazzan, staged a one-day protest strike by refusing to attend a meeting of his own cabinet that day.

I had inherited a difficult and heartrending problem from Sharon: soldiers who were missing in action. Five Israeli soldiers—Hezi Shai, Zacharia Baumel, Zohar Lifshitz, Yehuda Katz, and Zvi Feldman—had been missing in action since an engagement with Syrian forces at Sultan Yakoub in the eastern Beka'a Valley. One Israeli pilot, Gil Fogel, who had been shot down over Syria, was in prison in that country. And eight Israeli soldiers—Eliyahu Abutbul, Dani Gilboa, Rafi Hazan, Reuven Cohen, Avraham Motevaliski, Avraham Kornfeld, Yosef Gros, and Nissim Salem—had been taken prisoner in an ambush by the Palestine Liberation Organization (PLO) at an outpost near Bahmadun on the Beirut–Damascus highway. In Israel, a small country in which the soldiers are considered to be the "children" of the whole nation, MIAs are a concern not only of the immediate family but of the whole nation. Finding them and returning them to Israel is one of the most important tasks of the defense minister. I asked Shmuel Tamir, a friend and a former minister of justice, to oversee the effort of bringing them home. At least once a week I met the families, who naturally asked not only that I share with them any information regarding their children that was available to me but also insisted that everything possible be done to bring them home. I had a close connection with the families of two of the MIAs and the family of the pilot who was a prisoner in Syria. Zohar Lifshitz was the son of Dr. Israel and Dvora Lifshitz, who were longtime friends; and Zecharia Baumel's brother was married to my wife's cousin. The pilot, Gil Fogel, was the son of Bernard Fogel, a close friend of our family. It was an indication of how close-knit Israeli society is. Bernard Fogel, a Holocaust survivor, came to my home to tell me that he and some of his friends were planning to help his son escape from prison. I managed to discourage him from such a dangerous adventure.

The work of Shmuel Tamir and his team eventually led to prisoner exchanges with the PLO and the Syrians that brought an initial group of our MIAs and the pilot home. In September six of the eight soldiers captured by the PLO were returned in exchange for 4,700 Lebanese detainees held by the Security Services at a temporary detention facility in Ansar in southern Lebanon and 65 Palestinian terrorists being held in Israel. The soldiers in the hands of the PLO were not really prisoners of war in the usual sense, but rather hostages held by a terrorist organization. That raised the principal question of whether we should negotiate with terrorists and what kind of a deal to strike with them. Nevertheless, they were soldiers who had been captured under wartime conditions. I agreed to this disproportionate exchange with a heavy heart, but finally gave my consent. I was not particularly concerned by the release of the large number of Lebanese detainees, who I believed were going to be released shortly in any case. More problematic was the release of sixty-five Palestinian terrorists in return for six Israeli soldiers. After some soul searching I gave my consent. Two of the soldiers captured by the PLO had been turned over by them to Ahmed Jibril's Popular Front for the Liberation of Palestine; they would be returned almost two years later in a controversial exchange when Yitzhak Rabin was defense minister.

In June 1984, in a prisoner exchange with the Syrians, Gil Fogel and two other Israeli soldiers and also the remains of five Israeli soldiers were brought home in return for the release of 291 Syrian soldiers, 13 Syrian civilians, and the remains of 74 Syrian soldiers. One of the bodies of the Israeli soldiers that were returned was that of Zohar Lifshitz.

Shultz was still trying to save the May 17 agreement, banking on the Lebanese government and the Lebanese army, believing that if given a few more days they could establish order in the Shouf. Unfortunately, this was a pipe dream. I had given up on the agreement weeks before, convinced that it would not work. I did not want to expose our soldiers to additional casualties by delaying the planned evacuation. At this point Shultz, probably having given up on me, decided to appeal to Begin. He asked Reagan to write a letter to Begin asking that the Israeli withdrawal be delayed so as to give the Lebanese army a chance to take over the area to be evacuated. But Druze and Christian militias were active in the areas to be evacuated, prepared to fight over control of them. The Druze were backed by the Syrians and were likely to overpower the Christian militias, while the Lebanese army was impotent. Before the American ambassador in Israel, Sam Lewis, had a chance to deliver Reagan's letter, Begin announced his retirement. It was August 28.

"I can't anymore," Begin said at the cabinet meeting that day, announcing his decision to resign. The ministers were stunned and pleaded with

Begin to reconsider, or at least to delay his move. "I can't anymore," Begin repeated. He looked tired and wan, and yet determined.

Begin offered no further explanation beyond that short phrase. Numerous explanations for his move have been offered. The most obvious is the way he related to the great responsibility that rested on his shoulders as prime minister. Like Israeli prime ministers before him—Ben-Gurion, Levi Eshkol, Golda Meir, and also his successor, Yitzhak Shamir—he felt that being prime minister was a mission that had been entrusted to him; leading the people of Israel was a heavy burden he carried on his shoulders from the day he entered the prime minister's office. Now he had reached the decision that he could not carry that burden anymore.

No doubt the death of his wife, Aliza, in November had been a big blow to him. They had been very close and he had relied on her. The Peace for Galilee operation—originally envisaged as a campaign that would last no more than a few weeks but instead had continued month after month—and the resulting Israeli casualties had caused him great grief. The time had come to transfer the responsibility of being prime minister to someone else.

When the stunned ministers realized that he was not to be dissuaded, they pleaded with him to at least wait until his successor could be chosen, so that the Likud would continue to head the coalition. He acceded and held off his resignation for a few days.

Now the race began. Who was going to be the next prime minister? It had to be somebody from the ranks of the Herut Party, the senior component of the Likud. The Herut Central Committee would have to make the choice. As defense minister I was the senior Herut member of the government and might have been the natural choice, but I was not a member of the Knesset, having resigned from the Knesset when I left for Washington. According to the law the prime minister has to be a member of the Knesset. That left me out. I had no feelings of regret. It had not been my ambition to become prime minister of Israel. The next obvious choice was Shamir, the foreign minister. However, David Levy, the minister of housing, announced that he would contest the election.

Levy, who had immigrated to Israel from Morocco, had succeeded in elbowing his way to the front ranks of Herut and creating a camp of followers who saw him as a rising star, but to my mind he could not compare with Shamir. Shamir had been one of the leaders of the underground who fought against British rule in Palestine. He was an old-timer, solid and dependable—a little stubborn guy whose one mission in life was serving the Jewish state. Levy asked to meet with me to obtain my backing, but did not succeed in changing my mind.

The election was held at Herut Party headquarters, the Jabotinsky House in Tel Aviv, at 2:00 a.m. on September 2, and Shamir won, 436 votes to 302. Now Begin submitted his resignation to the president, Haim Herzog. Shamir, heading the previous coalition, presented it to the Knesset, obtained the approval of a majority, and was sworn in as prime minister on October 10. I continued as defense minister in his government.

Earlier, on September 4, the IDF pulled out of the Shouf, and the Druze militias promptly began an offensive against Christian positions there. The United States was trying to shore up the Gemayel government, which was being hammered by the Druze, supported by the Syrians, and by Amal, the Shia militia. It was a hopeless task. On occasion the U.S. Marines, part of the Multinational Force deployed in the Beirut area since the Sabra and Shatila massacre, now came under fire. The United States intervened by supplying the Lebanese army with military equipment and by bombarding Syrian and Druze positions in Lebanon from U.S. Navy ships lying off the Lebanese coast.

On the morning of October 23, two suicide bomb trucks simultaneously struck a building housing U.S. Marines at the Beirut airport and the French paratrooper barracks in Beirut. Two hundred forty-one America servicemen and fifty-nine French paratroopers were killed. I immediately called Shultz offering our assistance, but there was little we could do. The Shia Islamic Jihad claimed responsibility. In time it became clear that the man who had engineered these acts of terror was Imad Mughniye, who for years had headed Shia terrorist activities. In later years these included the blowing up of the Israeli embassy in Buenos Aires in 1992 and of the building housing the offices of the Argentine Jewish community in 1994. He was probably also responsible for the bombing of the U.S. embassy building in Beirut in April. His murderous career was brought to an end in 2008 when his SUV was blown up in Damascus.

The U.S. response to the attack on the Marines in Beirut was desultory bombing of Syrian positions by attack aircraft and shelling of Syrian targets from Navy ships. But Washington was hit by a "get out of Lebanon" fever, and in February 1984 the Marines were withdrawn. It was the first encounter by America with Middle Eastern terrorism, and it did not end well.

I decided to make one more attempt to extricate our forces completely from Lebanon by approaching the leader of the Shia militia, Amal, in southern Lebanon. The majority of the population in southern Lebanon were Shia Muslims. They suffered during the years that the PLO operated freely there and enthusiastically greeted the IDF as liberators when they first entered the area, chasing the PLO forces before them. It was a mistake that Israel had ignored them and had placed sole emphasis on the connection with the Christians in Lebanon. By now Amal was allied with the antigovernment forces in Lebanon and saw the IDF as an occupation army. I had appointed Uri Lubrani, our former ambassador in Teheran, to deal with political problems in Lebanon. He identified Muhammad Ghadar, living in the village of Al Ghaziye near Sidon, as commander of the Amal militia in the south, and succeeded in making an appointment for me to meet with him. We flew near there by helicopter, and protected by a detail of IDF soldiers I entered his house. He shooed his children into another room and we sat down and talked.

Ghadar had spent some years studying at Texas A&M, and spoke perfect English. No interpreter was needed. "Look," I said, "we want to clear out of southern Lebanon and return our forces home. We have only one requirement: that after we depart no terrorist acts be committed against northern Israeli towns and villages from there. If you can guarantee that, we will be out in no time. We are prepared to assist you—to train and equip your forces and make you the most powerful militia in Lebanon. Do we have a deal?"

He had listened attentively, and after a moment he said, "I cannot make such an agreement." Whatever else I said did not convince him. "I can't do it," he repeated.

If the carrot did not work, I thought I'd better bring out the stick. "If we can't reach an agreement, then we will stay and we will fight you," I threatened. "You know that the IDF is stronger than your militia and you are bound to lose," I continued.

"I know," he replied, "but you forget one thing—we Shia enjoy suffering." We shook hands and I departed. It looks like we're going to stay in southern

Lebanon for a while, I said to myself. Shortly Hezbollah pushed Amal to the sidelines and engaged the IDF in southern Lebanon for many years.

On November 4 it was our turn to be hit by a suicide bomber. At six o'clock in the morning a man drove a small truck loaded with explosives to two adjoining buildings in the Lebanese town of Tyre that housed Israeli interrogation facilities. The man set off the explosives, blowing himself up in the process. Twenty-eight Israelis and thirty-one Lebanese were killed. This attack, too, was probably the work of Imad Mughniye.

That month I accompanied Shamir on his first visit to Washington as prime minister. My efforts during my tenure as ambassador to dramatically raise the level of U.S.-Israel cooperation in defense matters were now bearing fruit. Prior to the visit Reagan signed National Security Decision Directive 111, which reinstated the concept of strategic collaboration with Israel and provided a basis for the development of a formalized structure of strategic cooperation. This opened the way for discussions on joint military exercises, the stockpiling of U.S. military equipment in Israel, the sharing of intelligence data, the use of Israeli ports by the Sixth Fleet, and joint planning for military contingencies. During the visit the United States and Israel agreed to establish a Joint Political Military Group, which would convene every six months as an official forum for discussions of military issues. Following his meeting with Shamir and me, Reagan, speaking to reporters, called on Congress to approve the use of U.S. military assistance funds to develop the Lavi. A few days later the *New York Times* headlined its front-page story "House and Senate Vote $550 Million to Help Finance Israeli-Built Fighter." The bill authorized the use of $250 million of U.S. aid money for the Lavi in Israel and $300 million for Lavi-associated developments in the United States. With that kind of support from the president of the United States and the American Congress, the Lavi aircraft now seemed safely on its way. It was up to Israel's engineers to do the rest.

In December the Druze militia was about to complete its conquest of the Shouf, placing in acute danger the Christian civilian population still there and the fighters of the Christian militia protecting them. After receiving frantic appeals from Lebanese Christians I agreed to evacuate them from the region under the protection of IDF units. On December 15, after a temporary truce had been arranged, IDF units reentered the Shouf, after which a long convoy, escorted by units of the IDF flying the Israeli flag, came down the mountain and brought them to safety in southern Lebanon.

I spent Christmas Eve that year in Bethlehem as the guest of Elias Frej, the mayor. He had approached me some months earlier and asked whether I could annex the town of Bethlehem to Israel. He was looking for protection from the increasing number of Muslims in his city. I told him that, regretfully, it was not in my power to do so. We had been friends since then. Next days' newspapers showed me walking hand in hand with Frej past a Christmas tree in Bethlehem. By now Frej is gone and Bethlehem has become a Muslim city.

In 1978, as a response to PLO terrorist attacks against northern Israel, the IDF had conducted an eight-day operation in southern Lebanon, code-named Operation Litani, and had created a small security zone bordering Israel to provide protection for Israel's northern villages and towns. Major Saad Haddad, a Greek Catholic officer in the Lebanese army, assumed control of a militia he named the Free Lebanon Army, composed mainly of Lebanese Christians, and assisted the IDF to keep the area clear of PLO forces. Now that the IDF was redeploying into a wider security zone in southern Lebanon, I had hoped that Haddad and the Free Lebanon Army, allied with the IDF, would help control this security zone. But Haddad was felled by cancer and died at Rambam Hospital in Haifa in December. I visited him there, when he was on his deathbed. A continued alliance with the local population seemed essential if we were going to stay in the area for some time. Now we needed to look for a replacement for Haddad.

One day in January Colonel Meir Dagan appeared in my office, bringing with him a Lebanese general named Antoine Lahad. Dagan was an outstanding officer—courageous, a daredevil full of ideas. He had been awarded a medal for bravery. In time he was to become a legendary head of the Mossad. Now he had gone to Lebanon looking for a replacement for Major Haddad. He had gotten into a jeep and driven all the way to Beirut, crossing areas held by the different militias; had found Lahad, a retired Lebanese Lieutenant-General; had talked him into heading a military force in southern Lebanon; and had brought him back to me. I spent some time interviewing him and agreed that he was the man we needed. A Maronite Christian and a Lebanese patriot, opposed to Syrian domination of Lebanon, he was prepared to fight for a free Lebanon. He renamed the force in southern Lebanon under his command the South Lebanon Army. It was composed of a few thousand Lebanese soldiers of all denominations—Christians, Druze, and Shia and Sunni Muslims. His headquarters were at Marjayoun, not far from the Israeli border. He cooperated with the forces of the IDF in securing the security zone for the next sixteen years, until the unilateral withdrawal ordered by Prime Minister Ehud Barak in May 2000.

On April 12 four Arab terrorists from the Gaza Strip hijacked the number 300 Eged bus on its way from Tel Aviv to Ashkelon and diverted it to the Gaza Strip. Holding the 40 passengers hostage, they threatened to blow up the bus if Israel would not release 500 Arab terrorists imprisoned in Israel. The incident became a cause célèbre and had far-reaching consequences for Israel's Security Services.

When I heard about the incident I rushed to the scene, arriving about midnight. The bus had been stopped near Dir el Balah in the Gaza Strip. It was surrounded by police and a number of onlookers. Avrum Shalom, the head of the Security Services, and some of his men were on the spot, and negotiations had begun with the hijackers. Moshe Levy, the IDF chief of staff, had given instructions to Brigadier General Itzik Mordechai, the IDF's chief infantry officer, to make preparations to storm the bus, and the elite reconnaissance unit of the IDF had been rushed to the scene and was preparing for action. Mordechai had also arrived.

We had no intention of meeting the hijackers' demands, and I gave permission to storm the bus. At dawn the unit went into action. Within a matter of seconds they had taken control of the bus. Two of the terrorists were killed, and one of the passengers, a young girl soldier, Irit Portugesi, lost her life. Two other terrorists had been captured and were in the hands of the Security Services. Interviewed by radio on location in the morning before I left the scene, I announced that one passenger had lost her life, the others had been freed, two terrorists had been killed, and two had been taken prisoner. Weary from the night's events, I nevertheless went directly to my office for a meeting with the Finnish defense minister, who was visiting Israel. In a few hours it was announced on the radio that the four terrorists had been killed. I was puzzled by the announcement. Something must have happened after I left.

That day Shamir asked to see me. When I sat down opposite him in the prime minister's office, he said, "Avrum says that you gave the order to kill the two terrorists who were captured alive."

I was astonished. "That is not true," I replied. I hurried back to my office and called Avrum Shalom, told him what Shamir had related to me, and added that he knew that that was not true. For a moment there was silence on the line, and then he said, "I'm sorry, I was mistaken." It was the beginning of an attempt to cover up what really happened. Shalom had given his people the order to finish off the two captured terrorists. But that became clear only much later.

It took an investigating committee whose conclusions were inconclusive, a media campaign, the defection of senior members of the Security Services, and the intervention of the government's legal adviser to finally get at the truth: Shalom had ordered some of his men to kill the two captured terrorists. In June 1986 Shalom resigned as head of the Security Services. Thereafter President Haim Herzog pardoned him and three other members of the Security Services in anticipation of criminal charges that were to be brought against them.

It was an earthquake for Israel's Security Services. Until this event, Shalom had been considered an excellent head of the Security Services. I held him in high regard. It seemed that that day in Dir el Balah he had acted in what he considered to be the tradition of this service until then— that terrorists should not be allowed to survive acts of terror, and that the public should be spared the details. Ami Ayalon, a former navy admiral, was appointed to replace Shalom as head of the Security Services to bring order to an organization that had been badly shaken. Things were not going to be the same from then on.

In March a majority of the Knesset approved a motion by the Labor Party to hold early elections; the date set was July 23, 1984. For the next four months the country was seized by election fever. The outlook for the Likud was not auspicious. The economy was undergoing runaway inflation, and many were disappointed with the results of the operation in Lebanon. Peres, the Labor candidate for prime minister, promised the public that if elected he would pull our forces out of Lebanon.

The Herut Central Committee now had to elect the list of Herut's candidates for the Knesset. In the race for the top spot, the person to be the Likud's choice for prime minister, Sharon, challenged Shamir. In the vote Shamir beat Sharon easily. I was elected to the third spot on the Herut list, after Shamir and David Levy.

In the Knesset elections the Labor Party came in ahead of the Likud, receiving forty-four Knesset seats to the Likud's forty-one, but neither party was able to put together a coalition government. The only possible government in light of the election results was a national unity government, in which the Labor Party and the Likud shared power, something that had never happened in Israel before. As for the person to head this government—the prime minister—a unique Israeli solution was invented. The position would be rotated, Peres for the first two years and Shamir for the following two years.

A condition put forth by the Labor Party was that Yitzhak Rabin would be the defense minister throughout the tenure of the government. Now it was up to me. I did not hesitate. Concerned with the deep divisions in Israeli society regarding the war in Lebanon, I felt it was imperative to seek national unity. I wanted a national unity government to be formed, and had no problem with turning the Defense Ministry over to Rabin if that would facilitate the establishment of such a government. Three years later I deeply regretted that decision, when Rabin brought to the government a motion to cancel the Lavi aircraft program. I had never imagined that possibility. Had it not been for my "excessive patriotism" when the national unity government was formed, the Lavi would be flying in the Israel Air Force to this day.

During the negotiations surrounding the composition of the government I told Shamir that this was an opportune moment for me to retire from politics. I felt that I had done my share of public service and was eager to get back to aeronautical engineering. He objected strongly and asked me to stay on, telling me he needed me at his side, insisting that I could have my choice of any of the ministerial positions allotted to the Likud in the new government. I was not interested, and finally agreed to serve in the new government as minister without portfolio, a member of the cabinet without responsibility for one of the ministries.

NINE

National Unity Government

The election results of July 23, 1984, provided a demonstration of the complications resulting from Israel's system of proportional representation. Neither of the two large parties was able to form a coalition government. Although the Labor Party had a three-seat lead over the Likud, it was not able to form a coalition. The distribution of votes among the smaller parties gave the Likud the possibility of leading a coalition on condition that a small faction, Yahad (with three members of the Knesset), were to join. Yahad had been formed prior to the elections by Ezer Weizman, a former defense minister and a former leader of the Likud. He had waged a grandiose American-style election campaign, confident of coming to the next Knesset as head of a faction large enough to be the balance of power, able to dictate the formation of the government. The results were a disappointment to him. He was in a position to permit the Likud to form the next government, were he to join such a government. But even if he were to decide to join a Labor-led government, that would not be sufficient to permit Labor to form a government. In other words, he could be a spoiler and prevent the Likud from forming a government and force the formation of a national unity government.

The unique Israeli solution to the political impasse created by the election results was the formation of a national unity government with the participation of both Labor and Likud was rotation. Shimon Peres (Labor) would officiate as prime minister for the first two years, to be followed by Yitzhak Shamir (Likud) as prime minister for the next two years.

Having been a leading member of the Likud in the past, even claiming on occasion that he had been the architect of the Likud's victory in 1977, Weizman might have been expected to help the Likud to form the government, but that was not his way. He took some pleasure in spoiling the Likud's chances, although he gained little from it. He seemed to be driven not by ideology but by ego. Some even considered him to be an egomaniac. He ended up a minister without portfolio as an ally of Labor's contingent in the government, which gave Peres the opportunity to precede Shamır ın the rotation of prime ministers.

Rabin's desire to be defense minister in the government might have served as an obstacle to the formation of this Labor-Likud government—it would require me to vacate that post. I had no hesitation about doing so. I thought that Israel needed a government of national unity and that Rabin would make a good defense minister, and volunteered to turn the post over to him. I was to rue that decision three years later, when Rabin unexpectedly introduced a motion in the government to cancel the Lavi fighter program.

On September 9 the Knesset voted confidence in this government: Peres as prime minister, Shamir as deputy prime minister and foreign minister, and Rabin as defense minister. Weizman and I were both ministers without portfolio, without ministries to manage, but with an equal voice in making government decisions. And the prime ministers would "rotate."

Lebanon continued to be cause for concern. Hezbollah, the Shia militia rival to Amal, was becoming a dominant force there. Funded and trained by the Iranians, Hezbollah attacked American targets in Beirut, the Israel Defense Forces (IDF), and the positions in the southern Lebanon security zone held by the South Lebanese Army (SLA), now commanded by Antoine Lahad. On September 13, 1984, a Hezbollah suicide bomber drove a truck into the U.S. embassy in Beirut. Twenty-three people were killed. Originally the embassy had been located in West Beirut, but after the bombing of the embassy in West Beirut in 1983 it had been moved to East Beirut, which was considered more friendly territory. Now it had been hit there as well. The Iranian vendetta against America continued. This attack, too, was the work of Imad Mughniye, the mastermind behind the bombing of the Marine compound in Beirut. But America had withdrawn the Marines from Lebanon, and Israel was withdrawing its forces from most of Lebanon. Lebanon was being abandoned to the Syrians and the Iranians. Poor Lebanon. Nobody was ready to fight for it, and it was incapable of fighting for itself.

In the government of national unity, two longtime political rivals, Labor and Likud, sat together, but each still had its eye on the next election, eager for political gain. This was especially true of Labor, which was out to prove that the Peace for Galilee operation had been a mistake, and that as a result the IDF was now stuck in the Lebanon quagmire. During the election Peres had promised that if elected he would extricate the IDF from Lebanon, a call that resonated with much of the public, grieving for the more than 600 soldiers who had fallen in Lebanon. Now that Peres was prime minister and Rabin defense minister, he wanted to make good on his promise.

In the vain hope that the IDF could be extricated from Lebanon without endangering the people living in northern Israel, negotiations with the Lebanese were conducted between November 1984 and January 1985 at Nakura, near the Lebanese-Israeli border, under the auspices of the United Nations Interim Force in Lebanon. Israel was seeking an arrangement that would permit it to withdraw its forces from Lebanon but insisted on assurances that the area to be evacuated must not become a staging ground for terrorist attacks against Israel, leaving Israel exposed to terrorist attacks as it had been before the Peace for Galilee operation. Israel proposed that upon an Israeli withdrawal to the international border, the SLA should control the area from the border up to the Zahrani River, that the areas between the Zahrani and Awali Rivers would be under the control of UN forces, and that the area north of the Awali River would be left to the control of the Lebanese army. The talks were doomed to failure. The United States did not want to get involved, remembering well the fate of the Israel-Lebanon agreement negotiated by George Shultz. Behind the scenes, though, the Syrians were involved. They were out to scuttle this agreement. Prompted by the Syrians, the official position of the Lebanese was that the entire area in question was sovereign Lebanese territory and that no one but the Lebanese army would be allowed to operate there. And no Israeli of any political stripe was prepared to trust the Lebanese army to prevent attacks from southern Lebanon against northern Israel.

The failure of the negotiations did not cool Peres's ardor to bring about a withdrawal of the IDF from Lebanon. On January 14 Peres and Rabin brought to the government a proposal for a unilateral withdrawal of IDF forces to the international border, leaving the SLA to secure a narrow zone five to fifteen kilometers wide north of the international border, even though this would bring northern Israel again within range of Katyusha rockets fired from Lebanon. Rabin claimed that the SLA would only require instruction, training, and occasional support from the IDF, but that no permanent presence of the IDF there would be needed, thus fulfilling Labor's promise for a complete withdrawal of the IDF from Lebanon. The Labor ministers mustered a majority in the government in support of their proposal. The Likud ministers, insisting that the proposed plan did not provide the necessary protection for the civilian population in northern Israel, voted against it. David Levy broke ranks with the Likud ministers and supported it.

Although the initial impression that was presented to the government by Rabin was that the IDF would finally be extricated from Lebanon, it shortly became clear that the SLA on its own was not capable of defending the security zone without active help from the IDF, so the IDF stayed in southern Lebanon. For the next fifteen years rockets were again fired against Israeli towns and villages in the north, and the IDF and the SLA, fighting shoulder to shoulder, fought off Hezbollah's attacks, both suffering losses month after month.

In fact, the withdrawal put Israeli civilians in the north in danger, just as they had been prior to the Peace for Galilee operation, and fueled a debate on Israel's national security policy that has continued to this day. Must the IDF risk Israeli soldiers' lives to secure the safety of Israel's civilian population, or should the civilian population share with the soldiers of the IDF the burden of sustaining fire from the enemy? In other words, are there circumstances when civilians should be allowed to be exposed to enemy fire in order to avoid casualties among the soldiers, or must soldiers be exposed to enemy fire with the express purpose of protecting civilians from that fire?

In late 1956, Prime Minister and Defense Minister David Ben-Gurion had conditioned Israel's participation with Britain and France in the Suez Campaign against Egypt on the French Air Force's taking control of the skies over Israel and providing protection for Israel's civilian population against the possibility of bombardment of Israel's cities by the Egyptians. His doctrine was that in any conflict the safety of Israel's civilian population must be assured. Similarly, the Peace for Galilee operation was initiated by the Begin government to secure the safety of Israel's civilians in the north, who had come under fire from rockets launched from southern Lebanon. Now, after the many losses Israel had sustained in Lebanon during the past year and a half, the painful question arose again.

The depth of the debate might be difficult to comprehend in countries where there is no compulsory military service for young men and women—where the soldiers are men and women who have volunteered for military service, well knowing that it entails risks to their lives. It is generally understood that they will be in harm's way in order to serve the national interest—that is a part of their mission.

In Israel, a small country with compulsory military service, most adults have children or grandchildren doing military service. A soldier who has fallen is to them a child lost, a feeling also shared by their friends and neighbors. When the picture of a fallen soldier is published it is almost as if the whole country shares in the grief of the bereaved family. Thus the loss of a soldier may well touch many more of Israel's citizens than does the loss of a civilian to enemy action. The nation's concern for the lives of its children serving in the IDF is the reason why successive Israeli governments have staged unilateral withdrawals, have hesitated to bring military operations to a decisive victory, or have failed to take preemptive military action that might ensure the safety of Israel's civilian population.

Ben-Gurion's doctrine of protection for civilian lives was gradually, almost imperceptibly, abandoned. The first step was the shrinking of the south Lebanon security zone, according to Rabin's proposal, which again exposed the Israeli population living in Galilee to rocket fire from Lebanon. In the years to come, Ehud Barak's unilateral withdrawal to the international border with Lebanon in 2000, and the failure to take preemptive action as the range of rockets in the Hezbollah armory steadily increased, eventually led to all of Israel being in the range of rockets in the hands of Hezbollah in Lebanon while Ariel Sharon's unilateral withdrawal from the Gaza Strip in 2005 put all of southern Israel in range of the rockets launched from there by Hamas.

Before the withdrawal to the narrower security zone had been completed, Israel received a painful reminder of the danger of letting terrorists get too close to the Israeli border. On March 10, 1984, a suicide bomber driving a truck loaded with explosives drove his truck into a convoy of Israeli soldiers near the northern border town of Metulla, killing twelve and injuring fourteen.

Shortly after the decision to reduce the southern Lebanese security zone we were faced with another dilemma created by our concern for the fate of our soldiers. This time it was the fate of three soldiers—Yosef Gros, Nissim Salem, and Hezi Shai—who had been taken prisoner during the Peace for Galilee operation. They were being held in Lebanon by the Popular Front for the Liberation of Palestine (PFLP) General Command, headed by Ahmed Jibril. Jibril's organization was prepared to release them in exchange for a very large number of terrorists held in Israeli prisons. Negotiations had been going on for many months through intermediaries with Jibril's organization. They had begun during my tenure as defense minister and continued when Rabin took over from me. Leading the negotiations, which took place in Geneva, was Shmuel Tamir, whom I had appointed to deal with Israeli MIAs and prisoners of war and who continued working for Rabin after the National Unity government was formed. The parents of the three soldiers, led by Miriam, the mother of Yosef Gros, had been in my office at least once a month during my last months as defense minister, and continued to knock on Rabin's door with even greater frequency, pleading for the return of their sons.

On May 21 Rabin brought an agreement for an exchange of prisoners to the government. It was unprecedented. For the three Israelis he held, Jibril demanded the release of 1,150 terrorists being held by Israel and the right to select some of the terrorists to be released. They included many terrorists with the blood of innocents on their hands, including Kozo Okamoto, one of the three members of the Japanese Red Army who in May 1972 had perpetrated the Lod Airport massacre for the PFLP, which had killed twenty-six and injured eighty (Lod Airport is now Ben Gurion Airport).

It was a difficult decision. Military action to free the three soldiers was not possible. As for the price demanded by Jibril, it was a take-it-or-leave-it proposition. Concern for the three soldiers, whose families had been very active pleading their case with the decision makers, trumped the disadvantage of the precedent that was being set for future cases that were surely to come. The government approved the deal, with one dissenting voice. It was Yitzhak Navon, our former president and the minister of education, who correctly added up the pluses and minuses of the deal. I voted for the agreement—and regret it to this day. I felt I had a debt of loyalty to Rabin and thought that I should support him. A bond of friendship had developed between us in recent months, and the relief of the immediate release of our boys took precedence over the consequences of the deal in the future. As it turned out, many of those we released formed the backbone of the first Palestinian Intifada and were responsible for the future loss of life and injury of many Israelis. The decision was to haunt us for years to come. The immediate sense of relief that accompanied the release of our prisoners always seemed to take precedence over the potential long-term dangers.

Tamir, who had been responsible for the negotiations, was against accepting Jibril's conditions, and resigned once the government had accepted them. I assume that loyalty to Rabin prevented him from confiding his opinion to me. If he had shared his opinion with me, I might have changed my vote, although it would not have made any difference—the majority approved it.

The National Unity government had inherited a disastrous economic situation. As a result of excessive government expenditures inflation had taken hold of the economy over the last few years, and inflation seemed to be getting worse as the months went by. The linkage between the consumer price index and wages that had been negotiated between the Manufacturers Association and the Labor Federation (the Histadrut) years earlier seemed to provide protection to employees, and a linkage between the consumer price index and a host of other economic parameters seemed to provide the illusion that everybody could ride along the wave of inflation as it grew.

By 1984 inflation in Israel had reached 450 percent on an annual basis and was projected to reach 1,000 percent by the end of the year. It had become a runaway inflation that made rational economic planning impossible and could endanger the foundations of the country's economy. It had stalled the country's economic growth, while government expenditures soared. Many in Israel lived in a fool's paradise, believing that the system of linkages provided protection that would permit living with inflation. There was one man who saw disaster at the end of the tunnel: George Shultz, the U.S. secretary of state. He was an economist by profession and a great admirer and friend of Israel. For him as secretary of state the economy was really not his business, but he made it his business.

During my tenure as ambassador I had attended a meeting Shultz held with Israel's minister of finance, Yoram Aridor, and his director general, Ezra Sadan, when they visited Washington. They tried to convince him that inflation in Israel was not as bad as it seemed, but he told them in no uncertain terms that it was an intolerable condition that would lead Israel to disaster if not corrected.

Toward the end of 1983 Shultz gathered a group of American economists to seek their advice on how to deal with Israel's runaway inflation. In a series of meetings they worked out a plan to halt Israel's inflation. By June 1985 they had finalized a program that included a cut in government expenditures, temporary price controls, a sharp devaluation of the shekel, Israel's currency, to be followed by a fixed exchange rate, and a U.S. aid package of $1.5 billion to stanch the outflow of Israel's foreign-currency reserves. U.S. aid was to be conditional on Israel's adopting the economic stabilization plan. Shultz and his economic advisers had maintained contact with Israeli government officials and convinced them of the urgent necessity to adopt their Israeli Economic Stabilization Plan.

Absolutely essential to the plan's success was the support of both the Bank of Israel and the Labor Union (Histadrut). The government's deliberations on the plan took place in a stormy session that started on June 30 and lasted through the night. The plan had been kept secret, and most ministers had seen it for the first time that day. Nobody seemed to be sure that it was going to work. The director general of the Finance Ministry said that it was gamble.

"That means that it might not succeed," Rabin interjected.

"That also means that it might succeed," Peres responded.

Peres was relentless in pushing for approval. It was he who had gotten both the Bank of Israel and the Histadrut on board. In the early hours of the morning of July 1, 1985, a majority of the Cabinet approved the plan. Many Likud ministers, including myself, voted against it. I felt that I had not had sufficient time to study the plan. Although convinced that the inflationary spiral had to be stopped, I was not certain that the plan as presented would work. I turned out to be wrong. Within a year inflation was down to 20 percent, and the government's budget deficit shrank from 15 percent of GDP to zero. Getting this plan adopted was one of Peres's great achievements. Paradoxically, it spelled the beginning of the end of the Histadrut-dominated socialist economy, a hallmark of the Labor Party's economic policy for many years.

On November 21, 1985, Jonathan Pollard was arrested by the FBI as he and his wife tried to enter the Israeli embassy in Washington. He had worked as an intelligence analyst with the U.S. Navy and was caught transferring secret information to his Israeli contact. Realizing that he had been exposed, he tried to storm into the Israeli embassy but was denied entrance there. I happened to be in Washington at the time, as a guest of the Washington Institute for Near East Policy, and was surprised to find that our embassy was closed and I could not enter it. When the reports came out of Pollard's arrest I was shocked. Although I had been defense minister during some of the time that Pollard had been busy collecting secret information, I had no knowledge of the man or of his activities. My policy during my tenure at the Defense Ministry was that nothing should be done that might in any way endanger Israel's relations with the United States.

It turned out that the Pollard operation had been managed by Rafi Eitan, who headed the Scientific Liaison Unit in the Ministry of Defense. This was a small organization that over the years had been collecting scientific and technical information. Rafi Eitan, a friend of Ariel Sharon's, had been appointed by Sharon to head the unit when Sharon was defense minister. He had evidently decided to enlarge the scope of the unit's operations far beyond its original mandate. He did not ask for my permission for this kind of activity and had not reported it to me.

The Israeli government, headed by Peres, looked for a way to untangle itself from this very unpleasant affair. Peres announced that "spying on the United States stands in total contradiction to our policy." But this was hardly enough. He counted on my close relationship with Shultz to smooth things over, and asked me go to Washington to try to get out of this mess. To accompany me he sent Ram Caspi, a noted lawyer who seemed to have Peres's trust. On arrival in Washington I met with Shultz, who invited Abe Sofaer, the legal adviser to the State Department, to the meeting. I pleaded our case: It had been a rogue operation, unauthorized by the government. The desire to contribute to Israel's security by those involved had led them to disregard authorized channels. Knowing Israel's security problems, you might understand how such a thing could happen. The French say: *Tout comprendre, c'est tout pardoner*—to understand all is to forgive all. "I am not suggesting that this illegal act be forgiven," I said, "but your anger should be tempered by understanding the circumstances." Shultz listened but did not respond. We parted friends, but I realized that the situation was out of his hands. It was now in the hands of the FBI and judicial authorities. I also met with attorneys friendly to Israel, but saw immediately that nobody wanted to touch this case.

I returned to Israel and briefed the government on my meetings in Washington. Now it was in Peres's hands. He tried to reach an arrangement with the American authorities while attempting to protect the Israelis involved, but was not successful. The case left a scar on Israeli-U.S. relations for many years to come. In Washington, suspicion lingered that this was not the only case of Israeli espionage activities in the United States. And such suspicions surfaced on a number of occasions.

Pollard was sentenced to life imprisonment, an unprecedentedly severe punishment for espionage conducted in the United States on behalf of a friendly nation. Secretary of Defense Caspar Weinberger wrote to the sentencing judge: "It is difficult for me . . . to conceive of a greater harm to national security than that caused by the defendant." Undoubtedly this letter influenced the judge when he passed sentence on Pollard, although no great harm to the national security of the United States caused by Pollard's spying has ever been substantiated. Numerous attempts made over the years to have Pollard pardoned by the president were unsuccessful. He was released in November 2015 under severe parole conditions after serving thirty years of his sentence.

In Israel the question was, who was responsible for this fiasco? Who authorized this operation? Was it I, defense minister when Pollard began his nefarious activities, or was it Rabin, defense minister when Pollard got caught? The Foreign Affairs and Defense Committee of the Knesset set up a special subcommittee headed by Abba Eban to investigate this matter. After long deliberations they concluded that "beyond all doubt the Scientific Liaison Unit headed by Rafi Eitan decided to recruit and handle Pollard without any check or consultation with the political echelon or receiving its direct or indirect approval." Both Rabin and I came in for criticism for insufficient supervision of the activities of this unit, which was under the jurisdiction of the defense minister.

I deserved this criticism, since I really had paid no attention to it during my time as defense minister. Busy with the problems associated with the IDF's deployment and redeployment in Lebanon, and the reforms I instituted in the IDF, I found no time to spend on a small unit whose activities I considered of little importance.

Rafi Eitan was known in Israel for his part in the Mossad action to locate and capture Adolf Eichmann in Buenos Aires in 1960 and bring him to Israel to stand trial. I believe that Eitan had hoped to be appointed head of the Mossad. Disappointed at not getting that position, he was tempted as head of the Scientific Liaison Unit to prove that this small unit under his direction could provide intelligence information that would outshine the work of the Mossad. The damage his activities caused far outweighed any benefit that Israel may have gained from the information he obtained through Pollard.

On October 20, 1986, the rotation agreement between Labor and Likud took effect, and it was Shamir's turn to take over as prime minister. In the preceding weeks doubt had been expressed as to whether Peres would abide by the rotation agreement and turn the job of prime minister over to Shamir. But he really had no choice. He was not in a position to form another government to be headed by him. The political arithmetic that had led to the rotation agreement was still valid, and when the day came he followed through. Shamir was duly sworn in as prime minister in the Knesset on the appointed day, and Peres took over Shamir's post as foreign minister.

But Peres was not about to take a backseat in the government. While prime minister he had been holding secret meetings with King Hussein of Jordan regarding a peace initiative, and as foreign minister he continued these efforts. In April he had arranged for a secret meeting in London with King Hussein of Jordan; Peres was accompanied by the director-general of the foreign ministry, Yossi Beilin. He reached an agreement with King Hussein for the holding of an international conference that would include the Soviet Union, to be hosted by the UN, in order to bring about a peaceful solution of the Arab-Israeli conflict and a resolution of the Palestinian problem. The holding of such an international conference had never been brought up for discussion in the government. He knew that Shamir and all the other Likud ministers were opposed to such a conference, where Israel was most likely to find itself under pressure by a majority of the participants. Before revealing the contents of the agreement to Shamir, Peres sent Beilin to meet Shultz in Helsinki, where he had stopped on the way to Moscow. There he presented the agreement to Shultz, asking him to take the initiative to launch the international conference. Peres's diplomatic activity behind the back of the prime minister and the government was without precedent in Israel's history, or for that matter in the history of diplomacy. When Peres finally reported to Shamir on the agreement, he read parts of it out loud to him but would not leave him a copy of the agreement.

It was clear that an effort had to be made to keep Shultz from endorsing the Peres-Hussein agreement. Shamir asked me to go to Washington to meet Shultz and convince him to not get involved in the brew that Peres had cooked up. I found Shultz interested in the idea of an international conference that might get negotiations with the Palestinians and the Arab world moving. I told him that Shamir and the Likud were opposed to such a conference, that there would not be a majority for this agreement in the government, and that if he were to get involved he would be involving himself in internal Israeli politics. Shultz decided not to get involved.

Over the years it has been claimed that Israel missed an opportunity: that the Peres-Hussein agreement presumably called for Hussein to assume responsibility for the Palestinian population in Judea and Samaria, and this could have gone a long way toward resolving the Israeli-Palestinian conflict. But nobody except for Peres, or possibly Hussein, has ever seen the agreement. To this day a copy of the agreement has not been found. Its contents were never brought for discussion to the government. Peres's initiative may have been part of a plan to bring down the government. If that was the intention, it failed.

The rotation had brought another change, seemingly minor, but of some importance to me. When Weizman was minister without portfolio he had been put in charge of dealing with Israel's minorities; now this job was passed on to me. It was a seemingly inconsequential assignment, since there was no ministry attached to the job and no budget allocated to it. Minister in charge of relations with Israel's minorities seemed like little more than a formal title. But I had plans.

This was my chance to advance my belief in the importance of integrating Israel's minorities into Israel's social fabric. It came as a surprise to many that a leading member of the Likud, considered a nationalist party, which in the past had paid little attention to Israel's minorities, should attempt to promote such an idea. An indication of the view held by some came when Gil Sadan, a reporter for Israel TV, asked an Israeli Arab for his reaction to my assuming the post of minister in charge of relations with Israel's minorities. His answer: "Everybody knows that Arens hates Arabs."

My approach to Israel's minorities was based on the premise that they had to be assured equal rights unconditionally, but that in time we should also achieve an equality of obligations of all Israel's citizens. The highest obligation of Israel's citizens was to participate in the defense of the country against its enemies. In other words, we should aim for military service for all of Israel's minorities equal to the service of Israel's Jewish and Druze citizens.

As might have been expected, the most outspoken objections to my call for military service for Israel's Arab citizens came from left-leaning parties. They clung to the idea that it was "natural" that Israel's Arab citizens would be loyal to their Arab "brethren," even when these brethren were enemies of Israel, and therefore they should not be asked to bear arms in Israel's defense. On the other hand, I found among Israel's Arab citizens many who did not reject the idea of military service and some who were eager to take upon themselves this obligation, realizing that it would pave the way to full integration into Israel's society.

Actually, Israel's Druze youths had been subject to obligatory military service for many years. During my first tenure as defense minister I had insisted on opening all branches of the IDF to them, and they were beginning to make their way into the highest ranks of the officer corps. The Druze are ethnically Arabs who adhere to a religion that differs from Islam. If the Druze Israelis could serve, why shouldn't Israel's Muslim and Christian Arab citizens serve in the IDF? Obviously, expanding the opportunity for military service would have to be a gradual process, but I wanted that process to begin. My visits to Israel's Arab communities where I explained my desire to see them integrated into Israel's society, and the importance to them and to Israel of their participating in the defense of the country, resulted in groups of Arabs who volunteered for short courses in basic military training that would allow them to be called up for reserve duty in the IDF.

The response was even more positive among Israel's bedouins in the Galilee and the Negev. Some bedouin tribes had a long tradition of serving as trackers in the IDF. Among them an increasing number of youngsters began volunteering for the full military service period of three years. In time a bedouin infantry battalion was formed, which has done excellent service and in recent years has been commanded by a bedouin battalion commander with the rank of lieutenant colonel. But most important, I had the feeling that I was beginning to break down a barrier of isolation that existed between Israel's Jewish and Arab citizens, and that they appreciated the interest I showed in them and the respect I showed them. It was a good beginning.

I also tried to approach the Druze residing in the Golan Heights. The area had been annexed to Israel in December 1981, and it had been assumed that the approximately 10,000 Druze inhabitants there would eagerly accept Israeli citizenship and follow their coreligionists in Israel in expressing loyalty to the State of Israel. But that was not the case. They insisted that they were Syrian citizens and maintained their loyalty to Syria. Subsequent Israeli negotiations with Syria based on an agreement that would return the Golan Heights to Syrian sovereignty only reinforced this sentiment among them, in the expectation that sooner or later they would again be living under Syrian rule. Even though they prospered under Israeli rule and enjoyed the benefits of a democratic society providing security and the rule of law, they maintained that position until recently. The turmoil in Syria since 2011 and the subsequent dismemberment of Syria, foreboding danger for the Syrian Druze community, has brought about a radical change in their position. Increasing numbers of Druze in the Golan Heights are applying for Israeli citizenship, and their young men are beginning to serve in the IDF. My own efforts had been premature.

My work with Israel's minorities was interrupted peremptorily on August 30, 1987, when I resigned from the government in protest against the government's decision to cancel the Lavi fighter aircraft program. It was an indication of the many friends I had made among Israeli Arabs during the past ten months that hundreds of Arabs from all parts of the country assembled on the lawn of my home in Savyon on the night of my resignation and pleaded with me to reconsider my decision. I tried to explain to them that despite the importance I attached to my work with them and the great satisfaction that accompanied these efforts, I could not reverse my decision.

Thirteen months earlier, on July 21, 1986, the Lavi fighter aircraft had its rollout. It was rolled out of a hangar at Israel Aircraft Industries in a very impressive ceremony attended by members of the U.S. Congress and presided over by Defense Minister Yitzhak Rabin, who had inherited the project from me and who seemed to take great pride in this Israeli technological achievement. As the hangar doors opened and the Lavi was rolled out, a burst of applause greeted the appearance of the sleek canard delta aircraft, painted for the occasion in Israel's colors, blue and white. It was an important milestone in the Lavi program.

On December 31 of that year the Lavi had its first flight test. Thousands, I among them, watched the sleek aircraft take off and land at Ben Gurion Airport as Menachem Shmul, Israel Aerospace Industries' (IAI) chief test pilot, a seasoned air force ace with a number of downed MiGs to his credit, took it aloft for a twenty-six-minute maiden flight. I thought that now the program had passed the point of no return, but I was mistaken.

The Lavi had a die-hard opponent at the Pentagon, Secretary of Defense Caspar Weinberger, who on several occasions had demonstrated his hostility to Israel. Killing the Lavi project had become an obsession with him, and he remained undeterred by Reagan's and Shultz's support for the Lavi program and its solid backing in the U.S. Congress. The hit man he chose for this mission was Dov Zackheim, a medium-level official at the Department of Defense. Zackheim was a financial analyst who knew nothing about fighter aircraft but was charged with the mission of proving that the Lavi project was financially unsustainable. His being Jewish in no way seemed to cool his enthusiasm to follow the directions he was given by Weinberger.

In March 1985 Weinberger ordered Zackheim to develop and implement a plan to terminate the Lavi. In a number of trips to Israel Zackheim presented calculations to the Ministry of Defense that presumably showed that Israeli cost estimates for the program were far too low. His projections for the cost of the program reached astronomical figures. Rabin, rather than sending him packing, agreed to cooperate with his efforts to review the cost of the program.

Rabin had never been a proponent of Israeli weapon development. "We have never won a war with Israeli-made weapons," he once told me. Impressed by the Lavi program when he first came into office, he was nevertheless easily swayed by voices in the higher echelons of the IDF who were concerned that the program would consume an inordinate part of the defense budget.

A week after the Lavi's first flight Weinberger decided to take his crusade against the Lavi public. On January 7, 1987, Zackheim held a press conference in Tel Aviv where he announced that the Pentagon estimated that the Lavi would cost 45 percent more than the $15.2 million per plane that Israel had projected. Such overruns would endanger other Israeli programs, he said, emphasizing that U.S. military aid to Israel would be limited to the present level of $1.8 billion in the years to come.

Now Weinberger and Rabin headed a coalition with the aim of canceling the Lavi program. Weinberger had been on the warpath against the

Lavi since becoming secretary of defense. Rabin was at first hesitant but came increasingly under the influence of IDF generals concerned for the future funding of their own programs. Leading those generals was Major General Avihu Ben-Nun, a well-known fighter ace, who had participated in the downing of five Soviet-piloted MiGs over the Sinai in July 1970, and had been designated to be the next commander of the Israel Air Force.

And there was also a personal element: Ben-Nun had expected to follow David Ivri as air force commander but Ivri had chosen Amos Lapidot as his successor. Ivri and Lapidot were ardent supporters of the Lavi. Now Ben-Nun, finally in line to become air force commander, was going to show up his former superiors.

The race was on. The Lavi's capabilities, demonstrated in a succession of flight tests, had to compete with what became a growing campaign calling for the Lavi program's cancellation before the point of no return was reached. First to join the anti-Lavi coalition were the economic wizards. Michael Bruno, the governor of the Bank of Israel, prognosticated, "Israel cannot afford the luxury of producing fighter aircraft, and it will harm economic growth." Many economists, who knew little about aircraft or the aircraft industry, chimed in.

Most of the media joined the race. A highly technical issue with long-range ramifications on Israel's defense posture suddenly became the subject of public debate, in which many of the participants understood little of what they were talking about.

Ben-Nun managed to mobilize many of the senior air force officers to support his position. To them dealing directly with U.S. aircraft manufacturers and choosing a ready-made aircraft seemed preferable to committing to an aircraft that was still in development in Israel and making Israel Aircraft Industries, whom they saw as a competitor for budgetary allocations, a partner in future decisions regarding aircraft procurement.

The second Lavi prototype made its first flight on March 30, 1987. It reached a speed of 350 knots (403 miles per hour) and an altitude of 20,000 feet. By this time the first prototype had gone through twenty-three flights, reaching a speed of Mach 0.75 and an altitude of 43,000 feet. By June the two prototypes had accumulated more than forty flight hours and had reached a speed of Mach 0.9. By August the two prototypes had flown more than a hundred hours and had gone supersonic, reaching a top speed of Mach 1.45 at an altitude of 41,000 feet. A third prototype was being readied for flight testing.

As part of what had become a sales campaign, a few senior air force pilots were given a chance to fly the Lavi. One of them was Danny Halutz, a future air force commander and thereafter the IDF's chief of staff. His reaction appeared in a book he published some years later: "I was enamored of the plane. . . . It was similar to the F-16, but in some areas it was superior to it. . . . After installation of all the systems scheduled for it, it was going to be the best fighter airplane in the world."

The public campaign against the Lavi was leading up to a debate in the cabinet, where a decision would have to be made. There, at first sight, there was room for optimism. The cabinet was chaired by Yitzhak Shamir, who should be expected to bring all the Likud ministers into line in support of the Lavi as well as to steer the discussions so as to defeat the motion for the plane's cancellation. On top of that, Peres had been a patron of IAI while at the Ministry of Defense and was a friend of Al Schwimmer, the founder of IAI, so he could be counted in the camp of the Lavi's supporters. Furthermore, Shoshana Arbeli-Almozlino, the minister of health and a member of the Labor Party, had on a number of occasions publicly expressed her support for the Lavi. It looked like Rabin's attempt to ground the Lavi was heading for failure.

But the fly in the ointment was Al Schwimmer. Schwimmer had become friends with Peres during Israel's War of Independence, when Schwimmer had been instrumental in bringing aircraft and pilots to Israel from the United States. On his return to the States he had started an aircraft maintenance depot in Southern California. Peres convinced him to transfer the operation to Israel, with Schwimmer installed as the manager, and that became Israel Aerospace Industries. For the next twenty-five years Schwimmer managed IAI and led it to a number of successes in the development of missiles and aircraft. It was he who convinced me in 1962 to move from the Technion to IAI to head its Engineering Division. In 1977, when the Likud formed the government, Ezer Weizman, the new defense minister, terminated Schwimmer's appointment as manager of IAI. Schwimmer may have harbored some rancor toward IAI's management since then, and that might have influenced his position regarding the Lavi program.

Schwimmer was a lifelong aviation enthusiast and an avid reader of *Aviation Week*. He had worked in the past as a flight mechanic but did not have engineering training. To Peres he was an oracle on anything to do with aviation. Now Peres turned to Schwimmer for advice on the Lavi. I was amazed when Peres told me that Schwimmer had told him that the project should be canceled and that he intended to follow Schwimmer's advice and vote for cancellation of the Lavi.

What turned Schwimmer against the Lavi? What made him oppose his former teammates at IAI? At the time he explained it by saying, "If we were to get eighty or ninety Lavis, they would contribute nothing to our defense capabilities, and a production run of eighty or ninety aircraft is nothing at all. . . . It's competing with the F-16, of which 3,000 or so will be sold, and even if it were a better aircraft, it's too late. The market for this generation of aircraft is over, and the next generation is going to be a very different type of aircraft." He called instead for the development of a "next-generation" fighter. "Within six or seven years we could have an aircraft that would be in front of the buying cycle rather than behind it. The Israeli air force could support it with a purchase of 250 or 300 aircraft, and we could start to look for export customers."

I could tell that Schwimmer was under the influence of recent articles that had appeared in *Aviation Week* regarding an ongoing competition in the United States for a next-generation fighter aircraft, the ATF (advanced tactical fighter). It was to be an aircraft capable of cruising supersonically. The program never realized its promise and has been overtaken by the F-35 in the meantime. Today, twenty-nine years after government debate on the Lavi, the U.S. Air Force fields fewer than 200 F-22s, while F-16s are being sold to this day. Schwimmer's idea that Israel should cancel the Lavi and launch the development of a fighter similar to the ATF was sheer fantasy, but Peres bought it, hook, line, and sinker. And that was the position he took at the government debate on the Lavi.

Peres's move to the camp of the opponents of the Lavi was a turning point. He had decided not only to vote against the Lavi but actually to lead the opposition to the Lavi in the cabinet. Now it was clear that it was going to be a fight down to the wire. Peres tried to line up all of the Labor ministers in the government against the Lavi. He had turned it into a political battle—Labor against Likud—as opposed to a debate on the merits of the project. Was Shamir going to line up all the Likud ministers in support of the Lavi?

The final debate in the cabinet on the Lavi project, held on August 30, 1987, was lively, almost fierce, but there was a feeling that reason was not going to determine the outcome. Instead, behind-the-scenes political maneuvering would determine the fate of the Lavi and the fate of tens of thousands of engineers, scientists, and technicians who were engaged in a frantic effort to provide the Israel Air Force with the best aircraft and establish Israel as an aerospace power in the world.

Rabin, leading the offensive, misled the assembled ministers. First he put to rest the fear of all ministers that the cancellation of the Lavi would lead to massive layoffs among Israel's brightest engineers. Not at all, he insisted. The Ministry of Defense presented a list of new projects, code-named "Lavi replacements," which he claimed would absorb all of the personnel working on the Lavi. He presented to the cabinet a chart that, with mathematical precision, showed the number of engineers to be employed on these new projects—it added up to just the number of engineers working on the Lavi. His presentation completely disregarded the high degree of specialization required in many disciplines for the design of a fighter aircraft. In fact, the chart was sheer nonsense. There was no real basis for it, and within a year it became clear that the "Lavi replacements" were the figment of someone's imagination and never came into being. When the Lavi was canceled, thousands of Israel's best engineers were laid off.

Next, Ben-Nun threw a bombshell. The air force was about to be downsized, he told the cabinet, and would require no more than 80 Lavis. All of the economic calculations of the Lavi project had been based on the air force acquiring 120 Lavi aircraft, a requirement set by the air force itself. Naturally this downsizing by a third of the projected production of the aircraft increased the projected cost of each airplane considerably and threw into doubt the economic justification of the project. Actually, in the years to come the air force procured hundreds of F-16 aircraft, contrary to the projections presented by Ben-Nun to the government.

To this projection he added another one that was sure to rattle the ministers. He said the Israel Air Force was planning to acquire the American ATF (now called the F-22), a fighter superior to the Lavi, a decision that would make the whole Lavi project superfluous. In fact, not until

2005, twenty-two years later, would the U.S. Air Force begin acquisition of its first F-22 aircraft. Procurement has now ceased at aircraft number 187, the assembly line has been shut down, and the last plane was delivered to the U.S. Air Force in 2012. Israel has not and will not acquire the F-22. The plans for Israel's procuring the F-22 that Ben-Nun brought to the government discussion of the Lavi was a red herring, pure and simple.

Representatives of the Finance Ministry told the assembled ministers that in their opinion not only could Israel not afford the Lavi, but that unless the program was canceled, Israel was heading for bankruptcy. That was enough to scare the pants off some of the ministers who did not know better.

Most bizarre were the arguments for canceling the Lavi program advanced by two ministers who, unlike most other ministers, were presumed to have a degree of acquaintance with military aircraft programs: Shimon Peres and Ezer Weizman. Peres, repeating the advice Schwimmer had given him, claimed that the Lavi was not a sufficiently advanced aircraft, that the program should be canceled, and that a new fighter development program should be launched of a more advanced fighter, which he dubbed Lavi 2000. Weizman, on the other hand, insisted that the Lavi was too advanced an aircraft and that what he had in mind when he originally backed the program was no more than a replacement for the A-4 Skyhawk. The program having veered so far from his original conception, it should now be canceled, he argued.

I valiantly defended the program, citing its many advantages: giving Israel a quality edge over aircraft in the inventory of Arab air forces, some of whom flew the latest U.S.-manufactured fighters; providing the foundation for an advanced aerospace industry in Israel; establishing the precedent of a high degree of cooperation with the U.S. aircraft industry that was an integral part of the program; plus gaining the intangible benefits of fielding an Israeli-made fighter, which was the best of its kind in the world.

Not appeals to reason, but behind-the-scenes arm twisting were to determine the cabinet's decision. The outcome of the vote depended on two ministers, Shoshana Arbeli-Almozlino (Labor), the minister of health, and Moshe Nisim (Likud), the minister of finance. Arbeli-Almozlino had been an enthusiastic supporter of the Lavi all along. If she stuck to her guns and broke ranks with her Labor colleagues, the Lavi would be home safe. Moshe Nisim had become minister of finance almost by accident. A lawyer by training, he had no business or financial experience. He inherited the position that had been held by his Likud colleague Yitzhak Modai when Peres during his tenure as prime minister had forced Modai out of the position. Being a newcomer to the world of finance and economics, and knowing nothing about aircraft development and production, Nisim was following the advice tendered to him by the bureaucrats of the Finance Ministry. And they were against the Lavi. To assure the Lavi's survival, Shamir now would have had to bring Nisim into line with the rest of the Likud ministers. For reasons not clear to this day, he made no attempt to do that. Nisim was going to vote for the cancellation of the Lavi.

Now everything depended on Arbeli-Almozlino. Peres decided to take care of that. He cornered her in a room and browbeat her. He made her a minister he said, and now she had to follow his orders and vote for the cancellation of the Lavi project. She protested, broke down and cried, but Peres persisted. These are orders, he told her. During the vote, tears running down her face, she abstained. The Lavi, the crowning achievement of Israel's defense industry, was downed by a vote of 12 to 11.

I was shocked. A dream, created and nurtured by me, had been shattered by a one-vote margin. A bad decision had been taken. Bad for Israel, bad for Israel's security, bad for Israel's economy. My former students and teammates had been abandoned. I could not be party to such a decision. Since in the Israeli system of government all ministers in the government bear collective responsibility for decisions taken by the government, regardless of their vote, staying a member of the government would mean that I, too, would bear responsibility for this decision. This I was not prepared to do. No sooner had the vote's outcome had been announced than I slipped Shamir a note that I was herewith resigning from the government, and walked out of the cabinet meeting.

According to Israeli law, a resignation from the government or the Knesset only takes effect after forty-eight hours. This leaves you time to think it over and change your mind. But I needed no further reflection; my mind was made up. One person who appealed to me to go back on my decision was Menachem Begin. Ever since his resignation he had withdrawn to an apartment on Tzemah Street in Jerusalem, never venturing out, and not participating or intervening in the day-to-day goings-on. Now he sent me a message that he wanted to see me.

I found him sitting on a chair, dressed in a bathrobe. He seemed in good spirits, no different than he had been when we were close associates during his tenure as prime minister. After a few opening remarks he came to the point: he suggested that I withdraw my resignation from the government. I had the difficult task of explaining to him why I could not do that. When I told him that the decision to cancel the Lavi passed by a one-vote majority, he noted that in 1793 the French National Convention decided to execute King Louis XVI by a single-vote majority. Obviously, his memory was as good as ever.

Even though he had left the political arena three years before, he was evidently following events closely. I assume that he saw me as a future leader of the Likud, possibly the future head of the Likud, and did not want me to abandon my political career. I felt sorry that I had to disappoint him.

After the cancellation of the Lavi, Rabin thought he still had a cleanup job to do. He saw the IAI Engineering Division as a breeding ground of ideas that might well bring forth more projects like the Lavi. Understanding little of the functioning of an aircraft industry and the central importance of the Engineering Division in that industry, he ordered IAI management to disband the Engineering Division. It was a body blow to IAI, from which it never recovered.

Out of the cabinet, but still a member of the Knesset, I also held the position of chairman of the Herut Party secretariat, the executive body of the party. Five months earlier, at the Herut Party convention in March 1987, I had been elected by a sizable majority to that post, running against Yoram Aridor, a former minister of finance who was backed by David Levy.

The 1987 convention was a continuation of the convention held a year earlier, in which Levy and Sharon challenged Shamir. It had broken up in chaos. Levy had decided to continue his challenge of Shamir's leadership of the party. At the opening session of the convention, held in Jerusalem, he anointed himself as Begin's heir with the announcement: "Menachem Begin, you have an heir!" Modesty was not one of his attributes. He had mobilized a camp of supporters from development towns, populated mostly by new immigrants, who saw him as their representative. They in turn were joined by young politicians who hoped to ride to positions of importance on Levy's coattails. One of them was "Ruby" Rivlin, who was to become Israel's president some years later. When Sharon decided to lend them his support, they became rowdy and broke up the convention.

It took a year, and Shamir's assumption of the premiership as part of the rotation agreement with Labor, to patch up the quarrel and reach a unanimous agreement to elect Shamir as head of the party. Levy was elected deputy head of the party—a meaningless position—by a small margin; Sharon was elected chairman of the party's central committee; and I was elected chairman of the secretariat. Levy swallowed his pride, but it was clear to everyone that we had not heard the last of him.

I backed Shamir throughout. I did not consider Levy to be a suitable candidate to lead Herut. During the 1986 convention, what is referred to as the Shamir-Arens camp took shape. Its adherents backed Shamir and considered me to be his successor. Opposed to us was the Levy camp, and straddling the middle, maneuvering to take advantage of opportunities as they arose, was Sharon, who had built himself a following among the settlers in Judea, Samaria, and Gaza who were Herut members. Conflicts between these three political camps were to accompany Herut, and after the Liberal Party merged with Herut, they bedeviled the Likud for the next five years.

As chairman of the secretariat I threw myself into preparations for the coming elections, which were scheduled to take place in about a year. If the Knesset completed its full term, then in November 1988 simultaneous elections would be held for the Knesset and for Israel's municipalities, and I was aiming for a double header—success in both the Knesset and the municipal elections.

I searched for Likud candidates for some of the major municipal contests, expecting them to lead the mobilization of our supporters in the Knesset elections as well. As I began lining up promising candidates for a number of large municipalities, the Labor Party leadership caught on to my game plan and decided to postpone the municipal elections, separating them from the elections to the Knesset. Allied with a number of other parties who were afraid of losing their positions in a number of municipalities, they marshaled the votes necessary to pass such a motion through the Knesset. Nevertheless, my strategy paid off—we did well in the coming Knesset elections and swept almost all the important municipal elections when the time came. The Knesset elections were scheduled for November 1, 1988, and Shamir appointed me to head the Likud election campaign.

In September I returned to my position in the cabinet to resume my work with Israel's minority populations, who were glad to see me return.

The following year was a time of intensive preparation for the coming Knesset elections in November. It was up to me as chairman of the Likud election campaign to bring home a victory for the party. This I successfully accomplished.

TEN

Foreign Minister

Likud beat the Labor Party in the November 1988 elections for the Knesset, 48 votes to 47. The narrow win gave Yitzhak Shamir, the leader of the Likud, the choice of forming a narrow-based government without Labor or leading a national unity government, but this time without rotation. Shamir chose to form a national unity government. Yitzhak Rabin continued as defense minister, I was named foreign minister, and Shimon Peres was shifted to the Finance Ministry. Shamir's decision led to great difficulties in the year to come.

Astute observers of the election results noticed that for the first time, the Likud had succeeded in attracting a substantial number of voters among the Druze community as well as in Arab villages and bedouin towns in the Negev. In fact, these new votes had delivered to the Likud the margin needed for the additional Knesset seat and thus were the key cause of the victory over Labor. It came as a surprise to many, who found it hard to believe that Israel's minorities would vote for the Likud with its hard-line image. The result was the fruit of my work among Israel's minorities and my appeals to them during the election campaign. I hoped that this outreach and the resultant electoral participation would be the beginning to the entry of minorities into the ranks of the Likud, which I considered advantageous not only for the Likud but, more important, for the process of integrating Israel's Arab population into the fabric of Israeli society. Unfortunately, in later years the Likud leadership invested little effort in this direction.

Driving up to the Foreign Ministry in Jerusalem for the changing-of-the-guard ceremony with Peres, I listened on the radio to his farewell speech to the assembled crowd of senior foreign ministry staff and reporters. It was another opportunity for him to deliver his well-worn lecture about the importance of arriving at peace with the Arabs. I arrived at the foreign ministry in time to respond. In my response I talked about the important task awaiting him in the Finance Ministry. "You, Shimon Peres, are now moving to one of the most important jobs in Israel, that of finance minister," I began. "Israel's future depends first and foremost on the state of our economy. If we do well economically we will do well in all other areas. Conversely, if Israel is in bad shape economically we shall be in trouble in all other areas, including our foreign relations. Israel could be one of the richest countries in the world," I went on. "In an age where population quality is all-important, we have a highly talented and skilled population. And yet Israel is a poor country because of the Bolshevik economy that was imposed on Israel by the Labor Party. Wherever you look there is government interference and control. More than half the business sector is under either government or Histadrut ownership. Many of our best entrepreneurs and professionals are leaving Israel because they cannot find an outlet for their talents." And then I let him have it. "Go to the Finance Ministry, forget your socialist doctrines and the Labor Party's vested economic interests, and remove the shackles that suffocate our economy. That is the necessary condition for the solution of most of Israel's problems. Good luck!"

We clinked glasses of fruit juice, wishing each other well, and he was off to the Finance Ministry, while I ascended to the second-story office located in one of the prefabs that constituted Israel's foreign ministry at the time. It was the office that had been occupied by my illustrious predecessors: Moshe Sharet, Golda Meir, Abba Eban, Yigal Alon, Moshe Dayan, Yitzhak Shamir, and, for the past two years, Shimon Peres.

Benjamin Netanyahu had returned from his post as Israel's ambassador at the UN in order to run in the Likud primaries. He had achieved considerable popularity by his impressive appearances at the UN, and had no trouble being elected to the Likud's Knesset list. We had been in close contact ever since he had been my deputy in Washington, and now that he had been elected to the Knesset he urged me to appoint him as my deputy at the Foreign Ministry. I was glad to do it.

I assumed the post of foreign minister at a difficult time. For close to a year, since December 1987, the Intifada had been raging. There were daily demonstrations, and Palestinians in Judea, Samaria, and Gaza threw rocks and Molotov cocktails at cars on the roads. Rabin had decided on a brutal response. "Break their bones," he instructed the Israel Defense Forces (IDF). The violence only increased. Many of the demonstrators were injured and killed, and Israel came under international pressure to take steps to end the violence. It was clear to me that it was high time to address the aspirations of the Palestinian population living next to us, almost among us, in Judea, Samaria, and Gaza.

I knew that the George Bush administration taking over in January was not going to be as friendly to Israel as the Ronald Reagan administration had been. Compared to Reagan and his secretary of state, George Shultz, Bush and his secretary of state, James Baker III, were rather cool to Israel. I had met Bush a number of times when he was Reagan's vice president. He had been strongly opposed to Israel's operation in Lebanon. Baker, who had been the White House chief of staff while I was ambassador, had declined a number of my requests to meet with him. I told Shamir that the honeymoon with Washington that had characterized the Reagan administration, a period during which the U.S.-Israel relationship had blossomed as never before, was over and that the new team in Washington was going to play hardball with Israel.

Before facing the new administration in Washington I attended a conference of foreign ministers on the prevention of chemical warfare, held in Paris on January 9, 1989, under the auspices of President François Mitterrand, although it had been President Reagan's initiative. It was eleven days before the inauguration of George Bush, and George Shultz was finishing his term as secretary of state just as I became Israel's foreign minister. We met as old friends, saying good-bye. We could have worked well together and I was sorry to see him leave.

Addressing the conference I said, "As foreign minister of Israel I come to the conference with a greater sense of concern and urgency than any other delegate on the issues being discussed here. Not only because millions of Jews were killed in gas chambers during World War II, but also because the two countries that have used chemical warfare in recent years—Libya in the fighting in Chad, and Iraq on a massive scale against the Iranians as well as against their own Kurdish villages—are located in the region in which we live and insist that they are in a state of war with Israel."

My words obviously made little impact. In the years that followed, the Iraqis continued developing their chemical warfare capability, not only without hindrance from the world but with the active assistance of industries and specialists from some of the countries represented at the conference whose representatives spoke so eloquently about the need to ban chemical weapons.

In Paris I had the opportunity to meet the Egyptian foreign minister, Ismat Abd el-Meguid, an urbane, elderly gentleman and a veteran diplomat of the old school. He had also attended the conference. He invited me to a meeting at the ornate Egyptian embassy to discuss Israeli-Egyptian relations. Actually, what was on his mind was Taba, a one-square-kilometer area in Sinai next to Elat that Israel had not evacuated, claiming that it was on the Israeli side of the international border with Egypt. Holding on to Taba, where in the meantime a luxury hotel had been built, had been Sharon's idea at the time of the Israeli withdrawal from the Sinai in 1982. Egyptian protests had brought the issue to international arbitration, as required by the Israeli-Egyptian peace treaty. On September 29, 1988, the arbitration panel, which had convened in Geneva, announced, after lengthy discussions, a majority decision in Egypt's favor. Abd el-Meguid was concerned that Israel might not comply with the arbitration decision. He had good reason, since some Likud ministers had voiced the opinion that Israel did not have to implement the decision, and Shamir's position on the issue was not clear.

Abd el-Meguid was friendly and courteous when he met me at the entrance to the Egyptian embassy. I thought it best not to discuss the chemical warfare conference, and the Egyptian army's use of chemical weapons in its operation in the Yemeni civil war during the sixties. So I let him plunge right into the Taba issue, which I knew was on his mind. He seemed greatly relieved when I told him that I would try my best to have the Israeli government implement the decision of the arbitration panel. A further expression of his appreciation was his visit to my suite at the Hilton Hotel the next morning. He talked to me about the future of Israeli-Egyptian relations. "If you solve the Taba issue," he said, "then the sky will be the limit in the relations between our two countries." I sensed that he thought that I was a coming star on the Israeli political scene, and that it was worth investing effort with me. He promised to follow up on my invitation for him to visit Israel, and we parted like old friends.

The ways of politics are strange. I had voted against the Camp David agreement that Menachem Begin had signed, which turned over all of the Sinai Peninsula to Egypt. I thought it was a bad deal that had no precedent in history. Egypt, which had attacked Israel four times—in 1948, 1956, 1967, and 1973—was recovering all of the territory it had lost in these wars of aggression. It was my view that Begin should have been prepared for a territorial compromise, but should not have thrown in everything but the kitchen sink. He held the cards: Anwar Sadat, after the defeat he suffered in the Yom Kippur War, was not prepared for another war. But Begin, eager to bring home a peace treaty, under pressure from Moshe Dayan and Ezer Weizman (who accompanied him to Camp David), and supported by Ariel Sharon, had played his hand badly. And now I had the task of completing, down to the last inch, the withdrawal I had so strongly opposed.

But now I had no doubts about my course of action. Having paid so egregious a price for a peace treaty with Egypt, it made no sense to me to impede the establishment of good relations with Egypt because of Taba, a minuscule postage stamp of territory.

Upon my return to Israel I presented a motion to the cabinet that Israel would abide by the decision of the arbitration panel. Sharon was strongly opposed, insisting that the Egyptians had not fulfilled all their obligations under the peace treaty and that therefore Israel was free to disregard the decision of the arbitration panel, but my motion was passed by a majority vote.

Now the time had come to face the Palestinian issue. The Intifada was an urgent reminder that time was not to be lost. I was sure that the Bush administration was not going to let us ignore this festering wound, and that an Israeli initiative was called for that would provide a start of negotiations with the Palestinians and relieve the pressure on Israel.

After six weeks in the job as foreign minister I had formed in my own mind the outline of a peace initiative. It consisted of five points:

1. A call for a meeting of the signatories to the Camp David Accords (Egypt, Israel, and the United States) to review the status of the Israeli-Egyptian peace treaty.

2. A call for meetings between representatives of Israel and representatives of each and every Arab country claiming to be at war with Israel.

3. A conference of representatives of countries supplying arms to the Middle East and the recipient countries to discuss ways of moderating the ongoing arms race in the region.

4. A conference of the major industrialized nations to discuss ways of alleviating the conditions of the Palestinian refugees.

5. Elections to be held among the Palestinians in Judea, Samaria, and the Gaza Strip for representatives who would negotiate with Israel the Palestinians' status and that of the areas in which they resided.

The initiative attempted to address the host of problems weighing on Israel, the Palestinians, and the Middle East: the absence of normalization in Egypt's relationship with Israel, despite the great concessions Israel had made and the promise of normalization of the relationship implied in the treaty; the continued state of war between most of the Arab world and Israel; the heightened tension in the area due to the introduction of large quantities of weapons; the economic burden weighing on the countries in the region as a result of increased tensions; the plight of the Palestinian refugees, which could be relieved only by an organized international effort; and the initiation of negotiations between Israel and Palestinian representatives to be elected by a democratic process.

I discussed the initiative with Shamir a number of times and urged him to adopt it as Israel government policy. I found him at times reticent, at other times taciturn, and on occasion favorably inclined, although it was clear to me that he was far from enthusiastic. I found him hesitant, overly cautious, risk-averse—preferring to do nothing rather than proceed on a course that might entail risks. I should not have been surprised at this, having seen him abstain in the Knesset vote on the Camp David Accords, even though he was opposed to them. Again, during the debate on the Lavi, he had opposed the cancellation but had failed to get all of the Likud ministers on board to oppose cancellation, unlike Peres, who had done the necessary arm twisting of the Labor ministers to mount an effective opposition to the project that mobilized a one-vote majority for canceling the project. It seemed completely out of character with the image I had had of Shamir in the past: He was one of the leaders of the underground Stern Group during the days of British rule in Palestine, who had risked his own life innumerable times and sent others to risk theirs. When had he become so cautious? Was it his age? Or the heavy responsibility he felt on his shoulders as prime minister of Israel? I was to be frustrated by his cautiousness on a number of occasions in the years to come, although we continued to work closely as a team in the Likud.

Shamir decided to discuss the initiative with Defense Minister Yitzhak Rabin. Trying to get Rabin's support before bringing the initiative to the government was the right thing to do but, keeping his cards close to his chest, he did not consult with me beforehand, nor did he ask me to participate in this meeting. Shamir reported to me that Rabin had vetoed the third point of the five-point initiative, the one that called for a conference of countries supplying arms to the Middle East and the recipient countries. I assumed that Rabin, knowing that after the cancellation of the Lavi Israel was totally dependent on the United States for the supply of fighter aircraft, was concerned that such a conference might lead to a reduction of arms supplied by the United States to Israel. To my mind Rabin was mistaken. An attempt to moderate the regional arms race would probably be viewed favorably in the world, and any reduction of arms supplies to Israel would have to be matched by a reduction of arms supplied to the Arab countries. But I saw that Shamir accepted Rabin's position and decided to defer to him. So now it became a four-point initiative.

The proposal to hold elections for Palestinian representatives to negotiate with Israel was meant to begin a process of negotiations with the

Palestinians while bypassing the Palestine Liberation Organization (PLO), headed by Yasser Arafat. The PLO laid claim to being the representative of all Palestinians, including those who had left Palestine during the War of Independence and their descendants, and demanded for them the right of return. It was a terrorist organization responsible for a series of atrocities committed in recent years. My intention was that Israel negotiate with the Palestinians living in the area under Israeli control—Judea, Samaria, and the Gaza Strip.

That left open the question of the modalities whereby the Palestinian interlocutors would be chosen. I told Shamir that the best solution was to hold mayoralty elections in the major Palestinian towns in Judea, Samaria, and the Gaza Strip, and to accept the elected mayors as the negotiation partners. The alternative of holding elections for delegates in these territories who would represent the Palestinian population there would require establishing the modalities for a separate election of negotiators, and that itself would then become a subject for negotiations with the Palestinians. I thought it would be best to avoid such an ill-defined scenario.

But Rabin told Shamir that he rejected my proposal. As defense minister he had the responsibility for the territories. The Palestinian towns were currently run by officers of the IDF, and he objected to the elections of Palestinian mayors in these towns to take the place of these IDF officers. Shamir again accepted Rabin's position, and the subject of establishing the modalities for the election of Palestinian delegates became the major sticking point in advancing the initiative.

I had not yet succeeded in convincing Shamir to adopt the initiative when I was notified that Arye Levin, head of our consular office in Moscow, had been called to the Foreign Ministry and informed that Eduard Shevardnadze, the Soviet foreign minister, would be visiting the Middle East the following week, but had no intention to visit Israel and would like to meet me during his stay in Cairo. Obviously, such a meeting in Cairo would have to be approved by the Egyptian government. Before I had a chance to request such an approval the Egyptian ambassador to Israel, Mohammed Bassyouni, called me to tell me that I was invited to Cairo to meet Shevardnadze and that a meeting with Abd el-Meguid had also been scheduled for me. The Soviets must have informed the Egyptians of their desire for Shevardnadze to meet me in Cairo, and Mubarak evidently gave his consent to hold this meeting. When I asked whether I could also meet with President Hosni Mubarak, he called back within an hour to inform me that a meeting with Mubarak had been scheduled for February 20. Getting the Israeli government to approve the Taba arbitration decision had evidently opened some doors for me in Egypt. Here was an opportunity to explore the possibility of advancing our relations with Egypt, and to find out what the Soviets under Mikhail Gorbachev wanted to tell Israel.

As I stepped off the El Al plane at Cairo airport with my wife, Muriel, I could see that I was getting the red-carpet treatment. Abd el-Meguid and his wife were there to greet us, his wife carrying a bouquet of flowers for Muriel. Together we drove to the Sheraton Hotel in Heliopolis. Hoping to have a frank discussion with Mubarak, I asked Abd el-Meguid to find out if I could meet with Mubarak privately, without note takers. When I arrived at Mubarak's palatial quarters he told me that Mubarak had agreed to a private meeting.

Mubarak had inherited the presidency from Anwar Sadat when Sadat was assassinated by an opponent of the Israeli-Egyptian peace treaty. Like Sadat, Mubarak ruled like a dictator, supported by the Egyptian army. After Sadat's assassination there was great concern in Israel that his death would lead to the abrogation of the peace treaty—that all of Israel's concessions had been in vain. Clearly there were risks involved in making agreements with dictators. But Mubarak, now largely dependent on U.S. aid, was determined to uphold the treaty. Begin and Sadat had had a personal connection, but that personal connection had not been translated into full normalization of relations between Egypt and Israel after the signing of the peace treaty. It had been a disappointment to Israel. Now even some of the warmth of the Begin-Sadat relationship had disappeared. Under Mubarak it had become a very cold peace. Was the removal of the Taba roadblock going to change that, I wondered.

Mubarak was elegantly dressed in a business suit. The conversation between us flowed easily. I thanked him for arranging the meeting with Shevardnadze, and then we got to talking about the peace process with the Palestinians. "Talk to the PLO," he said. I tried to explain to him that we wanted to negotiate with representatives of the Palestinian population living in Judea, Samaria, and Gaza, and not talk to a terrorist organization that claimed to represent the "Palestinian diaspora" and their "right of return to Palestine." He obviously did not like my idea of holding elections among the local Palestinians. Why would he? Holding elections in Egypt was the farthest thing from his mind, and he did not warm to the idea of elections being held nearby.

When I spoke to him about our security concerns, and the threat of Scud missiles emplaced in Iraq with a range to reach Israel, he told me that as far as Saddam Hussein was concerned we had nothing worry about. "He knows what you have in your possession and he will not dare to attack you," he said emphatically. (He was to be proved wrong within a few months, when, during the First Gulf War, Scud missiles launched from western Iraq began landing in Israel.) He rejected my suggestion that he meet with Shamir on the occasion of the tenth anniversary of the Egyptian-Israeli peace treaty. "This is not the right time," he said. "I had wanted to meet with him, but he keeps making these statements about not giving up an inch of territory. Under these circumstances I cannot meet with him." I could see that he was limited by his concern for Egyptian public opinion— drawing closer to Israel at this time was not one of his priorities.

My meeting with Shevardnadze two days later at the Soviet embassy was one of the many small steps that were part of a slow process that led to the reestablishment of diplomatic relations with the Soviet Union more than two and a half years later, shortly before the dissolution of the Soviet Union. The Soviet Union had broken off diplomatic relations with Israel in June 1967, during the Six-Day War. Reversing that decision seemed to be a painfully slow process for the Kremlin, preceded by minuscule steps such as the permission to open an Israeli consular office in Moscow and, now, Shevardnadze's visit to the Middle East that did not include Israel, but did include meeting me in Cairo.

At the Soviet embassy, with its broad view over the Nile panorama, Shevardnadze waited for me outside at the top of the steps leading to the building. I took them two at a time, we shook hands, and we stepped inside. He was accompanied by an interpreter and two other gentlemen who remained silent throughout the meeting. For openers I said, "Well, if Mohammad does not come to the mountain, the mountain comes to Mohammed," alluding to his decision not to meet me in Israel.

Then he came forth with his prepared message: "The Middle East is a powder keg, and war could break out at any minute, and therefore it is imperative to bring peace to the region."

I retorted by explaining to him the dangers that Israel had faced in the past and the heavy price we had paid defending ourselves against aggression. "The vast quantities of Soviet arms that are being shipped into the region are not helping matters," I concluded. I saw that I was talking to a wall. He seemed to have only superficial knowledge of the Middle East and was evidently speaking from a prepared text.

He urged me to negotiate with the PLO and suggested that such talks could be held in the Soviet Union, an obvious attempt to bypass the United States and get the Soviet Union involved in these negotiations. He must have known of our close relations with the United States and that we were not likely to take up such an offer. After I explained to him that we Israelis needed to talk with representatives of the Palestinian population in Judea, Samaria, and Gaza, we seemed to have nowhere to go from there.

Taking the initiative, I suggested that we set up an Israeli-Soviet committee of experts so as to facilitate an exchange of views on the Middle East, which might lead to finding common ground. To my surprise, he agreed.

When he broached the subject of renewing diplomatic relations, I told him that that decision had to be taken in Moscow, since they had broken off relations. The primary subject of interest to us was Soviet Jewry and their immigration to Israel. He did not respond, and I saw that it was time to go. Talking to reporters on the steps of the embassy as we parted, he announced that we had a good meeting and that we had agreed to set up an Israeli-Soviet committee of experts to exchange views on the problems of the Middle East. Within weeks it became clear that Moscow had no intention of setting up such a committee. The idea must have received a cold shower back at the Kremlin upon his return. Shevardnadze was evidently being controlled from there.

Shevardnadze's interest in meeting me was one of the many signs of the imminent collapse of the Soviet Union. The Soviet satellites began demonstrating their independence. On September 1 I had been invited to Budapest for the renewal of diplomatic relations with Hungary. On February 9 I was in Prague for the renewal of diplomatic relations with Czechoslovakia. Poland and Bulgaria were to follow suit in the coming months.

On November 9, 1989, the Berlin Wall had come down. Within two weeks the West German chancellor, Helmut Kohl, announced a program for eventual reunification of the two Germanys. In early February 1990 we received a message at the Foreign Ministry that the German Democratic Republic (East Germany) wished to establish diplomatic relations with Israel. On February 14 Kohl announced that all obstacles to German reunification had been removed. Obviously, reunification of the two halves of Germany would seem to make meaningless the establishment of diplomatic relations with the GDR. Under these circumstances it was not clear to me how to respond to the feeler from the GDR government, and I decided to travel to Bonn immediately and get Kohl's opinion on the matter.

I met with him on February 15, and I got straight to the point. "We have a request from the East German government to open negotiations leading to the establishment of diplomatic relations," I told him. "Shall we be entering negotiations with a ghost?"

I was surprised by his reply: "Go right ahead. Reunification is going to take considerable time." Despite this prognosis, it was already clear that after forty-five years of separation the two Germanys were well on their way to unification. I had sent one of our senior Foreign Ministry officials to meet an emissary of the GDR in Copenhagen, but there seemed little point in pursuing this contact. Indeed, the German Unification Treaty was signed only half a year later, on August 31.

In Israel there were mixed feelings about a unified Germany. While in Bonn I was interviewed on German television and asked to give my view. The previous week Shamir had called a unified Germany "a deadly danger to Jews," but that was not my opinion, even though it was difficult to be enthusiastic, considering the bitter memories we had retained of a united German state a generation ago. On the other hand, the GDR had been hostile to Israel and had cooperated with Palestinian terrorism, so that unification with the Federal Republic, a democracy that had for some years maintained good relations with Israel, could be seen as a positive development. So I told the German audience, "If a united Germany is democratic and fully conscious of the responsibilities it has toward the Jewish people, I don't think there is a danger to be concerned about." In subsequent years I was proved right.

That week the Likud won a sweeping victory in the municipal elections. Over a year of organizational work in preparation for these elections and the selection of suitable candidates had paid off. The Likud won in Petah Tikvah, Ramat Gan, Holon, Ber Sheva, Hadera, Tiberias, and many other cities and towns across Israel. It was the second political upset in Israel, the first having been the Knesset elections in May 1977. Now, thirteen years later, the Likud was victorious in most municipal elections.

My next stop was going to be Washington, to face the Republican administration that followed Ronald Reagan's eight years at the White House. Reagan's had been the friendliest American administration that Israel had known since it came into existence. Primarily, this stemmed from Reagan's deep feeling of friendship and admiration for Israel, a feeling shared by his two secretaries of state, Alexander Haig and George Shultz. Of course, there had been inevitable differences of opinions and even crises, but they had been overcome because Reagan and Schultz wanted to overcome them.

From our point of view, Reagan's administration had brought a change to the American political scene. Over the years, support for Israel had come primarily from the Democrats. Among Israel's outstanding supporters over the years had been two Democratic senators, Daniel Inouye of Hawaii and Henry (Scoop) Jackson of Washington. On the whole, the Republicans had been cool to Israel. Most of them saw it as a small country that tended to interfere with America's desire to maintain close relations with the Arab world. After the combined British-French-Israeli operation in the wake of Gamel Abdel Nasser's nationalization of the Suez Canal in 1956, which brought Israeli troops to the banks of the Suez Canal and chased the Egyptian army out of the Gaza Strip, President Eisenhower had applied brutal pressure on David Ben-Gurion to withdraw from the Sinai Peninsula and the Gaza Strip. His secretary of state, John Foster Dulles, was considered downright unfriendly to Israel.

It wasn't until Reagan's presidency that support for Israel in Washington became truly bipartisan. George Bush, Reagan's successor, although not unfriendly to Israel, did not share Reagan's admiration for Israel, and like previous Republican administrations saw Israel as a small country that made life difficult for the United States in its relations with the Arab world. Now that the Cold War was over, Israel also seemed to have lost its importance as an ally in the conflict between the West and the Soviet Union.

The Bush administration, which saw the Israeli-Palestinian conflict as the major impediment to the pursuance of good relations between the United States and the Arab world, set its sights on resolving that conflict. The ongoing Intifada aroused considerable criticism of Israel in much of the world, and in the eyes of Bush and his secretary of state, James Baker, it set the stage for applying pressure on Israel to begin negotiations with the PLO and its leader, Yasser Arafat, in order to bring the conflict to an end.

I knew that it was not going to be easy to disabuse them of some of their ideas on the conflict, but I felt certain that the way to meet the oncoming pressure was to launch a preemptive initiative of our own. That was the initiative that I had presented to Shamir. Because of some of Rabin's objections it had been abridged, yet Shamir still had not approved it.

I wanted Shamir on his upcoming trip to Washington to present the initiative, and I planned on preparing the ground for that during my own meetings there. But I was not prepared for the reception awaiting me.

As I arrived in my hotel room in New York on Sunday morning, March 12, a report on the front page of the previous day's *New York Times*, entitled "PLO and Israel to get Bush Ideas on Mideast Peace," greeted me, It was from the *Times*'s diplomatic correspondent, Thomas Friedman. It began: "The Bush Administration plans to ask Israel and the Palestine Liberation Organization to take steps to ease tensions in the Israeli-occupied West Bank and Gaza Strip to lay the foundations for peace talks, a senior Administration official said. The official said the Administration's suggestions for Israel will be presented on Monday when Israel's Foreign Minister, Moshe Arens, meets with President Bush, Secretary of State James A. Baker 3rd and the national security adviser, Brent Scowcroft." I had no doubt that the "senior Administration official" was none other than Jim Baker. This was his way of letting me know that from now on it was going to be a new ball game. I was no longer the Washington media star that I had been during my tenure as ambassador, and the chummy relationship that I had developed with George Shultz and the Reagan administration had been replaced by a game of hardball with Israel. There was no need to extend the courtesy that would ordinarily be expected by a new foreign minister representing a newly elected government in Israel, and to listen to what he had to say, before opening up with both guns. It was better to forewarn him before he had a chance to open his mouth. It was a preemptive blow below the belt. Welcome to the Bush administration.

What was the use of taking the shuttle to Washington the next morning, I thought, where there seemed to be little interest in what I had to say? But of course I went nevertheless. In his office Baker greeted me courteously.

"I received quite a welcome with that story that was leaked to the *New York Times*," I opened. Baker denied that he had had anything to do with that report, but added that he saw nothing particularly wrong with it.

Getting to the heart of the matter, I emphasized the importance of the United States and Israel working in concert in order to bring stability to the Middle East, which was a common objective. The new Israeli government was in the process of formulating a peace initiative, I said, and we needed a little more time. Baker nodded here and there and made a few comments that expressed some doubts, but left me with the impression that he would await our initiative.

In my meeting with President Bush I explained the need for finding interlocutors among the Palestinian population in Judea, Samaria, and Gaza, rather than entering negotiations with the PLO, which was continuing terrorist activities. This evidently ran counter to Washington's view, which was that the PLO was an organization that had forsworn terrorism. Bush asked if I could substantiate my remarks regarding continued PLO terrorism, and suggested that we send an Israeli counterterrorism expert to Washington to present the evidence. On my return to Israel we were informed by the State Department that there would be no need to send our expert to Washington. No need to confuse them with the facts— their mind was made up. It was clear that Bush had already decided, before meeting with Shamir, and knowing full well that Shamir's government did not see the PLO as a partner for negotiations with the Palestinians, that negotiations with the PLO should be the next step.

The March 13 *New York Times* provided further clarification of the position taken by the Bush administration: "The senior State Department official said Mr. Baker had made it clear to Mr. Arens that when Prime Minister Yitzhak Shamir comes to Washington in the first week of April, the Administration expects him to bring specific proposals for improving the atmosphere in the occupied territories, as well as general ideas about how Israel sees the 'final status' of the West Bank and the Gaza Strip." In other words, start talking to the PLO and start thinking about the establishment of a Palestinian state in the "occupied West Bank and the Gaza Strip."

They knew that this was contrary to the policy of the Shamir government but decided to press ahead, no doubt taking account of the views of the Labor members of the Shamir-led national unity government, which differed from the views of its Likud members and those of Shamir himself. This attempt to play off one side of the Israeli government against the other was to become apparent in the following months.

The basic concept, now to be vigorously pursued by the Bush administration, was that the Israeli-Palestinian conflict was the major obstacle to improving America's relations with the Arab world and that that conflict could be resolved through Israeli negotiations with the Palestinians, leading to Israel's agreeing to the establishment of a Palestinian state in the West Bank and the Gaza Strip. This concept continued to be the basis of U.S. Middle East policy for many years. From that point of view Israeli settlements in the West Bank and the Gaza Strip were seen as a major stumbling block to the realization of the administration's plans and aroused the ire of succeeding administrations in Washington. In due time it became clear to all that most Arab rulers have only superficial interest in the Palestinian problem, that turmoil in the area has nothing to do with the Israeli-Palestinian conflict, and that resolution of the Israeli-Palestinian conflict is not attainable in the foreseeable future.

On my return to Israel I reported to Shamir on the situation in Washington and the pressure we could expect from there, and urged him again to adopt the peace initiative I had put together and to present it to Bush during his upcoming visit to Washington. Sometimes I felt that I was talking to a wall; at other times he seemed to be vacillating between moods of gloom and defiance, leaving me in doubt as to just what he was going to say when he got to Washington.

I was to find out on Sunday, April 2, after the weekly meeting of the cabinet. Shamir invited Peres, Rabin, and me to his office in order to brief us on what he intended to present during his upcoming visit to Washington. Without referring to it as a peace initiative, he told us that he was going to present four of the five points I had proposed to him. The arms-control point was missing, evidently vetoed by Rabin. I think Rabin was wrong on this. The idea would have drawn attention to the arms race in the Middle East, but would probably not have brought about any change—the vested interests of those who were supplying arms to the Middle East were too powerful.

But then came the mistake that was to haunt us over the next few months. I had proposed that Palestinian interlocutors be elected by the Palestinian population in the West Bank and Gaza. I was fully cognizant that the PLO was attaining recognition in the world as the representative of the Palestinian population and that the Bush administration was intent on having us negotiate with this terrorist organization. My proposal of holding democratic elections among the population was intended to bypass the PLO and establish contact with representatives of the Palestinian population directly concerned. It would have been difficult for the United States to oppose. But Shamir suggested instead that Jordan and/or Egypt put together a list of Palestinians as partners for negotiations with Israel.

The result of settling on this option should have been clear. Neither Egypt nor Jordan, both autocratic regimes, was interested in having democratic elections among the Palestinian population. Both had already recognized the PLO as the representatives of the Palestinians, and they were not about to veto PLO participation in negotiations with Israel. The composition of the list was to become a source of argument among Israel, Egypt, and the United States. It was a contest we were not likely to win. But that was yet to come.

In a meeting with Bush on April 6, Shamir presented the four-point peace initiative and also mentioned the possibility of holding elections among the Palestinian population in Judea, Samaria, and Gaza. It was the election proposal that drew everybody's attention. There was little interest in a conference to review the status of the Israeli-Egyptian peace treaty. Why antagonize Mubarak at this time, they were probably thinking in Washington. As for a call for meetings between Israel and Arab countries in a state of war with Israel, Washington considered it premature: the accepted dogma was that resolving the Israeli-Palestinian conflict was a precondition to any relaxation of tensions between Israel and the Arab world. Nobody could deny that dealing with the Palestinian refugee problem was important and urgent, but this ran counter to the position of the

PLO, which insisted that Palestinian refugees must be able to return to their former homes in Israel. The United States, promoting negotiations with the PLO, did not want to touch this issue, nor were countries standing in line to contribute to an effort to resettle the refugees elsewhere.

The PLO lost no time to declare that they were opposed to the Palestinian elections suggested by Israel. And no wonder. They had declared themselves to be the representatives of the Palestinians and were not eager to be replaced by a democratically elected Palestinian leadership. In this they were supported by Jordan and Egypt, for the reason previously alluded to: both were themselves autocratic states and had no use for democratic precedents next door. Baker too saw the PLO as the negotiating partner, and was looking for ways to introduce them into the process despite the position of the Israeli government. Moreover, he was already concentrating on a final solution, that would involve large-scale Israeli withdrawals from territories that would be turned over to the Palestinians. He gave expression to these views in his speech to an AIPAC conference in Washington on May 22: "For Israel, now is the time to lay aside once and for all the unrealistic vision of a Greater Israel. . . . Forswear annexation. Stop settlement activity." He left little doubt as to the direction in which he intended to push Israel.

Shortly it became clear that attempts were being made to subvert the Israeli peace initiative from a number of quarters. Baker was trying to get the Egyptians to come on board, and they in turn were not prepared to move without PLO acquiescence. In addition, the Egyptians tried to exploit the tensions between Labor and Likud in the Shamir-led government and Labor's inclination to accept proposals emanating from Egypt as a way of undercutting Shamir's leadership. Baker was prepared to play along with this and established contact with Rabin. But the major onslaught came from the Likud itself.

The trio of David Levy, Ariel Sharon, and Yitzhak Modai, each one seeking to advance himself, each believing that he could be and should be prime minister, banded together in an attempt to topple Shamir and sweep me aside—they saw me as a potential rival, most likely to succeed Shamir. They knew that they could not succeed if they attacked Shamir from the left, as they would find little support for that in the Likud, so they chose to attack him from the right. They claimed that he was prepared to make concessions that were endangering Israel, that he was not dealing adequately with Palestinian terrorism, and that he had to be "constrained" from taking steps that would involve great risks to Israel. These three became known as the "hishukaim," "the constrainers."

This was the height of hypocrisy—ambition taking a front seat, leaving principles behind. In addition, it was ludicrous. Shamir was probably the most hawkish of Israeli politicians. He wasn't prepared to give an inch when it came to conceding a part of the Land of Israel. There was no way you could pass him on the right. Yet they tried. Sharon had his followers among the members of the Likud who were settlers in the territories and who saw him as their patron. Levy had support from the development towns populated mostly by recent immigrants to Israel. Modai had the support of some of the former members of the Liberal Party.

Actually, as became clear within a few years, these three weren't ideologically on the right at all. Sharon, when he became prime minister, uprooted the Gush Katif settlement bloc in the Gaza Strip and was never forgiven by the settlers. Levy in due time left the Likud and joined the government of Ehud Barak, then the leader of the Labor Party. And Modai left the Likud, forming his own party, only to be defeated at the polls and leave the political scene.

But they could sure cause a ruckus. Not satisfied with a vote in the government approving the peace initiative, they called for a debate and vote on the issue in the Likud Central Committee. Sharon was the chairman of the committee and tried to dictate its agenda. Shamir wanted a vote of confidence, while Sharon insisted on a vote on the need to fight terrorism. He grabbed the microphone from Shamir, and a shouting match ensued. The meeting ended in disarray. What might have seemed to an uninformed observer as no more than a sideshow actually turned out to be the beginning of the countdown of a process that led to the fall of the national unity government.

Peres and his Labor colleagues in the government concluded that this kind of opposition to Shamir within the Likud made it unlikely that he would go along with Baker's efforts to assemble a Palestinian delegation that would suit the Egyptians, who in turn were coordinating their position with the PLO. Shamir, not enthusiastic about meeting with any kind of Palestinian delegation, played into their hands by rejecting Baker's attempts to come up with a compromise formula regarding the composition of the Palestinian delegation. Peres, by pointing out that Shamir was unwilling to proceed with the peace initiative that Shamir himself had promoted, hoped to be able to convince the ultra-Orthodox (Haredi) members of the government to abandon Shamir and join him in forming a new government, to be led by him. The first step in that direction would be to introduce a no-confidence motion in the Knesset, which if successful would bring down the Shamir-led government, and then to form an alternate coalition.

And so an ugly political maneuver began taking shape whereby the Labor members of the government plotted the downfall of the government of which they were members, and inexorably brought it about.

After Peres's plot failed, Rabin, Peres's rival in the Labor party, was to call it the "dirty trick." After negotiations with the religious parties in the coalition, Peres on Monday, March 12, 1990, felt confident that he could mobilize a majority in the Knesset for a no-confidence motion in the government. It was scheduled to come to a vote on Thursday, March 15. Preempting the no-confidence motion in the Knesset, Shamir decided to use his prerogative as prime minister to fire Peres from the cabinet at the cabinet meeting to be held on Tuesday, March 13. By Israeli law the dismissal takes effect only after forty-eight hours, so that by the time the no-confidence motion were to pass in the Knesset on Thurday afternoon, the dismissal would already have taken effect.

As the ministers assembled in the cabinet room that morning, they seemed to realize that they were witnessing something unprecedented in Israel's political history. Peres, the deputy prime minister and finance minister, was being fired. Shamir accused Peres of having plotted the downfall of the government. Then Shamir pushed the letter of dismissal over to Peres. Peres, visibly shaken, accused Shamir of responsibility for dissolution of the government. Then the remaining ten Labor ministers handed in a collective letter of resignation from the government. Then they left the room, leaving Shamir as head of a reduced government that might not command a majority in the Knesset, but that would continue, according to Israeli law, as a caretaker government until such time as a new government could be formed.

By gaining the support of the ultra-Orthodox parties for his maneuver, Peres succeeded in obtaining a majority in the Knesset on Thursday for a no-confidence vote on the Shamir-led government. It passed by a vote of 60 to 55; five of the six members of the religious Shas party had simply absented themselves from the vote. Now the president, Haim Herzog, had to charge a member of the Knesset with forming a new government; in accordance with Israeli law, he began a series of consultations with the Knesset factions, each of which recommended its favored candidate.

The Labor party naturally recommended Peres. Who was the Likud going to recommend? Shamir again? The decision rested with the Likud Knesset members. They held prolonged consultations. Levy had brought along many of his supporters, who demonstrated their support for him. There were rumors that I was going to throw my hat into the ring. Shamir, back in Jerusalem, became a little nervous and called me to ask if I was going to abandon him at this critical moment. I had thought of it, but decided not to do it. The majority of the Likud Knesset members, including me, voted for Shamir. So it was Shamir again, and Herzog had to decide between Peres and Shamir. Each was recommended by sixty members of the Knesset, the Shas Knesset members having chosen Shamir. Herzog chose Peres.

Now a drama ensued that shortly developed into a comedy of errors. If we could maintain the support of the bloc of sixty that had recommended Shamir, Peres would be one vote short of the majority he needed to confirm his government. The answer was to come the following week, on Monday, March 26, when Rabbi Eliezer Schach, the ninety-one-year-old leader of Degel Hatorah, an ultra-Orthodox faction in the Lithuanian religious community, addressed a capacity audience of his followers at the Tel Aviv basketball stadium in Yad Eliyahu. The venerable rabbi spoke in a mixture of Hebrew and Yiddish. The whole country was listening. But what was he saying? When he denounced Labor's kibbutz movement for not knowing what Yom Kippur or Shabbat were and for eating nonkosher food, his followers got the message—he was supporting Shamir. Peres remained one vote short of the majority he needed.

Now Peres, counting on the support of Agudat Yisrael, the other ultra-Orthodox party, asked for the Knesset to be called into session on April 11 so that he could present his new government. He arrived dressed for the occasion, expecting to be sworn in as Israel's next prime minister, only to be sorely disappointed. Two members of the Agudat Yisrael Party by now had decided to disregard the edict of the Council of Sages, which dictated the party's policy, and Peres was dumbfounded to find that he was two votes short of a majority. He asked the president for a twenty-one-day extension to give him additional time to form a coalition. He put his hopes on Modai, who headed a five-member faction in the Knesset that had deserted the Likud. The negotiations dragged out while we in the Likud tried to convince Modai to support Shamir.

On April 25, a day before Peres's mandate to form a government was to expire, President Haim Herzog gave a festive dinner in honor of the Czecholovak president Vaclav Havel on a visit to Israel. Both Peres and Shamir were in attendance. Modai's impending decision was the subject of all conversations. Even Havel, who had caught on to the political drama sweeping over Israel, inquired about Modai's decision. Modai, ever the showman, decided that he would announce his decision on the nine o'clock evening TV news. He chose Shamir, and dashed Peres's hopes of forming a government.

Peres's attempt to bring down the government was the end of our attempt to begin negotiations with an elected Palestinian delegation. The PLO's insistence that it was the legitimate representative of the Palestinian people, the acceptance of that position by the Arab states, the growing international recognition of the PLO, and the halfhearted position of the Labor Party on this issue all doomed our efforts to failure.

It was the beginning of a process that led to negotiations between Israel and the PLO by Rabin's Labor government; the Oslo Accords in 1993; the entry of Yasser Arafat and his cohorts, who had been chased out of Jordan by King Hussein and out of Lebanon by the IDF, into the West Bank and Gaza; and the imposition of their rule on the Palestinian population there. It led to the Second Intifada, in which more than a thousand Israelis lost their lives and disabused most Israelis of the dream that peace could be concluded with the PLO. Rabin, whom Peres had pulled into making a deal with Arafat, had the best of intentions, but it was a misguided move. Rabin, Peres, and Arafat were awarded the Nobel Peace Prize for their efforts. The Accords did not pave the way to peace with the Palestinians. Chaperoned by President Bill Clinton, supported by most of the Israeli public, cheered on by many around the world, the Accords led Israel and the Palestinians into a blind alley. The process was fueled by

Israel's desire for peace, a desire so strong that it blinded many to the reality that the PLO was not seeking peace with Israel at all.

PLO rule over the Palestinian population has been marked by corruption and mismanagement. In 2006 Hamas, the Islamic fundamentalist party, pledged to the destruction of the State of Israel, won the Palestinian legislative elections, beating the Fatah Party, associated first with Arafat and then with Mahmoud Abbas. Hamas subsequently took control of Gaza, leaving Fatah in charge of Judea and Samaria. Hamas does not want peace with Israel, while the Palestine Authority, the successor to the PLO, is incapable of making peace with Israel. What should have been clear then, and hopefully is clear to all by now, is that an accommodation, if one can be reached, must be reached with the Palestinian population in the West Bank and Gaza, not with those who claim to speak not only for them but also for the Palestinian diaspora, demanding the "right of return" for the Palestinians who fled their homes during Israel's War of Independence, and their descendants.

On June 11, 1990, almost three months after Peres had brought down the Shamir government, Shamir presented his new government to the Knesset. It was approved by a vote of 62 to 57.

ELEVEN

Defense Minister Again

Yitzhak Shamir had struggled to form a new coalition government that would not include Labor. After endless negotiations with the religious parties, he finally managed to put all the pieces together on June 6, 1990, the deadline given him, in accordance with Israeli law, by President Haim Herzog. Failing that, we would have gone to early elections.

It turned out that the religious parties were not his biggest problem. It was one of our own, David Levy, one of the "constrainers," who insisted that he should be the foreign minister in the new government. And Shamir, cautious as ever, decided to give in to him, hoping it might put an end to Levy's troublemaking in Likud Party forums.

As for the Ministry of Defense, Shamir put it to me straight: "If you don't take on the Defense Ministry, we don't have a government." Having given in to Levy's demand, he was not prepared to appoint Ariel Sharon to the post of defense minister. I was not enthusiastic. I didn't think Levy was a good choice as foreign minister. I knew that I would be facing a tough task at the defense ministry. I would be inheriting the Intifada from Rabin, who had handled the situation ineptly. It was raging, rocks were being thrown at travelers on the roads, and whatever I did I was most likely to be criticized by Sharon. But it had to be done.

As I moved over to the Defense Ministry, Benjamin Netanyahu, who had been my deputy, decided to stay at the Foreign Ministry and be Levy's deputy there. He was soon to regret that decision.

On June 12, 1990, I reviewed the Israel Defense Forces (IDF) troops lined up in the Defense Ministry compound in Tel Aviv and was greeted there by Chief of Staff Lieutenant General Dan Shomron and Director General David Ivri. I knew them both well. During my previous tenure as defense minister I had passed over Shomron when I appointed Moshe Levy chief of staff, and had asked Shomron to continue his army service so that he would have a chance to be chief of staff the next time around. Rabin had appointed him to the position when Levy completed his four-year tenure. Shomron had supported cancellation of the Lavi aircraft when Rabin brought the issue to the cabinet. His claim that canceling the Lavi would make it possible to initiate a number of advanced sophisticated weapons programs in its stead came to nothing. Ivri, a former illustrious air force commander and Levy's deputy chief of staff, had been a fervent supporter of the Lavi all along.

But the Lavi was now in the past. I saw little chance of reviving the program. We could not expect from the Bush administration the kind of support we had received from the Reagan administration. My immediate challenge was to put an end to the Intifada. It was now in its nineteenth month and showed no signs of abating. On the Palestinian side hundreds were dead, many thousands injured, and tens of thousands imprisoned. On the Israeli side many had been killed and hundreds, injured. The Palestinians had suffered grievously; more than 100,000 Israelis in the territories now traveled on roads at considerable risk to their lives. Rabin had used severe measures—all of the schools and universities in Judea, Samaria, and Gaza had been closed, and most Palestinian cities were now run by IDF officers. But to no avail. I knew that bringing about an improvement in the security of the Israeli settlers while trying to establish a dialogue with the Palestinians was not going to be easy. On my second day in office, I scheduled a visit, accompanied by Shomron, to the two largest Israeli settlements in the territories: Ma'aleh Adumim in the Judean desert, a five-minute ride from Jerusalem, with a population of close to 10,000; and Ariel, a half-hour ride from Tel Aviv, in central Samaria, with a population of 7,000.

We arrived by helicopter and were greeted by Major General Yitzhak Mordechai, head of the Central Command, and by the local mayors. I was amazed to learn that Rabin, throughout his five-year tenure as defense minister, had never visited these towns, and that it was Shomron's first visit as well. Rabin had been in the habit of disparaging the settlements, once referring to the Ariel settlement as "Ariel, Shlomiel." The IDF under Rabin and Shomron had treated the Intifada as something of secondary importance and had assigned little priority to providing for the security of the settlers in the territories. They saw the preparation of the IDF for the possibility of another war as their primary mission.

I told Shomron that dealing with the Intifada was now the IDF's primary mission. "Provide safety for those traveling on the roads," I instructed the army. "Do whatever is necessary, whether it means stationing soldiers along the roads, increasing the number of patrols, or even seizing buildings that control stretches of the roads." Although providing safety for the tens of thousands of Israeli vehicles traveling on thousands of kilometers of roads, many of them running through Arab villages, was no simple matter, rock throwing at passing cars soon was significantly reduced. The army had reset its priorities.

Simultaneously I began establishing contacts with Palestinians. During my first two weeks in office I met with Elias Frej, the mayor of Bethlehem, who was an old friend from my previous tenure as defense minister. In 1983 he had come to my office, asking that Bethlehem be annexed to Israel. It was one of many indications of the sorry state of the Arab Christian population, which feels threatened by the Muslim majority surrounding them. They are caught between a rock and a hard place—persecuted by the Muslims and yet feeling the need to demonstrate their loyalty to the Palestinian cause. Frej saw Bethlehem—a Christian town, the town where Jesus was born, the site of annual Christian celebrations—gradually being turned into a town with a Muslim majority, and thought that annexation to Israel could preserve its Christian character. I had told him that, unfortunately, I did not have the authority to annex Bethlehem. Since that time Muslims have taken control of Bethlehem. That has been the fate of all Christian towns and villages in the West Bank. The higher birthrate among Muslims and the emigration of Christians are gradually reducing the Christian presence in the West Bank. Only in Israel do Christian Arabs feel safe and stay on.

I met with the mayors of Bet Sahur and Bet Jalla; with Fayez Abu Rahme, a well-known Gaza lawyer; and with Dr. Akram Matar, who ran the Gaza eye clinic, and his brother, who was head of the Gaza architects association. It was the first time that they had been invited to the office of the defense minister. I explained to them that even though Israelis and Palestinians differed strongly on the terms of the settlement to the conflict, it was not a zero-sum game and therefore we should identify those steps that would be of mutual benefit. I urged them to help stop the violence and make it possible for me to reopen the schools and the universities, withdraw the army from populated areas, and set the stage for the holding of elections and subsequent negotiations between us. They seemed to appreciate my attitude, but it was clear that they would be afraid to present themselves as candidates in an election. In the Palestinian society the rules of the game were unlike those of democratic societies—political opponents were simply assassinated. The influence of the Palestine Liberation Organization (PLO) was strongly felt among the population, and the PLO was not interested in democratic elections. They had already appointed themselves the representatives of the Palestinians. Their policy was to eliminate all rivals.

The PLO was receiving increasing international recognition, Washington had established relations with it, and it was terrorizing potential political rivals in the territories. The prospects for holding elections were beginning to look dim.

At this point my attention was directed to the threat facing us from Iraq. On April 1, Saddam Hussein, the Iraq dictator, speaking in Baghdad, had announced that he now possessed a "binary chemical weapon." "By God, we will make the fire eat up half of Israel if it tries to do anything against Iraq," he boasted. We knew that mustard gas and nerve agents such as sarin and tabun were being produced at facilities in Samarra, Falluja, and Salman Pak that had been built using German and other western European technology. The Iraqis were also acquiring ballistic rockets with sufficient range to reach Israel. Named Scud by American intelligence agencies, they were the Soviet version of the German V2 rockets that had been launched against London in the last months of World War II. There was no way of intercepting them in flight—in that sense, nothing had changed in the intervening fifty-five years. Ballistic rocket interception technology was still in its early development stages in Israel at this time, as part of the Strategic Defense Initiative launched by President Reagan.

Saddam Hussein had rockets capable of reaching Israel. In addition to a 500-kilogram conventional warhead, it was known that Iraq had also developed a chemical warhead for this rocket, while pursuing the development of nuclear technology. Here was a clear and present danger for Israel. Although Hosni Mubarak had a few months earlier confided to me that Saddam Hussein would not dare to attack Israel for fear of an Israeli nuclear response, there was no way of being sure of that. The Iraqi dictator was known to be a gambler.

On July 20 I met with Dick Cheney, the U.S. secretary of defense, in his office in the Pentagon to present our concerns regarding the Iraqi dictator. I was accompanied by Major General Amonon Lipkin-Shahak, the IDF's head of intelligence, and Shabtai Shavit, the head of the Mossad. Cheney was joined by Undersecretary of Defense Paul Wolfowitz and Lieutenant General Harry Soyster, head of the Defense Intelligence Agency. In addition to reviewing the developments in Iraq's missile and nonconventional weapons program, I pointed to the close military relations that were developing between Iraq and Jordan. A combined Iraqi-Jordanian fighter squadron had been established and Iraqi aircraft were using Jordanian airspace.

Jordan's King Hussein was making his second mistake. The first had been when he decided to join Egyptian president Gamal Abdel Nasser in his attack on Israel in June 1967. Now he was allying himself with Saddam Hussein. If Iraqi forces were to enter Jordan, it would radically change the military situation and might require preemptive steps on our part. I emphasized the need for close coordination between the United States and Israel under these circumstances. Cheney thanked me for the presentation. It was a rather low-key response. Less than two weeks later Saddam Hussein occupied Kuwait, and the Gulf crisis was on.

On the night of August 2, 1990, the Iraqi army marched into Kuwait. It was a walkover. Within a week the United States began deploying military forces in Saudi Arabia. On August 14, President Bush publicly called for "the immediate, complete, and unconditional withdrawal of all Iraqi forces from Kuwait."

A few days earlier the American ambassador, Bill Brown, had arrived at my home one morning to inform me of the American deployment in Saudi Arabia and had requested that we take no preemptive action. My visit to Washington had evidently left the impression that we were gravely concerned by the developing situation and that we might be planning military action to forestall the oncoming danger. Such action on our part, it was felt, would interfere with their operational plans and their attempt to build a coalition to confront Saddam Hussein that would include Arab states. From that point on—as the Gulf crisis escalated, leading up to the American Desert Storm operation, which began on January 17—Washington was intent on keeping Israel from getting involved. Every effort was made to achieve this objective.

The argument presented to us was that Israeli involvement would lead to the breakup of the coalition that had been put together, and particularly to Saudi Arabia's leaving the coalition. Whereas the participation of some of the other Arab countries was of no more than symbolic value, Saudi participation was crucial, as Saudi Arabia served as the staging ground for the deployment of American forces in preparation for an attack on Iraqi forces in Kuwait and Iraq. American aircraft were taking off from and landing at Saudi air bases. Even though the Saudis, fearing that the Iraqi dictator might choose them as the next target after Kuwait, were eager to cooperate, this argument nevertheless carried weight with us. After all, the Americans were going after Saddam Hussein, an enemy of Israel, and we were not inclined to do something that might interfere with this operation.

The specter of the breakup of the coalition was continually held before us. The real objective of President Bush's policy was to cement an image that the United States was a friend of the Arab world. Israeli involvement might tarnish that image. This policy followed from a well-established theory in Washington that U.S.-Israeli relations, as important as they might be, constituted a burden on America's desire to maintain close relations with Arab countries, and particularly with Saudi Arabia, the wealthiest of them all and the supplier of much of the oil needed by the American economy. As the years went by it became clear that there was very little substance to this theory.

While burdened by my concern regarding a possible attack by the Iraqis, by rocket attacks or by ground and air forces through neighboring

Jordan, or possibly by both, I was suddenly faced by an assault from an unexpected quarter.

We knew that the Iraqis had large facilities preparing chemicals for military use. They had already used them in an attack on a Kurdish village in Iraq. We had to assume that they had prepared chemical warheads for their Scud rockets. An attack by Scud rockets carrying chemical warheads could not be discounted.

Years earlier the Israeli government had begun a program of acquiring gas masks to be kept in storage for distribution to the population in case of need. Now that the newspapers were carrying reports on Iraq's chemical warfare capabilities, calls were being heard to distribute the gas masks. I decided not to do so. First, we did not as yet have enough gas masks for the entire population, and distribution to part of the population was bound to arouse panic and rage among those who were left out. In any case, I did not consider the danger to be sufficient—neither the possibility that the Iraqis would use chemical warheads nor the damage that might be caused in case a few were launched against Israel—to warrant arousing fear and possibly panic by distributing gas masks to the civilian population.

At the weekly cabinet meeting on Sunday, August 19, 1990, Foreign Minister David Levy, without any prior warning, astounded the assembled ministers by accusing me of taking too lightly the mortal danger facing Israel's population from an impending Iraqi chemical attack. He demanded that gas masks be issued immediately to the public.

Shamir tried to placate him by telling him that this was not a suitable subject for the full cabinet and that he could raise it at the next meeting of the inner cabinet, which would deal with security issues. But Levy was not to be placated—he had a plan of action. He briefed reporters after the cabinet meeting, and the following day made a TV appearance where he repeated his accusations against me and demanded the immediate distribution of gas masks. He did not bother to speak to me, nor did he inquire whether there were enough gas masks available to make distribution to all possible at this time. It was a political move and damn the consequences.

Levy's offensive led to a feeling of unease among the public and increasingly calls were heard for the distribution of gas masks. My immediate objective was to make sure that we had enough gas masks to go around. After an intensive effort of ramping up production of gas masks and scouring

Europe for more, we eliminated most of the shortages. By then some of the tension regarding the chemical threat had subsided, and I concluded that we could begin the orderly distribution of gas masks to the public. On October 1 I issued an announcement that a trial distribution would begin in three small towns. I hoped that this would provide a clear signal that there were no indications of an impending attack, and therefore no need for an emergency distribution to the entire population. The public took the announcement calmly. In the following weeks gas masks were distributed gradually to the entire population, after we had solved specific problems such as gas masks that would fit religious men with beards and protection for babies. It went pretty smoothly. Since we still did not have enough, we decided not to distribute them to the population in Judea and Samaria: I considered it unlikely that the Iraqis would target the Arab population in Judea and Samaria. Gaza was in any case out of range of the Iraqi Scuds. But the Israeli settlers in Judea and Samaria demanded that they be given gas masks. When that was settled an attorney representing Arabs in Bethlehem appealed to the Israeli Supreme Court asking that they, too, be issued gas masks. The court ruled in their favor.

For the next three months, Israelis took the cardboard boxes containing their gas masks wherever they went. It was needless and cost a lot of money. We were prepared for a chemical attack that never came.

On a visit to Washington I met Dick Cheney on September 17. I told him that I was operating on the assumption that once the United States initiated military action against Iraq, there was a significant probability of the Iraqis attacking Israel in order to demonstrate to the Arab world that this was really a war against Israel. We were likely to be hit by Iraqi rockets, possibly with chemical warheads. The Iraqis might even strike at Israel prior to any American move being made. In any case we had to be prepared for a confrontation with Iraq sooner or later. Of all the countries involved in this crisis, Israel was the most exposed. Under these circumstances, I felt that the United States should make available to Israel intelligence information regarding Iraq, and a framework for operational coordination should be established between our armed forces to be used if the need arose. Cheney was reticent on both issues. He was not prepared to provide us with real-time satellite photos of Iraq, and the mention of operational coordination between the United States and Israel seemed to cause him considerable unease.

As the weeks went by it became apparent that the Bush administration was determined to distance Israel from the plans they were formulating regarding Iraq, and to prevent as far as possible any Israeli military initiative. Withholding satellite photos of Iraq, which Washington assumed might facilitate an Israeli attack on Iraqi rocket-launching sites, was part of that policy.

On November 29, 1990, the United Nations Security Council passed a resolution authorizing the use of force if Iraq did not evacuate Kuwait by January 15, 1991. Now it was up to Saddam Hussein. If he refused to budge there would be war.

Jordan's King Hussein was getting jittery. If Israel were to respond to an Iraqi attack by flying over Jordanian airspace, it might very well put an end to his kingdom. Using the Mossad's connections in Jordan, he asked to hold an urgent meeting with Shamir in London. They met there secretly on January 5. Shamir, accompanied by Major General Ehud Barak, the IDF's deputy chief of staff, told King Hussein that if Israel were attacked by Iraq, Israeli aircraft might have to fly through Jordanian airspace on their way to retaliatory missions in Iraq. Hussein responded that if Israel sent ballistic missiles through Jordan's upper atmosphere there was nothing he could do about it, but he could not countenance Israeli aircraft flying through Jordanian airspace—that would be a violation of Jordanian sovereignty and would require a reaction by Jordan. Passively accepting such an act by Israel would make it look as though he was collaborating with Israel. It was a friendly meeting that did not lead to any agreement.

Early in January we had the first sign of a willingness by Washington to establish a framework for cooperation. A secure telephone line had been set up between Cheney and me. The Israeli end, codename "Hammer Rick," was located in a hut in the Defense Ministry compound; it was staffed by a small group of American technicians and Israel Air Force officers. It was about a two-minute walk from my office. I could run the distance in one minute if it was something urgent. On Friday, January 4, I made a regular call to Washington and scheduled the inauguration of the secure line for the following Monday, January 7, at 3:00 p.m. Israeli time, 8:00 a.m. in Washington.

A meeting between Baker and the Iraqi foreign minister, Tariq Aziz, had been scheduled to be held in Geneva on January 9, in a last-ditch attempt to avoid war. When I spoke to Cheney on Monday he sounded very determined. He did not think that anything was going to come of the meeting. Cheney knew whereof he spoke. At the conclusion of the meeting Baker announced that Iraq would have to leave Kuwait by January 15 or else face the use of force. Aziz announced that Iraq would not submit to this ultimatum. When asked whether Iraq would attack Israel, Aziz replied, "Absolutely, yes." Now it was clear that Israel was in the crosshairs of Iraq's missiles, and Saddam Hussein was prepared to gamble that Israel would not reach for a last-resort weapon if attacked by Scud rockets.

The following day, Thursday, I called Cheney. "Now that the Baker-Aziz talks have ended in failure," I said, "it looks like the countdown to the initiation of hostilities has really begun. We have taken notice of Aziz's declaration that Iraq would attack Israel, and now have to consider the possibility of an Iraqi strike against Israel even before you initiate hostilities. This state of affairs makes it essential that we set up operational coordination between us immediately. In the absence of such coordination we would probably have to fly over Jordanian airspace to respond to an Iraqi attack on Israel, which might have serious consequences. I assume this is well understood by you in Washington."

Cheney had to hear me out, since the secure connection allowed only one party to speak at a time. Cheney tried to evade the issue by telling me that Baker's deputy, Larry Eagleburger, and Cheney's deputy, Paul Wolfowitz, would be arriving in Israel on Saturday and that they would discuss this matter with the prime minister. Cheney repeated that military coordination could be discussed with Eagleburger and Wolfowitz during their upcoming visit. Then he continued, "I want to emphasize that the targets in western Iraq will be dealt with by the U.S. Air Force, including all targets that could be a threat to Israel. From a military point of view there will be no need for you to respond; there will be no targets in western Iraq that will not be taken care of," he assured me.

"You know," I said, "that the Iraqi mobile launchers will be difficult to destroy, and even the stationary launchers might escape destruction by the U.S. Air Force. We have to be prepared to respond to an Iraqi attack on Israel." I repeated that it was essential to come to an arrangement where U.S. and Israeli aircraft might be operating in the same airspace. "Talk to Eagleburger and Wolfowitz about that," he repeated. "We are going to allocate a great part of our resources to deal with the threat against Israel. An attack on Israel will be considered a provocation that will call for a move by us." On that note our conversation ended.

The next day, Friday, Cheney called to tell me that Eagleburger, Wolfowitz, and Rear Admiral Merrill Ruck of the National Security Council would be arriving in Israel on Saturday in order to convince us not to get involved, not to retaliate even if we were attacked, and to leave everything to the American armed forces. "Let me emphasize the importance of Israel staying out of the conflict," he said. "It is important not only for Israel but also for the interests of the United States. There will be no targets in Iraq that will not be attacked by us, there will be no targets for you that we will not attack. We are in a situation where if Israel becomes involved it will influence some members of the coalition to cancel their military participation and it will increase the burden on the United States. We will have to take upon ourselves additional missions, and this will cause us more casualties. We will suffer casualties in order to destroy targets that threaten you." Getting a little hot under the collar, I told him that we had a long tradition of defending ourselves and had never asked anybody to fight for us.

Larry Eagleburger was a friend from my days as ambassador in Washington, when he worked for George Shultz. Paul Wolfowitz was Jewish and had a sister living in Israel. I assumed that they had been chosen to bring Washington's message to us in the belief that they would be seen by us as friends and inspire confidence. But of course they were the loyal messengers of the president of the United States. He wanted us to stay out.

They were going to work on Shamir, assuming that as prime minister he had the final word, and probably considered me to be a harder nut to crack. Before their arrival I urged Shamir to stand fast on our position that if attacked we would respond.

During their meeting Eagleburger urged Shamir to keep Israel out of the conflict, but Shamir stuck to his guns. Then Eagleburger said that the United States had a "fall-back" position. If Israel was attacked and decided that it had to respond, the United States and Israel would consult in order for U.S. forces to "stand down" in a mutually agreed area of Iraq and permit Israel to take action there. Shamir accepted this proposal, and assured them that we would not take preemptive action prior to a U.S. move.

When I met Eagleburger, Wolfowitz, and Ruck the next morning, Eagleburger referred to the "fall-back" position that had been agreed with Shamir, but emphasized that the United States was not prepared to undertake joint operations with Israel, nor to provide targeting information or to assist us in obtaining overflight rights. He assured me that the U.S. armed forces felt completely confident of their ability to eliminate the missile threat against Israel. He said that they planned to attack western Iraq and the missile-launching sites in the very early stages of their operation, so there was nothing for us to worry about. But I continued to worry.

Claims had been made that the Raytheon Patriot anti-aircraft missile also had the capability to intercept ballistic missiles. We had put in an order for such missile batteries that were supposed to have been delivered in September, but they had not yet arrived, so Israeli crews for these missiles had not yet been trained. When I reminded Eagleburger of that he said that they had been needed for U.S. troops, but he offered to deliver them now, together with U.S. crews who would stay as long as it took to train Israeli crews to operate them. That offer I refused. We had a long tradition of doing our own fighting and I did not want to deviate from it by having U.S. troops operate in Israel's defense.

The U.S. military had no prior experience in dealing with mobile missile launchers, and their confidence in their ability to fulfill this mission, evidently communicated to the president, was misplaced. The Israel Air Force had faced this problem during the Yom Kippur War when Soviet mobile anti-aircraft missile launchers had been deployed in Egypt, and they had learned the hard way how difficult a challenge they posed, their exact location being unknown at the time the air strike against them is launched. Some years later, during Israel's Lebanon operation, the Israel Air Force responded effectively to the threat of missiles launched from mobile launchers by the use of technology and tactics tailored specifically for this purpose.

At midnight on January 16 Cheney called to tell me that the American operation would begin in two hours. At 2:00 a.m., in my office, I watched Baghdad being bombed on CNN; two hours later I saw President Bush announcing the beginning of hostilities; and at 5:00 a.m. Cheney came on the secure line and provided initial information on the results so far, emphasizing that considerable airpower had been devoted to dealing with the ballistic-missile threat in western Iraq.

Forty-eight hours after the beginning of the American operation against Iraq, the first Scuds fell on Israel. Three landed in the Tel Aviv area, one in the northern outskirts of Haifa, and two fell into the sea. Only the one aimed at Tel Aviv hit a densely populated area, in the southern part of the city, causing considerable property damage but no fatalities. The Americans had obviously not been able to prevent these launches. So presumably the time had come for the agreed "fall-back" position to become operational: for the United States to stand down and clear the decks so that Israel could act.

I asked Shamir to call a meeting of the cabinet the next morning to discuss the situation. I had spoken to Cheney during the night and requested again that arrangements be made to coordinate the actions of Israeli and American forces. He continued to stall. "I'll check your request and get back to you," he said as he signed off.

It was a tense meeting at 8:30 a.m. the following morning. There was a general feeling that Israel had to respond to the Iraqi attacks. But how? Hundreds of U.S. and allied aircraft were flying over Iraq. For our aircraft to enter that airspace required coordination with the Americans, but I had still not heard anything from Cheney. I asked the air force commander, Avihu Bin-Nun, to present the operational plan for attacks on western Iraq that the air force had prepared. The pilots were in their fighter aircraft on the runways ready to take off the moment the cabinet signaled its approval. I told the cabinet that I hoped to hear from Cheney during the day, but in the meantime we had no choice but to wait.

Ariel Sharon's voice was the most forceful at the meeeting. "Notify the Americans and send our aircraft," he urged.

"Notification is not the same as coordination," I replied. I recommended that we not take the risks involved by sending our aircraft over Iraq without prior coordination with the Americans. Shamir, keeping calm, summarized the meeting: The actual operational plans presented were approved on condition that they were coordinated with the Americans.

Baker had spoken to Shamir during the night, emphasizing the importance of Israel's staying out of the conflict. It was the first of an avalanche of telephone calls and messages to Shamir from Washington, all reiterating the same thing: Stay out of the conflict.

From then on it became almost a ritual. As Scuds kept falling on Israel and American efforts to prevent these launches seemed to have no success, I would tell Cheney in my daily conversations with him that operational coordination between our air forces had to be established so that we could carry out our plans to attack the areas in western Iraq from which the Scuds were being launched against Israel; he would stall me time and again, telling me that the president had not authorized to arrange for such coordination. At the same time Bush was bombarding Shamir with telephone calls and messages asking Israel to stay out. To reinforce these appeals Bush had sent Eagleburger and Wolfowitz back to Israel to keep up the pressure on an hour-by-hour basis and keep Washington informed of the goings-on here. Bush's tactics were evidently based on the assumption that Shamir could be convinced and that he could be counted on to keep me from running wild.

At lunch with Eagleburger in Tel Aviv, he tried to work on me. "There's great appreciation for the restraint you have shown. You now have a lot of money in the bank in Washington—don't waste it," he admonished me. But knowing Washington and George Bush, I knew that that "deposit" was going to be depreciated very quickly once this war was over. Shamir was probably more impressed than I by the "credit" he was told he was amassing in Washington. He was going to be disappointed.

Saudi Arabia was also being hit by Iraqi Scuds. According to American reports the Patriot batteries there were successful in intercepting them. These reports led me to feel that I had no right to continue to refuse the American offer to supply Patriot batteries together with U.S. crews. I swallowed my pride and asked Cheney to send them. They arrived shortly and engaged incoming Scuds for the next few weeks, but with little success.

On the evening of Tuesday, January 22, the fifth day of the war, a Scud landed in downtown Ramat Gan, causing severe damage to a number of apartment buildings. More than fifty people were wounded, and three elderly people died of heart attacks. I rushed over to see for myself. What I saw reminded me of pictures I had seen of London in World War II during the Blitz: fire engines, stretcher bearers, ambulances, police, and special army evacuation units attempting to save people trapped in the rubble.

I decided to call Cheney to ask him to arrange for an aerial corridor to be cleared that would allow us to operate in the area in western Iraq from which the missiles were being launched. I told him that a plan for Israeli action would be presented to the cabinet for approval in the morning. He said he was at the White House and would have to consult with the president. "If you will operate there, we will simply leave the area west of forty-one degrees longitude," he said. I assumed that he had reconciled himself to an Israeli operation against the launching sites.

That conclusion, it turned out, was premature. Three hours later, at 2:40 a.m., a message was passed to me via the secure link by Rear Admiral T. Joseph Lopez, Cheney's executive assistant: "Lopez requests to transmit to Arens from Cheney that Eagleburger will transmit a message from the president to the prime minister. Till contact between the president and the prime minister is established, action on the matter raised by Arens in his conversation with Cheney is held up."

Seeing that American aerial attacks had not been effective in putting an end to the Iraqi missile attacks against Israel, I had asked the IDF to prepare for an action that would involve landing ground troops in the area from which the launches were being conducted to search for the missile launchers and destroy them. The action had been planned and rehearsed during the past few weeks, ever since I had ordered the IDF to prepare for the destruction of Iraqi missile launchers and launching sites in western Iraq. It was going to be a difficult and dangerous operation, to be carried out some 600 kilometers from our home bases. It was likely to involve casualties and possibly soldiers being taken prisoner, but I felt it had to be done. There had to be a response to the Iraqi attacks; every effort had to be made to stop these attacks. The next one might involve a large number of casualties or might even be chemical.

At 7:00 a.m., two hours before the cabinet was scheduled to meet, Shamir had received a telephone call from Bush. Bush asked him "not to do what Saddam Hussein wanted him to do," and get involved in the conflict. To reinforce the message Eagleburger had also brought Shamir a letter from Bush. The president wrote that he could imagine the pressure on Shamir, but he asked the prime minister to "show restraint in the face of aggression." Bush asked that we do nothing to relieve the pressure on Saddam Hussein—which Bush felt that Israeli retaliation, "be it most justified," would certainly do. Presumably, Israeli involvement would lead to Arab countries leaving the coalition, which would provide encouragement to Saddam Hussein. Bush wrote that in the view of the U.S. military the planned Israeli action did not have a "significant chance" of improving on the existing U.S. effort. The letter closed with an appeal that Shamir stand firm, despite the provocation, "for the greater good of Israel and the U.S."

At the cabinet I presented the plan, which involved overflying Jordanian airspace. Air Force Commander Bin-Nun laid out the complication to be expected: "We will have to shoot down any Jordanian aircraft that attempts to intercept us. Should they persist we will have to take appropriate measures." When he announced that weather conditions during the next two or three days precluded carrying out the operation, everyone relaxed.

I summarized the problems involved in the operation that was presented: "We are concerned over the possibility of a significant reaction from Jordan. There is the additional danger of a possible Syrian involvement, or that the Jordanians will ask the Iraqis to come to their assistance. If we decide to proceed it must be clear that we are taking these risks upon ourselves. There are two difficulties with this operation: One is determined by nature, the other by man. Nature's difficulty is the weather. The man-made difficulty is that the Americans must agree to clear the area for the required period of time. We would not ask them to arrange for a corridor, but rather to leave the area for three days in order to allow us to act—we do not have such an American commitment at the moment."

Shamir concluded the meeting: "The Americans are a very important political and military factor. It is most important, and we have to assure that they will help us and not hurt us. In every move of ours, we have to take this into consideration, their position and attitude toward us. . . . We don't have to take a decision today." I could see that the pressure from Washington had left its mark on Shamir.

The next day I went up to Jerusalem to talk to Shamir. I was concerned that he had in effect decided to accept Bush's demand that we stay out of the conflict. He must have thought that by giving in to them on this issue, seemingly so important to Bush, he would be compensated in the future by American support of Israel in its conflicts with the Palestinians and the Arab world. He felt that these were the major challenges facing Israel. But

I felt that I knew the Bush administration better than he did. Once the Gulf War was over I was sure that Bush would continue to pressure Israel on the Palestinian issue. Israel's responding to the Iraqi attacks was, I thought, important to maintaining Israel's deterrent posture—quite apart from the need to do everything possible to prevent additional casualties from Scud attacks.

The Scuds kept coming, most of them landing in unpopulated areas. Cheney kept stalling me on arranging coordination between U.S. and Israeli forces, and suggested that I send David Ivri, the director general of the Ministry of Defense, and Major General Ehud Barak, the deputy chief of staff, to Washington to discuss the matter. Off they went the next day. When they returned they reported to me on discussions with Cheney and General Colin Powell, the chairman of the U.S. Joint Chiefs of Staff, but brought back no agreement. They were told again that the United States objected to Israeli intervention in the war.

At the January 30 cabinet meeting I described the dilemma confronting us: "The question we face is whether to take action that is coordinated with the Americans, or whether to act even without such coordination. . . . We have presented an operational plan aimed at eliminating, as far as possible, the Iraqi missile threat. We can begin the operation tomorrow. . . . The plan exists, the capability exists, but the capability will be significantly greater if the plan is carried out in coordination with the U.S. . . . Since the war started, certainly since the first attack on us on January 18, we are in contact with the Americans in an attempt to achieve the coordination that will enable us to act. I think we are doing what needs to be done to convince them . . . and also to increase, day by day, night by night, their incentive to act as massively and as effectively as possible in the area. Since the initial attack on us, when we began discussing this question, there have been a number of changes for the better in the military sphere. First, the level of our intelligence on the area in question has improved tremendously. . . . Another change for the better over these past few days is the heavy destruction resulting from the American air attacks in the area. Eight days ago H-2 and H-3 were active air bases with their complex of anti-aircraft and SAM batteries intact. Had we entered the area then, we would have had to deal with them. . . . The task we face today is considerably easier than the one we would have faced a week ago."

Just then we received an unexpected blow. The recently acquired Apache attack helicopters were an essential part of the force preparing for our action in western Iraq. One evening we lost half of our Apache air crews. When they were returning from training exercises in the south, the light plane flying them back to Tel Aviv crashed and all aboard perished. We were left with half of the crews that were scheduled to participate in the planned action. I was assured by the army that we could carry out the action despite this tragic loss.

On February 1 the plan for the IDF's intervention in western Iraq was presented to me. It involved the air force and the landing of special forces in the area with the aim of searching for the Scud launchers and making it difficult for the Iraqis to get launches off while Israeli troops were roaming in the area. The units involved had already gone through many exercises in preparation for the mission. We all knew that it was going to be a dangerous mission—soldiers might be injured, killed, or taken prisoner—but all were optimistic about our ability to carry it out successfully. The action was to be led by Brigadier General Nehemia Tamari, a veteran paratrooper who had participated in the Entebbe airport rescue. Before approving the plan I turned to him and asked him how he felt about the mission. He did not hesitate. He said he was confident. I approved the plan.

Now I had to convince Shamir. It had become clear that Washington was counting on Shamir to keep Israel out of the conflict. By now, the danger that Israeli action could fracture the coalition the Americans had put together had receded. The Iraqis had been subjected to twenty-four-hour-a-day bombardment for two weeks since the American action had begun; American and allied ground forces were preparing to move against Iraqi forces in Kuwait, and success seemed assured. Still, Shamir hesitated.

I drove up to Jerusalem to convince him, and asked him to call Bush and tell him that he was sending me to Washington to present the case for an Israeli action aimed at putting an end to the Scud attacks on Israel. Not today, he said, maybe tomorrow. But it was not to be tomorrow, either. A week went by and he did not place the call.

On Saturday evening, February 9, a Scud hit a residential neighborhood in Ramat Gan. It was the thirty-first Scud to be launched against Israel so far, and the fourth to land in a populated area. It landed smack on the home of Moshe Meron, the Ramat Gan deputy mayor. When I rushed to the scene I saw Meron and his wife in their pajamas in front of the rubble that was all that remained of their home. Fortunately they had gone to the shelter when the alarm sounded.

Maybe that's what got Shamir to move. The next morning he called Bush and told him that I would be coming to Washington the next day bringing a message to the president from him. Bush said that he would be delighted to meet me. So off to Washington I went that evening, taking with me Ivri, Barak, and my aide, Salai Meridor.

By the time we arrived in Washington, Bush had already taken the decision to begin ground operations against the Iraqis. The United States had also learned that there was no need to be overly concerned regarding continued Saudi adherence to the coalition in case of an Israeli involvement, but that information was not passed on to us. On November 2 James Baker had met with Saudi Arabia's King Fahd to get his consent for additional deployment of American troops on Saudi soil. After receiving the king's assent, Baker posed the following question: "Suppose Israel became involved as the result of an Iraqi attack?" Fahd said it would be better for everyone if Israel stayed out, but then, to Baker's surprise, he added that he could not expect Israel to stand idly by if attacked; if Israel were to defend itself, the Saudi armed forces would still fight by America's side (this conversation was revealed by General Norman Schwartzkopf, who was present at the meeting, in his autobiography, published in 1992). Despite Fahd's reassurance, Washington continued to stubbornly insist that we stay out. Their primary concern, in my opinion, was that if Israel took action that would make it look like an ally in the American operation against Iraq, an Arab country, it might tarnish America's image in the Arab world. That did not fit in with their plans for resolving the Israeli-Palestinian conflict after completing the liberation of Kuwait.

On Monday, February 11, at 11:30 a.m. I was ushered into the Oval Office for what was to be a dramatic meeting with President Bush. He was joined by Vice President Dan Quayle; Jim Baker; Dick Cheney; Chief of Staff John Sununu; Brent Scowcroft, the assistant to the president for national security affairs; Robert Gates, assistant to the president and deputy for national security affairs; and Richard Haas, special assistant to the president and senior director for Near East and South Asian affairs. Facing this battery I was joined by the Israeli ambassador, Zalman Shoval, and by Ivri and Barak.

After I had introduced our team, making a point of mentioning that Ivri had planned the bombing of the Iraqi nuclear reactor in 1981 and that Barak was going to be our next chief of staff, Bush motioned me to the chair on his right next to him at the fireplace. We sat down, the Israelis facing the Americans. They knew why I had come and were prepared for what I had to say.

Bush opened: "I had a nice conversation with the prime minister. I also understand you'll be meeting with Dick Cheney later."

"Thank you for setting aside the time," I responded. "I bring greetings from the prime minister. He sends his admiration, as do all the people of Israel. We're not part of the coalition, and we understand that, but there is a feeling in Israel that we are at war. Thirty-one Scuds have been fired against Israel so far. They have caused thirteen fatalities, 237 injured, and 6,500 domiciles damaged or destroyed. The Scuds have a large blast effect, resulting in scenes not seen in the West since World War II. People in Israel feel that the threat is not gone."

Bush asked, "Do you feel that the threat is diminished?"

I said, "The Patriots have shown themselves to be of doubtful effectiveness against the Scuds. The last Scud hit has set people on edge, in part because it followed six days without attacks."

Scowcroft had been sitting quietly. In my occasional meetings with him I had gained the impression that his insensitivity to the problems Israel faced bordered on a dislike of Israel. Now he decided to come to the aid of the president, countering my description of the poor performance of the Patriot batteries by describing the success of the Patriot batteries in intercepting Scud missiles in Saudi Arabia. He implied that there was something wrong with my description of the Patriot's performance, or else we in Israel did not know how to operate them properly, even though they were being handled by American crews.

Replying to Scowcroft, I said that by our estimates the probability of a Patriot intercepting a Scud was no more than 20 percent. As it turned out, on the basis of postwar analyses it was concluded that in Israel there had not been a single Patriot intercept—but considerable secondary damage was inflicted by remnants of Patriot missiles falling to the ground after an attempted intercept. It was clear that the version of the Patriot originally designed to intercept aircraft was simply not capable of intercepting ballistic missiles. It was curious that the president had been led to believe that it was an effective weapon for this job. This was not the only case of American intelligence failures in connection with ballistic missiles and their launchers.

The tension rose visibly. The president now called on Cheney to refute my statement on the Patriots. Cheney came bearing charts that seemed to show a very high probability of Scud intercepts by Patriot missiles. You can see, he said, that your description of Patriot performance "is fundamentally at odds with our experience."

I saw little point in pursuing this argument. Their minds were evidently made up. Two weeks later a tragic confirmation of my point was provided by a Scud that hit a U.S. Army barracks at Dharhan in Saudi Arabia, killing twenty-eight U.S. soldiers and injuring many more.

Turning to the reason for my meeting with the president, I opened by reminding the president that we had been assured by Larry Eagleburger that U.S. air attacks would eliminate the threat of Scuds falling on Israel. That mission evidently turned out to be more difficult than had been anticipated. We in Israel now had to take an active part in eliminating that threat before we suffered severe casualties, or possibly were hit by a chemical warhead. Therefore it was important to improve the level of coordination between the IDF and U.S. forces operating in the area.

Bush seemed to be taken aback by my request. "What kind of things are you talking about?" he asked.

I did not want to spell out our operational plans, and just added that I believed that we could make a contribution to eliminating the Scud threat.

"What can you do better than what we're doing?" Bush asked, seemingly offended by what must have sounded to him like typical Israeli effrontery.

I was convinced that the IDF operating on the ground in western Iraq would be more effective in locating and destroying the Scud launchers and preventing further launching of Scuds, but saw little point in getting into an argument. "I don't want to be presumptuous," I replied. "We might do it differently—we could add another dimension," I said, hinting at our plans to conduct a ground operation in western Iraq. "We feel that this could be an important addition to your efforts to find and destroy the Scud launchers."

"But you would also contribute to Saddam's war aims," the president interjected. He was getting exasperated. "Tell us how to do it and we'll do it. I need to know why you believe you can do something we can't." Then he summed up the meeting: "I'm glad you'll be seeing Secretary Cheney and General Powell. I'm not brushing off your concerns, please convey this. But I have to keep in mind the big picture. This brings me to the fragility of this diverse coalition. I have the responsibility to see that we win, and when we do we will do an enormous favor for Israel and the region." As we left the Oval Office Baker approached me and asked to see me after my meeting with Cheney.

Our next stop was at the Pentagon to meet Cheney and Powell. There we were given an extensive briefing on the aerial campaign being conducted against Iraq. It was impressive, even though the allied aircraft were meeting almost no opposition from the Iraqis, and I assumed that the estimates of damage inflicted might be somewhat exaggerated. After the briefing I returned to the subject of coordination. "Let's establish a level of coordination so that we will have a real-time picture of the situation, so that we can contribute our suggestions on how to operate against the Scud threat, and so that we shall be able to go into action, when we so decide in coordination with you," I told Cheney.

Cheney's reply was, "If you intervene, we will break off contact and get out of the area—then we won't need coordination."

"That's not how I see it," I insisted. "If we get involved both of us will be operating against a common enemy, even though it may be in different theaters of operation. I don't think it will be good to carry out such an operation in an uncoordinated fashion. Many problems will surely arise that will require coordination." Cheney decided to kick the matter to a higher level: "I'm sure you understand that if you decide to intervene, the prime minister will have to speak to the president, and they will decide, yes or no, and under what circumstances."

From the two meetings I concluded that they did not want us to get involved, that they were counting on Shamir applying the brakes on my plans, but realized that they might have to reconcile themselves to an Israeli operation. "We will get out of the area if you intervene," Cheney had said.

In other words, they wanted to be able to tell their Arab friends that they had nothing to do with it.

Now, on to Baker. It was already past seven when I entered his office. "You were in the president's office this morning and you heard what I had to say—we may now have to act," I began the conversation.

Baker responded that "our boys are doing the job for you." Before I had a chance to express my anger at this remark, somebody brought me a message that a Scud had landed in Savyon, not far from my home. I excused myself and left the room to call my wife, who was at home in Savyon. I was relieved to learn that she was safe and sound, although our house had sustained some cracks in the walls. At that point there seemed little more to talk about with Baker, and I was in a hurry to return home.

When I got back to Israel I was determined to carry out our planned operation in western Iraq. By now I felt sure that King Hussein had lost whatever enthusiasm he may have had for Saddam Hussein and was not likely to respond to our overflying Jordanian territory on our way to Iraq. To confirm my assumption that such overflights were not likely to set off a conflagration with Jordan, I asked the army to present me with some flight profiles that would enter Jordanian airspace that would test the Jordanian reaction. They took their time about it. When they finally came up with a flight profile that was satisfactory, Shamir refused to approve it. When he approved it the weather was not favorable. The troops who were prepared to launch the western Iraq operation were straining at the bit. Eight more Scuds came down on Israel, but caused no damage. On February 28, a mere four days after the Allied ground operation had begun, forty-two days after the Allies began the aerial bombardment of Iraqi forces, Bush announced a unilateral cease-fire. "Quit while you are ahead" was his strategy. The window of opportunity for an Israeli operation in Iraq closed. The war was over.

The reasons for Bush wanting Israel to stay out of the war were obvious. He did not need Israel's assistance to win the war. He did not want Israeli participation that might anger his Arab allies, and he did not want to appear as if he was an ally of Israel. The Scuds that fell on Israel seemed to be of no great concern to him. So keep out, was his policy throughout the five weeks of the war. Shamir was ready to go along with this policy. He did not want to anger the Americans and hoped to find them on his side after the war. Was he right?

I was sure of one thing. We were not going to receive any compensation from Washington for staying out. As became clear after the first two weeks of the war, the coalition that Bush had put together was not going to break up if we were to undertake an action in western Iraq. Bush must have known this all along—to us it became clear as an Iraqi defeat became inevitable after the Allied aerial campaign really got under way. So what was there to lose?

The operation involved risks. Even though the Entebbe raid to free the hostages taken by terrorists in 1976 was carried out at a much greater distance from our home bases than our planned landing in western Iraq, the Ugandan soldiers at Entebbe probably constituted less of a challenge to the IDF than the Iraqis we would encounter. At the time there were conflicting opinions on whether Israel should carry out the Entebbe rescue operations so far from Israel. The chances of success had to be weighed against the risk of failure. Today there is no doubt that approving the IDF's plans at that time was the right decision. In planning the operation in western Iraq, I too had to take account of the chances of success and the risks of failure, but in addition also the pressure from Washington to keep out.

In this matter Shamir and I differed. Shamir believed that going along with the American demand that Israel stay out would stand him in good stead in Israel's relationship with the United States in the future. I thought the Bush administration was steering a steady course on the Israeli-Palestinian conflict but it ran contrary to Shamir's and my views, and it was not going to change. My concern was for the risks involved in the operation we were planning. We would probably take casualties, and we might not succeed in destroying the Scud missile launchers. But in any case Israel would still have gained: We would have shown the world, and especially our enemies, that Israel could not be attacked with impunity. The record would be clear that when Israel is hit, we hit back hard. Consequently I had no doubts about carrying out the planned operation, despite the risks involved.

Had we carried out the operation it would have taken place during the last days of the Gulf War. It most certainly would not have led to the breakup of the coalition, and the cease-fire declared by Bush would have found Israeli forces on the ground in western Iraq. For Israel that would have been a better ending of this war.

Aware of the danger to Israel's civilian population from rocket attacks, and having had to take into account that the IDF might at the same time be engaged in fighting on the ground, I concluded that a separate IDF command should be set up for dealing with safeguarding the civilian population. I instructed the IDF chief of staff to establish such a command, which would be added to the Northern, Central, and Southern Commands. The IDF brass was less than enthusiastic about it, in fear that it would encroach on their authority, but my orders were carried out. It was the second reform in the IDF structure carried out by me. The first was the establishment of the Ground Forces Command during my first tenure as defense minister.

As for compensation from Washington for our "good behavior" under extreme provocation, there was none. Six months after the Gulf War, Shamir turned to Washington with a request for $10 billion in loan guarantees that would help Israel absorb the wave of immigrants from the Soviet Union who were arriving in Israel. Bush insisted that settlement activity in Judea, Samaria, and Gaza cease as a condition for the United States to grant such guarantees. Shamir was not prepared to acquiesce to such a condition, and rightly so. There was wide-ranging support for U.S. assistance for the absorption of the immigrants from the Soviet Union that were reaching Israel. To counter this support Bush, at a press conference on September 6, linked approval of the loan guarantees to changes in Israel's settlement policy, saying that it was "very, very important . . . to do everything we can to give peace a chance" and asking "every single member of Congress" to defer "just for 120 days" consideration of the $10 billion loan guarantee for immigrant absorption in Israel. Baker chimed in: "Give peace a chance; 120 days, that's all we're asking for, 120 days."

Israel's friends in Congress, urged on by the American Israel Public Affairs Committee (the pro-Israeli lobby), were preparing to pass a resolution in Congress as an amendment to a continuing resolution. But Bush would not back down. "If necessary I will use my veto power to keep this from happening," he stated at a press conference, and went on, "We are up against some powerful political forces, very strong and effective groups that go up to the Hill." Referring to himself he continued, "We've only got one lonely little guy doing it . . . [but] I am going to fight for what I believe." And then came the bombshell: "Just months ago, American men and women in uniform risked their lives to defend Israelis in the face of

Iraqi Scud missiles . . . and while winning a war against aggression, also achieved the defeat of Israel's most dangerous adversary."

Bush refused Shamir's request for the loan guarantees. The credit in Washington that Shamir thought he had accumulated by accepting Bush's demand that Israel not respond to the Iraqi attacks had evaporated. In the June 1992 elections in Israel the Likud lost and Shamir was replaced by Yitzhak Rabin, while in the U.S. elections in November of that year Bush lost to the Democratic candidate, Bill Clinton. The loan guarantee imbroglio may have affected both outcomes. Rabin, on becoming prime minister, accepted Washington's conditions and the guarantees were provided. In retrospect they were not really needed. The absorption in Israel of about a million Jews from the Soviet Union went very smoothly. On the whole they constituted an economic asset rather than a burden.

During the Gulf War the Intifada had been relatively subdued, but now that the war was over it intensified. Youths threw rocks at cars on the roads, cars were ambushed in Judea and Samaria, and there were occasional incidents in the Gaza Strip. The deterioration of the security situation in Judea and Samaria had now become a matter of primary concern for me. On January 14 a bus traveling from Jerusalem to Shiloh, a settlement in Samaria, was ambushed near the Arab village of Ein Sinya. Seven people, including the driver, were injured. That evening a crowd of demonstrators assembled outside my home and called for my resignation. Sharon was quick to add his voice to that of the demonstrators. Accusing the government of responsibility for the wave of terror, he called for my resignation on TV: "Anyone who is not successful, who can't do this job, should leave and give the job to those who know how to do it. Let him go home," he concluded, meaning me. He probably expected a popular demand for his return to the Defense Ministry, but it did not materialize.

After an ambush on the night of January 15 against the ambulance of Itamar, the Samaria settlement near Nablus, I called in to my office Ehud Barak (whom I had recently appointed chief of staff to replace Dan Shomron) and the senior generals, and read to them the list of recent terrorist incidents. Putting an end to these terrorist attacks was now the IDF's first priority, I told them. The numbers of troops to be stationed in Judea and Samaria had to be increased substantially, and elite units and special forces had to be deployed there. Barak began to argue with me, Raising my voice, I said that if we were not successful in subduing this wave of terror, Barak himself and his whole headquarters staff would have to move into the area and participate in the task I had assigned to the IDF. That ended the argument.

Over the next five months we put an end to the Intifada, which had been raging for the past two and a half years. I spent a lot of my time inspecting the areas where terrorist incidents had taken place, interrogating the troops on the spot and their commanders, and deciding on the steps that had to be taken to prevent such incidents from occurring again. The key figures in suppressing the Intifada were Brigadier General Moshe (Bogie) Ya'alon, the commander of the troops in Judea and Samaria, and Gideon Ezra, who was in charge of the security services in Judea and Samaria. They, and the men and women under their command, deserve the credit for putting an end to the violence.

In late 1991 and early 1992, three of Likud's smaller coalition partners, who were to the right of the Likud politically, left the coalition one by one— leaving the government without majority support in the Knesset. This made it necessary to hold early elections. On February 4 an early-election law was passed by the Knesset, which set the date for these elections as June 23, 1992. It had the support of the Likud, the Likud's coalition partners, and the Labor Party. Those who had left the coalition and precipitated these elections had done so in the expectation that they would score substantial gains in the coming elections, but they were to be disappointed. The process they initiated ended up bringing the Labor Party to power.

Unlike the presidential system of government, in which the elected president has a fixed term of office, in the parliamentary system the government must have a majority in parliament in order to stay in office. If a party cannot get a majority, it must form a coalition with other parties. In Israel, where the Knesset is composed of a relatively large number of parties, some of them quite small, shifting party allegiances are a common occurrence, leading to a breakup of coalitions and the need for early elections. Dissatisfaction with this situation had led to the rise of a movement to change the system of government: the prime minister would be elected in direct elections, but otherwise the parliamentary system would be retained. Proponents of this change, spanning the spectrum of parties in the Knesset, claimed that it would bring political stability. The leading proponents were David Libai of the Labor Party, Uriel Lynn of the Likud, Amnon Rubinstein of the left-wing Meretz Party, and Yoash Tsiddon, a member of the party led by Rafael Eitan, a former general. Rubenstein was a highly regarded professor of constitutional law, Libai was one of Israel's leading lawyers, and Lynn, also a lawyer, headed the Knesset's Committee on Constitution, Law, and Justice. They were backed by a massive public campaign urging Knesset members to support the legislation that would bring about this change.

It was clear to me that the proposed hybrid presidential-parliamentary system would only further destabilize the Israeli political system. Although a large number of political parties were represented in the Knesset, its backbone was the two large parties, Likud and Labor. They provided the system with much-needed stability. If voters cast two ballots, as envisaged in the proposed change, it was likely that having cast their first ballot for one of the candidates for prime minister, voters might then cast their second ballot for one of the small parties. The result would be a decrease in the representation of the large parties and an increase in the representation of the small parties, further destabilizing the political system. I led the debate on the subject in the Likud Central Committee and called for the Likud to oppose the proposed change. A preponderant majority voted against the proposed change.

I also spent hours discussing the matter with Benjamin Netanyahu, and finally he promised me that if the outcome depended on him he would vote with the rest of the Likud members of the Knesset. When June 23 arrived, the vote in the Knesset was a cliffhanger. The operative section of the legislation was passed by a single vote—Netanyahu's. The outcome did depend on Netanyahu, and he voted for the change. I can only assume that his confidence in his ability to appeal to Israeli voters on the basis of his personality led him to believe that direct election of the prime minister increased his chances of attaining that position. Indeed, under that law Netanyahu in 1996 beat Shimon Peres in a very tight contest, and in turn was easily beaten by Ehud Barak in 1999.

Later, after I left politics following the 1992 elections, I headed an organization, the Committee for Parliamentary Democracy, that made the case for parliamentary democracy and called for repeal of the law for direct election of the prime minister. The law turned out to be a failure. It was a blow to the two large parties and increased the leverage of the small parties, thus destabilizing the political system. It was repealed in 2001 and Israel returned to the parliamentary system of governance. Ariel Sharon was the last to be elected in direct elections; he beat Barak in 2001.

In preparation for the June 1992 elections, the Likud was going to hold internal elections in February to choose its candidate for prime minister and its list of its Knesset candidates. Levy and Sharon, the two perennial challengers of Shamir's leadership, presented themselves. Shamir, although to my mind was preferable to both, was hardly the ideal candidate. He was seventy-three and would be running against a younger Rabin, who was seventy. His appeal to the public was limited. I thought that I would have been a better candidate, but Shamir was not prepared to pass the leadership on to me. Presenting myself as a candidate would have made it a four-way race, with no way to predict the outcome. I decided to back Shamir, and ran the Shamir-Arens camp to get him elected and to promote our candidates for the Knesset.

The Likud leadership elections were held on February 20. Shamir won handily, receiving 46 percent of the votes of the members of the Likud Central Committee, Levy 31 percent, and Sharon 22 percent. In the elections for Knesset candidates the Levy camp was almost wiped out. It was a complete victory for the Shamir-Arens camp. I was elected to head the list after Shamir, Sharon was second, and Levy third. Levy was a sore loser, hinting that he and his followers might leave the Likud.

After brooding on his defeat for a month, Levy called a meeting of his followers at the Daniel Hotel in Herzliya for March 29, and in a rambling speech he claimed that he had suffered discrimination in the Likud because of his Moroccan origin. Being appointed foreign minister and deputy prime minister was evidently insufficient recognition of his talents. After an oration lasting more than an hour he announced to his followers that he was resigning from the government.

He was counting on Shamir's panicking in the face of this threat, and he was right. Without consulting with me, Shamir concluded a deal with him that in return for Levy's withdrawing his threat of resigning from the government, Shamir promised Levy that he would be deputy prime minister and foreign minister and that he would have the right to appoint another minister in the next government, that four of his representatives would be appointed to the Likud Secretariat (which I headed), and that his followers would receive representation on the Jewish Agency Executive. It was a complete surrender.

In a meeting with Shamir, I told him that he did not have the authority to make such an agreement. He lost his temper, actually banged his fist on the table, and, glaring at me, insisted that that is what he had decided to do and that was all there was to it. At this point I decided that I had had enough of this kind of politics, and told him that I would be leaving politics immediately after the elections. "I too will leave politics after the elections," he replied enigmatically. And on that note we parted. For me it was no empty threat, and two days after the election results were made public I announced that I was resigning my seat in the Knesset and leaving politics. Shamir stayed on as a member of the Knesset.

As the election campaign swung into high gear, the immigration of Soviet Jews and the loan guarantees that Israel had requested from the United States to help in their absorption became a focal point of the campaign. Shamir had played a key role in directing the flow of Jews leaving the Soviet Union toward Israel. On a number of occasions he had explained to Reagan, Shultz, Bush, and Baker that they were not refugees, that they had a home in Israel, and had urged the Americans not to grant them refugee status in the United States. Now they were arriving in Israel at a rate of a quarter million a year, posing a great challenge to the government to provide them with housing and employment. If all their needs were not met immediately the immigrants directed their complaints against the government, and this was exploited by the Labor Party in the election campaign.

The Bush administration followed the campaign in Israel closely. Shamir was obviously not the favorite candidate of Bush and his advisers. While Shamir argued that the loan guarantees were essential for the absorption of the Soviet Jews arriving in Israel, Bush and Baker let it be known that they would support granting these guarantees only if Israel ceased all settlement activities in the "occupied territories" and East Jerusalem. They knew that this condition was unacceptable to Shamir, and of course he refused to accept it. The message to the Israeli electorate was clear—you have to chose between Shamir and the loan guarantees.

I pleaded with Shamir not to request the loan guarantees. I was convinced that this administration was not going to agree to provide them to a Shamir-led government. And I was not at all sure that they would really be required. Bush's denial of these guarantees to Shamir was ammunition for the Labor Party in its election campaign. Shamir stubbornly insisted that Israel's friends in the United States would force the administration to come through with the loan guarantees.

He was wrong. On February 25 Baker appeared before the House Appropriations Subcommittee on Foreign Operations and stated, "This administration is ready to support loan guarantees of up to $2 billion a year for five years, provided that there is a halt or end to settlement activity. From our standpoint it's up to Israel." And Bush added, "It is a proper policy and has been the policy of the United States government for a long, long time."

We went to the elections without having received the loan guarantees. The election was a disaster for the Likud. Rabin was elected prime minister. The failure to get the loan guarantees no doubt contributed to the Likud's loss. Labor increased its representation in the Knesset from thirty-nine seats to forty-four, while the Likud dropped from forty to thirty-two. We lost support everywhere except in Arab villages and among the bedouins in the Negev.

Two days after the election I announced my retirement from politics. I had reached that decision weeks earlier, after Shamir had made the deal with Levy behind my back, and had waited for the elections to be over before announcing it. Now the time had come.

I was swamped by calls urging me to reconsider. A group of bedouins camped out on my lawn and insisted that they would not move until I changed my mind. But my mind was made up. Enough was enough.

I had been in politics for eighteen years, interrupted by the year I spent in Washington as Israel's ambassador. I had never had political ambitions and had entered politics almost by chance. I had been defense minister twice, as well as foreign minister, and had served my country to the best of my ability. I had come close to becoming prime minister, but I had no regrets. It was time.

Four years later, in 1996, Netanyahu, having been chosen to lead the Likud, defeated Peres and became Israel's prime minister. By then I had become involved in the business sector, but naturally I continued to follow politics closely. I backed Netanyahu in the Likud contest and in the national elections. I thought he was the best candidate among Likud aspirants and was worthy of being Israel's prime minister.

The Oslo I Accord had been signed in 1993, while Rabin was prime minister. This was a departure from past Israeli positions, held by both Labor and Likud, that Israel would negotiate with representatives of the Palestinians living in the areas beyond the 1949 armistice lines, but not with the PLO. Thus Arafat and his cohorts, a terrorist gang noted for its corruption, were imposed on the local Palestinian population while the local leadership was sidelined, and the resolution of the Israeli-Palestinian conflict was held hostage to implementation of the "right of return," the unalterable demand of the PLO, which was the equivalent of the destruction of the State of Israel.

The Oslo I Accord was born of a yearning for peace in Israel after so many wars, an impatience that led to a faith that peace could be achieved if we only tried hard enough, Its supporters insisted that "Peace is made with enemies." Their romantic slogans, "Two States for Two People," "Land for Peace," and "Peace Now," were adopted by many in Israel and around the world. It brought the arch-terrorist Yasser Arafat into the Oval Office dressed in a military uniform of his own design and turned President Bill Clinton into an arbiter between democratic Israel, America's ally, and Yasser Arafat, who had no intention of making peace with Israel. As it turned out, Clinton's involvement as arbitrator between Netanyahu and Arafat, despite Clinton's best intentions, did not lay the foundations for direct negotiations. It gave Arafat reason to expect that the United States could force Israel to accept his demands. It was further proof, if any was needed, that the only path to an agreement was direct negotiations between Israel and the Palestinians.

The process gave birth to the myth that Israeli settlements beyond the 1949 armistice lines, the lines where the Jordanian Legion's attack on the nascent Jewish state was halted, were illegal according to international law and constituted an obstacle to making peace. Ignored, forgotten, and thrown into the dustbin of history was the League of Nations Mandate for Palestine, the international recognition of the "historical connection of the Jewish people to Palestine and the grounds for reconstituting their national home in that country," and the requirement that "close settlement by Jews on the land, including State lands and waste lands not required for public purposes" be "encouraged." This international recognition and the attendant provisions regarding Jewish settlement in all Palestine west of the Jordan River have never been revoked, and in accordance with article 80, chapter XII of the UN Charter have not been altered and are valid to this day. Jewish settlements in what is today referred to as the West Bank were established before the establishment of the State of Israel in accordance with these provisions of the League of Nations Mandate for Palestine, and were destroyed by the invading Jordanian army in 1948. There was nothing illegal in their establishment at the time, nor in their reestablishment after the Jordanian army, which had joined Egypt and Syria in their attack against Israel in 1967, was defeated. Nor is there anything illegal in the establishment of new Jewish settlements in the areas from which the Jordanian army was forced to withdraw.

Israeli leaders, in their eagerness to reach an agreement with the PLO, did not bother to insist on these internationally recognized Jewish rights in all of Palestine; and others, like the United States, no less eager for peace to reign in the area, were not about to remind Israel and the PLO of Jewish rights in Palestine.

On his election as prime minister Netanyahu found himself saddled with the Oslo I Accord, an international agreement, and with the obligation assumed by the previous government to comply with the provisions of this Accord, which called for substantial Israeli withdrawals and transfer of these areas to the PLO. Under pressure from President Bill Clinton and faced by opposition in his own government, he tried to square the circle. He managed to estrange some members of his own party, and went along with Clinton's arbitrating between him and Arafat, but did not bring an agreement any closer.

I was disturbed by the fact that senior members of the Likud were abandoning the party, and I thought that going along with Clinton's attempts at arbitration was a mistake. What's more, I did not believe that Netanyahu would be able to defeat Ehud Barak, Labor's candidate, in the coming election, and decided to challenge him in the internal elections in the Likud. But he had complete control of the party machinery and beat me easily.

A few days before the Likud elections he surprised me and asked me to return to the Defense Ministry to take the place of Yitzhak Mordechai, who had resigned from the government and now headed a rival list in the coming elections. That was a challenge I felt I could not refuse, but I did not want to commit myself until the votes had been counted in the Likud elections. I agreed, and on January 27, 1999, I was sworn in as defense minister for the third time.

It was to be a short tenure. Barak defeated Netanyahu convincingly in the elections held on May 17 and assumed the office as prime minister and defense minister on July 6. So I had a little over five months—the last few weeks in the knowledge that I would be replaced by Barak—to attempt to accomplish the objectives I had set for myself.

The principal problem I had to deal with was the IDF's involvement in the southern Lebanon security zone. Much of the burden of defending Israel's northern border fell on the shoulders of the South Lebanon Army (SLA) under the command of the Lebanese general Antoine Lahad, originally chosen by me during my first tenure as defense minister. Despite his able leadership and close cooperation with the IDF in the security zone, the IDF was losing an average of two soldiers a month in combat with Hezbollah there. Barak, during the election campaign, had promised that if elected he would pull the IDF out of Lebanon. His promise was in tune with the mood among many in the country who felt that we should get out of Lebanon and wanted to believe there must be a better way of protecting our northern border. It was an impatience born of many years of conflict and of being stuck in the quagmire of Lebanon. It was a natural yearning for a quick solution, characteristic of the mood of an embattled people.

I went up north to visit our commanders leading the battle against Hezbollah: Major General Gabi Ashkenazi, commander of the northern front, and Brigadier Generals Efi Eitam and Erez Gershtein, responsible for leading our soldiers on the northern border in coordination with the SLA, in the southern Lebanon security zone and for coordination with the SLA. They were among the best senior infantry officers in the IDF, with long combat experience under their belts. They were very optimistic, describing the tactics that they were using against Hezbollah and expressing confidence in being able to defeat it.

I was to disappoint them. "Look," I said, "I don't believe that we will be able to defeat Hezbollah in guerrilla warfare, fighting them on their home ground, especially since we are limited by the agreement, brokered by the United States between Israel and Hezbollah after the unsuccessful Israeli operation in southern Lebanon in 1996, while Peres was acting prime minister and defense minister. As you know it puts severe limitations on the IDF's freedom of operation in southern Lebanon."

"Moreover," I continued, "the Israeli public is losing patience with our losses, and unless there is a dramatic change we may yet be forced to withdraw by an impatient public at home."

Less than a month later, on February 23, Major Eitan Balahsan, the son of North African immigrants who was commander of the parachutists' reconnaissance unit, fell with some of his men when he ran into a Hezbollah ambush. And a few days later Gershtein, a member of Kibbutz Reshafim, who had been so confident that he would defeat Hezbollah, was killed by a roadside bomb laid by Hezbollah. I did not need any more convincing—there had to be a dramatic change in strategy and tactics.

The Syrians were running Lebanon and using Hezbollah as a proxy to harass Israel. In effect they controlled Hezbollah. If the Syrians could be hit, they might conclude that they had better rein in Hezbollah. Instead of trying to defeat Hezbollah on their home ground, could we get the Syrians to stop them? Could we accomplish this without starting an all-out war with Syria? That was the question. I reckoned that retaliating for Hezbollah Katyusha attacks against Israeli civilians in the north by striking at sensitive targets in Lebanon might produce the desired reaction in Damascus. The Lebanese public, reminded that Hezbollah was dragging all of Lebanon into a conflict with Israel, would call on the rulers in Damascus to stop Hezbollah from continuing its attacks against Israel, and the Syrians might consider that their rule in Lebanon was being endangered by Hezbollah's actions and get Hezbollah to cease sending rocket fire into Israel. Now I had to wait for the opportunity to test the validity of my assumptions.

The opportunity came, but at the last minute. On June 24 Kiryat Shmonah was hit by a heavy barrage of rockets. We were set to launch air force attacks against the Beirut electric power station and a number of other strategic targets in Lebanon. Barak had already been elected but had not yet formed his government and taken over as prime minister, and I thought it proper to advise him of my plans before authorizing the attacks. I went to see him and presented our plans to him. He did not like the idea, and I decided to hold off. A week later Hezbollah struck Kiryat Shmonah again. Two residents of the town were killed.

Now I decided to proceed. That night the Ministerial Defense Committee, still headed by Netanyahu, approved my plans for knocking out two power stations serving Beirut and the Beirut telephone exchange and some bridges on roads leading to southern Lebanon. After the attacks were carried out, the chief of staff, Shaul Mofaz, announced that we were prepared to increase the scale of the attacks should there be any further Katyusha attacks on Israel. But the Katyusha attacks ceased. Our strategy seemed to be working.

Four days later I turned the Defense Ministry over to Barak. He had other ideas on how to deal with southern Lebanon. Intent on a withdrawal of the IDF from the south Lebanon security zone, he was prepared to betray our allies, the SLA, and ordered the IDF to peremptorily withdraw, leaving the SLA behind. He was wrong. His betrayal of the SLA and the unilateral withdrawal of the IDF from the southern Lebanon security zone was interpreted in the Arab world as a sign of weakness and brought on the Second Intifada, which claimed more than a thousand Israeli casualties. It did not bring an end to Hezbollah's activity against Israel and was followed by the Second Lebanon War seven years later, with severe loss of life to Israeli soldiers and civilians.

The elections that brought Barak to power had also returned me to the Knesset, now as a member of the opposition. Actually, I had had little interest in returning to politics, and when the next election for the Knesset in 2003 approached I decided not to present myself as a candidate in the Likud primaries. My exit from politics was now really final.

TWELVE

Researching the Warsaw Ghetto Uprising

Leaving politics gave me time to look into something that had been on my mind for many years: the Warsaw ghetto uprising. The uprising had become the symbol of Jewish resistance to the Germans during the Holocaust. I had read fictionalized versions of the event—Leon Uris's *Mila 18* and John Hersey's *The Wall*. Is that the way it really happened? How had it been possible, in the Warsaw ghetto, to organize resistance against vastly superior forces?

In the generally accepted narrative, twenty-three-year-old Mordechai Anielewicz led a few hundred young people—members of youth groups that espoused Zionist and non-Zionist socialist ideology—in an uprising against German troops aided by Ukrainian units who had come to raze the Warsaw ghetto on the orders of Heinrich Himmler. Before the war, Betar, the youth movement inspired by Ze'ev Jabotinsky, the founder of Revisionist Zionism, had been the largest Zionist youth movement in Poland. Was it possible that members of Betar had *not* played a significant role in the uprising? My past association with Betar spurred my interest.

Not being a trained historian, before I began my search for the answers to some of the questions that puzzled me I decided to consult a recognized historian who had devoted his life to researching the Holocaust—Professor

Yehuda Bauer at Yad Vashem, the World Holocaust Remembrance Center, in Jerusalem. He was not encouraging. "You will learn nothing new. After all these years everything about the Warsaw ghetto uprising is known, including the degree of participation of members of the Betar youth movement," he told me. "You might want to talk to Professor Yisrael Gutman. He was there. He fought in the uprising," he added.

As it turned out, Gutman had been a member of the group led by Anielewicz in the Warsaw ghetto. He had belonged to the Socialist-Zionist youth organization, Hashomer Hatzair, and had joined a kibbutz on arriving in Palestine in 1946. After studying at the Hebrew University he became a professor of modern Jewish history there, specializing in the history of the Warsaw ghetto. His book *The Jews of Warsaw 1939–1943* is considered the authoritative work on that period. A number of students of the Holocaust studied under his direction and became his disciples. Now eighty years old, he had retired to a position as academic adviser at Yad Vashem.

I went to see him in his apartment in the Malha neighborhood of Jerusalem, where he lived alone. He seemed pleased to receive me, maybe impressed that a former minister of defense was taking an interest in his work. On hearing the purpose of my visit, he was quite straightforward. "It is true that the youngsters from Betar have not received full credit for their part in the uprising," he said. "The problem is that there is no documentation that attests to their activities during this period. You are not likely to find anything new." He was friendly but firm.

I was not to be put off so easily. I dived into the voluminous archives at Yad Vashem, and every time I found another book published in Poland that contained descriptions of the activities of the Jewish Military Organization led by youngsters from Betar, I would call Gutman to give him the good news.

"They are not reliable sources; you can't depend on them," was his response.

I searched the archives at Yad Vashem and the archives of the museum located in the Ghetto Fighters Kibbutz, the kibbutz founded by members of Anielewicz's fighting organization. Two of its leaders had been among them, Yitzhak (Antek) Zuckerman and Zivya Lubetkin. I searched the archives of the Jabotinsky Institute in Tel Aviv. I flew to Warsaw to search the archives of the Jewish Historical Institute there. Whatever material I found that dealt with the part played by members of Betar in the uprising was dismissed by Gutman as a fabrication or as not sufficiently reliable.

But then I hit the jackpot: I came upon the Stroop Report, a day-by-day account of the events in the Warsaw ghetto, prepared by SS Major General Jürgen Stroop, the man who had been handpicked by Heinrich Himmler to raze the Warsaw ghetto to the ground. "The Jewish Quarter of Warsaw Is No More!" (Es gibt keinen juedischen Wohnbezirk in Warschau mehr!) was a 125-page typed document, bound in black pebble leather, that included more than fifty photographs taken during the suppression of the uprising. It had been prepared by Stroop expressly for Himmler after being commissioned by Stroop's immediate superior, Higher SS and Police Leader in Poland General Friedrich-Wilhelm Krüger. It contained Stroop's daily and sometimes twice-daily communiqués issued during the suppression of the uprising and the razing of the ghetto, and a summary report for that period. Himmler's copy of the report fell into the hands of the U.S. Army as it entered Germany.

The Stroop Report and its contents were brought to the attention of the public when it was displayed on November 19, 1945, by the chief U.S. prosecutor, Robert H. Jackson, during his opening address to the International Military Tribunal at Nuremberg. Later, on December 14, 1945, Major William F. Walsh, special assistant to Jackson, quoted from the Stroop Report in his address to the tribunal. Referring to the battle at Muranowski Square, the central battle of the uprising, Walsh read from the Stroop report: "The main Jewish combat group retreated to Muranowski Square and there they raised the Jewish and Polish flags." Quotations from his address were picked up by the press throughout the world, including the Hebrew press in Palestine. The "main Jewish combat group" referred to by Stroop were members of the Jewish Military Organization, led by Pawel Frenkel and his comrades from Betar.

Copies of the Stroop Report can be found in all the major archives devoted to the Holocaust. They have been translated into English, Hebrew, and Polish. The prominent events of the Warsaw ghetto uprising are described there, and the major role of the Betar-led Jewish Military Organization is evident. Although written by the man who suppressed the uprising and destroyed the ghetto, it is the most reliable and explicit description of the uprising, written in real time as the events occurred.

I went to work analyzing the Stroop Report line by line, and examined the statement Stroop made to the American authorities after his capture and his testimony at his trial in Warsaw for war crimes he committed there. I interviewed the remaining survivors of the Warsaw ghetto, read the books published by them, and gathered whatever scraps of relevant information I could lay my hands on. I also pieced together all that happened in the Warsaw ghetto in the years before and during the uprising.

Since the establishment of the Warsaw ghetto in October 1940 by the German occupiers, the Jews there had been living for many months under intolerable conditions: humiliated, short of food, suffering from epidemics, forced to provide slave labor, and occasionally being subjected to attacks and killings. They heard rumors of the mass executions of Jews that were carried out as the German army invaded the Soviet Union on June 22, 1941, but did not want to believe that they would meet a similar fate. But on July 22, 1942—the ninth of Av, the day of mourning for the destruction of the Temple in Jerusalem—forced mass deportations from the Warsaw ghetto to the Treblinka gas chambers began. During the following seven weeks, 270,000 men, women, and children were shipped off to Treblinka. There was no resistance. Those who had been spared so far clung to the hope that they might yet survive. Fear that the least sign of resistance would result in destruction of the entire ghetto was widespread and even led to opposition to acts of resistance, which in turn kept the few who thought of organized resistance from taking action during that period.

It was the members of youth groups—who had continued their educational and cultural activities in the ghetto—who thought of resistance and began preparing for it. Continuing the tradition of the prewar years, they were highly ideologically motivated—fervent believers in their ideals and strongly opposed to those whom they saw as their rivals. The Communist and the Socialist groups, Zionist and non-Zionist, saw themselves as members of the proletarian class continuing the revolution that had begun in the Soviet Union. Their ideological rivals, their enemies, were considered Fascists, no matter whether German or Jew. The Socialist-Zionist groups—Hashomer Hatzair, Dror, Gordonia, Poalei Zion Left—considered Jabotinsky's followers, the Betar youth movement, Fascists. It was a projection and continuation of the deep ideological divide between Left and

Right in the Jewish community, the Yishuv, in prewar Palestine. The German onslaught on the Jewish people, the ghettos, and the death camps seemed to have left these ideological animosities unchanged in the Warsaw ghetto. Preparing for an uprising, daring to challenge the Germans, these young people were not willing to cooperate with Jews whom they considered their ideological enemies. And so it came about that the Jewish Fighting Organization—headed by Mordechai Anielewicz, a member of Hashomer Hatzair—included all the Socialist-Zionist groups as well as the anti-Zionist Jewish Socialist organization called the Bund and the Communists, but not Betar. The young followers of Jabotinsky in the ghetto organized the Jewish Military Organization, led by twenty-three-year-old Pawel Frenkel and his comrades from Betar.

Thus, two organizations, the Jewish Military Organization and the Jewish Fighting Organization—also known by the initials of their Polish names, ZZW and ZOB, respectively—each numbering a few hundred Jewish men and women, took part in the Warsaw ghetto uprising. They were well aware of each other, but fought their own battles in separate locations. The fighting organization led by Frenkel and his comrades was better organized, better trained, and better armed. It fought the main battle of the Warsaw ghetto uprising. Reading the Stroop Report and relating it to corroborative eyewitness reports makes that clear. But the generally accepted narrative of the uprising, as it was taught to Israeli schoolchildren or as it appears at the Holocaust History Museum at Yad Vashem in Jerusalem, the Holocaust Museum in Washington, D.C., or Polin, the museum in Warsaw devoted to the history of Polish Jewry, sidelines or ignores Frenkel and his fighters.

A version of what happened in the Warsaw ghetto uprising heard at Kibbutz Yagur, near Haifa, on June 7, 1946, was quickly accepted as the narrative of the uprising in the Yishuv—the Jewish community in Palestine—and thereafter was adopted by the State of Israel and, in time, by the rest of the world.

What happened at Yagur that day, in the foothills of the Carmel Mountains, was dramatic. Zivya Lubetkin, a fighter in the ranks of Anielewicz's organization who was newly arrived in Palestine from Europe, appeared before a crowd of thousands. They had come to attend a convention of the left-wing kibbutz movement HaKibbutz HaMeuhad, but their greater interest was in hearing what had really happened to the Jews in Europe during the Holocaust from someone who had fought back.

To Jewish youths in Palestine at the time, having no idea of the circumstances that prevailed during the Holocaust, the destruction of Europe's Jews was incomprehensible. Young men and women who were preparing to fight the British and the Arabs were stunned to learn that most of the Jews of Europe had gone to their deaths like the proverbial lambs to the slaughter. But not Lubetkin. And Lubetkin was one of their own—a leader of Dror, the Socialist-Zionist youth organization in Poland affiliated with the HaKibbutz HaMeuhad movement in Palestine.

Zivya Lubetkin was a good-looking woman in her early thirties who spoke fluent Hebrew. She told the rapt audience about what had happened in Europe, and she spoke about Jewish fighters and Jewish heroism. She told them about the Warsaw ghetto uprising—about Mordechai Anielewicz and his comrades of the Jewish Fighting Organization. But she told only half the story—actually less than half. She did not tell them about the four-day battle in Muranowski Square, about the flags raised there, about Pawel Frenkel and his comrades of the Jewish Military Organization.

Not that she did not know about them. She and Anielewicz had negotiated with Frenkel and his deputy, Leon Rodal, in an attempt to unite the two groups, but the negotiations were unfortunately doomed to failure. The flags flying high over Muranowski Square were seen in the ghetto and beyond its walls, and in the rest of the city of Warsaw, but Zivya decided not to tell the full story of the Warsaw ghetto uprising, realizing that there was a part of the story that her audience was not prepared to hear.

It was a time when members of the HaKibbutz HaMeuhad, in cooperation with the British in Palestine, were engaged in hunting down members of the Irgun who were fighting against British rule in Palestine, defying a policy set by the official leadership of the Jewish community in Palestine led by David Ben-Gurion. The Irgun (Irgun Zvai Leumi, or National Military Organization) was the parent organization of the Jewish Military Organization in the Warsaw ghetto. The ideological strife that had kept the two fighting organizations apart in the Warsaw ghetto (and that had no relevance there) was all too alive in the Jewish community in Palestine when Lubetkin arrived, and she quickly realized it. She knew better than to speak in Yagur about the heroism of fighters in the ghetto who were associated with the Irgun. Her narrative of the Warsaw ghetto uprising was quickly adopted by the governing institutions in the Yishuv, which were ruled by the Socialist-Zionist parties; later, in the State of Israel, it became the "official" narrative of this historic event.

Fifteen years later Lubetkin was called as a witness at the Eichmann trial in Jerusalem. Alongside the many witnesses who described the horrors of the Holocaust, her testimony bore witness to Jewish resistance and Jewish heroism during that tragic period. She retold the story of the Warsaw ghetto uprising. And although fifteen years had elapsed since her appearance at Kibbutz Yagur shortly after her arrival in Palestine, she told it again as she had then—leaving out the battle at Muranowski Square and the raising of the flags, the central event of the uprising.

Many of Lubetkin's comrades also had managed to survive the ghetto, arriving in Palestine after the war. They corroborated Lubetkin's narrative of the uprising. Pawel Frenkel and all of the senior fighters of the Jewish Military Organization had fallen in battle. There was no one left to speak for them and tell the full story of the uprising. There was, of course, the Stroop Report, but it was studiously ignored by politicians and historians alike in an attempt to manipulate history in the pursuance of political objectives. Lubetkin's narrative had by now become official history.

In George Orwell's dystopian novel *1984*, one of the slogans of the party that controlled society was "He who controls the past controls the future. He who controls the present controls the past." This kind of manipulation of events in the past for political purposes, characteristic of the rulers of the Soviet Union, was not foreign to the leaders of the socialist parties in Israel. In the seemingly never-ending battle against Jabotinsky and his adherents, they wanted to show that when it came to fighting, it was the youths educated in their youth movements who were the heroes, and not the "tin soldiers" of Betar; that at every important juncture in modern Jewish history it was *they* who had played the crucial role. And so they tailored the narrative of the Warsaw ghetto uprising to suit their ideological needs. During the almost thirty years of the Labor Party's rule in Israel, there was no chance to have the record set straight and to have the people of Israel pay homage to Pawel Frenkel and his comrades, who had given their lives for the honor of the Jewish people.

But what about the historians, Yehuda Bauer and Yisrael Gutman? They had both been educated in the Hashomer Hatzair youth movement, and evidently loyalty to that movement, and a dislike of Jabotinsky and his politics, affected their judgment. Gutman in his many publications provided the academic imprimatur to the doctored narrative of the Warsaw ghetto uprising.

I had summarized my research into the Warsaw ghetto uprising in a book, *Flags over the Warsaw Ghetto*, published in Israel in 2009. I went up to Gutman's apartment to show him the book. He leafed through it casually. "This is wrong," he pronounced. Some years later, at a conference at Yad Vashem not long before he passed away, he took me aside. Without any introduction he said to me, "It is good that you wrote your book." I was disarmed by his honesty. I knew it must have been difficult for him to say those words.

The book, by now also published in English and Polish, has been read by tens of thousands. Slowly the true story of the Warsaw ghetto uprising—that of Pawel Frenkel and his fighters, and that of Mordechai Anielewicz and his fighters—is taking its rightful place in the collective memory of the people of Israel. A wrong is being corrected.

Epilogue

I look back in wonder at Israel's sixty-nine-year history. In a few decades
it has developed into a country well able to defend itself with a dynamic
economy growing at a rapid rate, while simultaneously fulfilling its declared mission and absorbing millions of Jews in need of a haven. While
its fate hung in the balance when Arab armies invaded it in May 1948 and
victory seemed almost beyond reach, it has successfully defended itself
against recurrent aggression by a coalition of Arab armies. Its great victory
against the attacking Egyptian and Syrian armies during the Yom Kippur
War in 1973 brought Egypt to the peace table and has put an end to Arab
plans to attack Israel. It has over the years withstood waves of terror directed
against its civilian population. Beleaguered and embattled for many years,
its achievements are the result of the unending effort of the people of
Israel, old-timers and new immigrants, aided by Jewish communities around
the world. And it has paid a high price for its independence and security.
More than 23,000 men and women have given their lives in defense of
Israel. Israel is a bereaved nation. Hardly a family has not lost some member in Israel's defense over the years.

Knowing the cost of war, Israelis seek peace. But peace in the Middle
East is elusive. After Israel, in its War of Independence, defeated the

armies of Egypt, Jordan, Iraq, Syria, and Lebanon, whch had invaded Israel on May 15, 1948, and when the armistice agreements with Egypt, Jordan, Lebanon, and Syria were signed in 1949, it was hoped that they would serve as a basis for peace with the Arab world. But the Arabs saw their defeat as only a first round in their attempts to destroy Israel. Confident that they outnumbered and outgunned Israel, they believed it was only a matter of time before they would succeed. Later, Israel's dramatic victory in the Six-Day War in 1967 led to the infamous Arab response of the three nos at the Khartoum conference: no to recognition of Israel, no to negotiations with Israel, and no to peace with Israel.

It was Israel's great victory in the Yom Kippur War in 1973 (which began with a combined Egyptian and Syrian attack that caught Israel by surprise) that led to negotiations between Egypt and Israel, which culminated in the Israeli-Egyptian peace treaty of 1979. Egypt, the largest Arab nation, recognized Israel, negotiated with Israel, and made peace with Israel. Fifteen years later, in 1994, the Israeli-Jordan peace treaty was signed. There have been recurrent negotiations with Syria, but all of them have failed. Considering events in Syria in recent years, few Israelis regret the failure of these negotiations.

It is Israel's military prowess and economic vitality that has paved the way to progress toward peace with its Arab neighbors. Arab nations have come to realize that, like it or not, Israel is here stay. Egypt's president, Abdel Fattah el-Sisi, threatened by Islamic terrorists, sees Israel as an ally. Saudi Arabia's rulers, feeling threatened by a domineering Iran, recognize that Israel too is threatened by Iran and see room for cooperation with Israel. Jordan also looks to Israel for support. The chaos in the Middle East that followed the Arab Spring has brought about a reevaluation of interests among some Arab rulers and a more positive view of Israel. Developments that were unimaginable in the past may now lead in time to a widening of the circle of Arab countries at peace with Israel, even though the degree of popular support for such a peace in these countries is not at all clear. But Israel still has enemies who seek its destruction—foremost, Iran. Iran is a large country with an arsenal of ballistic missiles and is on the verge of being able to attain nuclear weapons capability. Its leaders regularly threaten Israel with destruction. Hezbollah, a Lebanese Shia terrorist militia, is armed and trained by Iran and follows orders from

Teheran. Its arsenal of more than 100,000 rockets and missiles constitutes a constant and imminent threat to Israel. Hamas, a Palestinian terrorist organization pledged to the destruction of Israel, rules the Gaza Strip and possesses thousands of rockets that are occasionally launched against Israel. And acts of terror are frequently committed by Palestinian terrorists against Israeli civilians. Against these threats Israel must be constantly on alert while preparing the appropriate responses or deterrent measures.

But it is the conflict with the Palestinians that is on the minds of most Israelis. It is a local conflict, and many in the international community who pressure Israel to take steps to resolve this conflict used to believe that resolving this conflict would bring peace to the entire Middle East. However, recent events in the region have made it clear that there is no connection between resolving this conflict and the tribal and religious rivalry at the root of the fighting and hostility that characterize the Middle East today.

Although a local conflict, much of the day-to-day attention of Israelis and the international community focuses on it. The recurrent acts of terrorism committed by Palestinians against Israeli civilians has saddled Israel with the burden of maintaining a military presence in Judea and Samaria (the West Bank). Israel is accused of "occupying" Palestinian territory while the Palestinians are left without the independence that its leadership seeks. Resolution of the conflict would presumably bring an end to this situation.

The conflict under different names has been around for a long time. It has evolved from being seen as a Jewish-Arab conflict to being considered an Israeli-Arab conflict after Israeli independence, and has reached its present form as an Israeli-Palestinian conflict after the Six-Day War in 1967. Clearly there are no easy solutions to conflicting claims and demands. There are two major roadblocks to progress in resolving the conflict.

First, there is the question of the Palestinian partner, one able to conduct negotiations with Israel to end the conflict and implement the provision of an agreement. For many years Yasser Arafat, the leader of the Palestine Liberation Organization who had signed the Oslo Accords, seemed the obvious partner. It was assumed that he had the authority to impose any peace agreement that he would sign on the Palestinian people. However, after a wave of Palestinian terrorist attacks against Israeli civilians that led to the killing of more than a thousand Israelis, it became clear that a peace treaty with Israel was not his objective. His heir as head of the PLO, Mahmoud Abbas, does not have the authority that Arafat had—it is contested by Hamas. If Abbas were to conclude a peace treaty with Israel, Hamas would probably reject it and continue its claims against Israel, and the conflict would continue. Most likely aware of this, Abbas is hesitant to engage in negotiations with Israel, so he turns to the United Nations, seeking international recognition for his claims against Israel.

The second roadblock to progress relates to Israel's security after the establishment of a Palestinian state next door to Israel. The neighboring Palestinian state, if it were to be established, must be capable of preventing acts of violence against Israel emanating from its territory. The peace treaties with Egyptian and Jordanian rulers have endured because leaders from those nations have shown that they can provide that security for Israel. It is highly doubtful that a Palestinian state would be able to meet that challenge.

Added to that is the insistent Palestinian demand for the "right of return," which for obvious reasons Israel cannot accept and the Palestinian leadership is not prepared to abandon.

Over the years, under Republican and Democratic presidents, the United States has attempted to mediate between Israel and the Palestinians in order to advance the peace process, but without success. Most outspoken and emphatic was Barack Obama, frequently telling Israel publicly what he expected from it. Rather than bringing the two sides closer, these demands brought about a hardening of the Palestinian side, which could not put forth positions more moderate than that of the U.S. president and believed that the United States could force Israel's hand. The end result of American mediation was negative and only reaffirmed that direct negotiations between Israel and the Palestinians were the only way to achieve an accommodation between the parties.

It is possible that as changes in the region unfold, it will be possible to reach an accommodation with the Palestinians, or possibly other solutions will appear on the horizon. The inevitable conclusion is that it will take time. The desire to arrive at a solution now is understandable, but evidently not achievable.

Index

Note: Surnames beginning with "al-" and "el-" are alphabetized by the subsequent portion of the name.